The Creatio Black Russian Terrier

Vol. 5: Moscow Families

Coming Up!

Vol. 6: Leningrad
Vol. 7: Experts' Descriptions 1952–78
Vol. 8: Care & Control

... and More!

Never Leave Infants and Children Alone with ANY Dog

For years animal behaviour experts have issued warnings that children should never be left unsupervised with dogs regardless of the size or breed. Dogs are pack animals that have a natural instinct known as prey drive: an instinct to hunt and take down prey. If triggered for any reason, serious consequences can occur, especially among large breed dogs.

Children under 10 years of age lack the maturity to see when this natural instinct has been triggered. Most adults are no wiser and at best, are untrained to recognized pending trouble: A dog's stiffened posture, forward lean, and straight tail are all giveaway signs which should be recognized by adults, and are generally missed by children.

That prey drive can be triggered by a child's rambunctious and unpredictable behaviour, such as running and screaming. An infant's crying, flailing arms, or cooing can trigger an aggressive response.

Dogs are not babysitters. When a dog places a paw or head over an infant or child, it is demonstrating an alpha controlling state — as within a pack situation with other dogs. This can be a sign of pending disaster.

Awareness and caution must always be exercised when young children are around dogs especially strange dogs.

In Canada, over a seventeen-year-period (1990–2007), eighty-five percent of fatal dog attacks involved children under the age of 12.

The average age was 5 years.

The Creation of the Black Russian Terrier

Vol. 5:

Moscow Families

Donald B. Anderson

Ottawa Canada
crowecreations.ca
info@crowecreations.ca

Designed by Crowe Creations
Text set in Arial, headings set in Belfast Heavy SF
Cover design copyright © 2016 by Crowe Creations

Both front cover and back cover photographs have been
graciously provided by Irina Nedeljko, Vladivostok, Russia

Front & back cover photographs © Svetlan Beolgurova, Novosibirsk, Russia

Crowe Creations
ISBN: 978-1-927058-32-9

CreateSpace
ISBN-13: 978-1532745447
ISBN-10: 1532745443

Dedicated to the Russian breeders of enlightened foresight, who took up the cause of building upon and advancing the foundation work of Red Star Kennel, collectively establishing the "Concept of Family" that ensured the creation of the Black Russian Terrier long before modern scientific insight and understanding of the canine genome.

Foreword

Family Hierarchy of the Black Russian Terrier

Principles and Procedures
Question: What best identifies a "purebred" canine Breed.
Answer: Family.

Hierarchy
Hierarchy is the building blocks creating Family — something engineered from a number of parts that are held or put together in a particular way, establishing inter-relationships or arrangements of parts [in a complex entity]. The original foundation "building block breeds" blended in a variety of mixes are what constituted the evolutionary creation of the Black Russian Terrier.

Steps to a New Breed
The creation of the Black Russian Terrier required a four-track approach:
1. Control: Red Star Kennel
2. Identification of the desired project results.
3. Professional knowledge, prolonged dedicated time, resolve to complete task, and financial and physical resources.
4. Selection of compatible building blocks: Breeds.

When the Russians began planning for the creation of a new canine breed, they already understood that the final outcome of their work would eventually be greater than the sum of its parts.

This new canine would be made up of a number of [evaluated] compatible parts [covered in Volumes 1–4 of *The Creation of the Black Russian Terrier*] that they, the originators, would combine in a particular evolving format. The interrelationships of these parts would be measured through quality control management, employing the concepts and principles of genetic diversification using the experience gained from like-experiments throughout the first half of the twentieth century.

Design

Simplicity in dog breeding was not the order of the day at Red Star Kennel. The practice of mating selected dogs with the intent to produce specific qualities and characteristics was taken to the *n*th power by canine geneticists at Red Star Kennel in the late 1940s through the 1950s with the stated objective of creating a new, powerful, independent-thinking guard and military dog breed. The purpose was to initially identify, select, then breed identified specimens from a variety of [somewhat compatible] breeds to produce a number of probably useful tracks. These tracks would enhance specific qualities and characteristics.

One pathway comprised combining the Great Dane and East European Shepherd; and a second involved adding the Rottweiler to that cross. The result was the creation of two distinct types. The first produced a breed that looked very much like a medium- to long-coated Great-Dane-sized German Shepherd with attributes of both breeds. The second produced a dog more representative of a Molosser/Great Dane type. Neither breed proved to be acceptable to the Russian Military and are reported to have been dropped from the program. [That premise may be open to question at a later time.]

Another pathway created the Moscow Waterdog with the crossing of Newfoundland male, Negus f. Mangeym, with the Caucasian Ovcharka female, Karabashka, and East European Shepherd, Rina, and possibly other undiscovered specimens of these two breeds. Offspring from these breedings were then bred together with Giant Schnauzer Roy and Newfoundland Lord, followed by the Rottweiler. This breed was also known by the names of Moscow Newfoundland Dog and Moscow Vodolaz. It was reported to be overly aggressive and unmanageable, and also became extinct as a specific breed. However, the Moscow Waterdog became a paramount factor in the creation of the Black Russian Terrier. [*See*, Vol. 2, *Moscow: Karabashka Group*].

Creating a New Breed

By definition, a Breed can be described as a unique group [family] of animals whose phenotype and genotype distinguish it from all others. Both are central to a Breed's identity. The primary goal is to design a sound animal by establishing and setting structure and temperament then follow with important but secondary requirements of expression, coat texture and colour, pigment or eye colour, and other desired characteristics. By its name, the Black Russian Terrier is black coated with a few sparsely placed white or grey hairs permitted. Although from the beginning, there was no all allowance for other colours, the genetic fact was [is] that other coat colours did and do exist. There is currently no allowance for a coloured coat variety.

Note

Should the future permit for a coloured coat variety, there would be no requirement for cross-breeding to attain that goal given that coloured coats' gene pool is fairly well established in Europe with a growing number in North America. Although there are some recognized Breeds with coat coloured varieties (Newfoundland Dog, Bullmastiff, Mastiff(s), Great Dane, Doberman, Irish Setters, *et al.*), major registering bodies have not allowed new varieties in the past fifty years. In order for a Breed, new or old, to be recognized, the breeders must be able to demonstrate several generations of pups that resemble one phenotype and be genetically similar to their parents. This means individuals can be distinguished based on their appearance and genetics. Colour-coated Black Russian Terriers will be presented in a future volume. Readers will note [newly identified] Giant Schnauzers added to the end of this volume.

How to Read This Volume

THE PRESENTATION FORMAT OF THIS study is one of a number of ways in which this complicated information could be shared and delivered, with this Volume being designed to follow specifically selected "Lines" as a guide to the structural construction(s) of the developing original Black Terrier toward becoming the officially recognized Black Russian Terrier.

Readers are invited to use this volume and others in the series as an information tool following general and specific pathways in the creation of the Black Russian Terrier. Readers will recognize many of the pathways followed by breeders utilizing a relatively small number of "subject dogs" in a large number of selected combinations, never losing sight of the final objective.

Every effort has been made to include emerging updated pedigree information in this volume with the aim of demonstrating consistency in the ownership and physical location of as many specimens as possible. The author also asks readers to take into account that some specimens were moved/shared between breeders in a variety of locations throughout Russia and bordering countries in the developing years.

The content of this [and other] volumes in this series is based on data obtained and interpreted by the author in his challenge to assemble and provide a portrait of the creation of the Black Russian Terrier in the English language. Every effort has been made to verify the information provided.

Hopefully, readers will understand and appreciate "the why" of repeats of some information and especially photographs. While seeking and compiling overlapping information, I found it so much easier to have photographs at hand as this reduced having to search all through the book to compare photos with pedigrees and data. Building easily available mental pictures as one reads documents like this can be very helpful with keeping the story grounded. For this volume, we have placed the pedigrees in Appendix A in order to have the photographs closer to their mention for more-easy comparing within the text.

Readers will note there is some overlapping/combining of pedigrees between Red Star/Moscow and St. Petersburg, again because of the uses/sharing of breeding stock. Likewise, repeat photographs are presented to facilitate the reading/comparing process.

In this volume, we have more information through Russian/English translation processes, so it contains additional information with regard to the growing breeder/owner relationships with Red Star Kennel when it began to allocate specimens to private owners. Readers can better appreciate the physical locations and movement of breeding stock within Russia, as well as the gradual spread of specimens to bordering countries.

Based on currently available information, it might safely be surmised that the use of breeding stock was much wider spread throughout Russia than could be confirmed through this study.

The structure of this research/writing exercise does not allow for the inclusion of the identification of private breeders. That is an exercise best left for Russian cynologists and researchers, and hopefully translated into English at a later time.

One section of this volume is organized and presented in a chronological time period of 1950–80 identifying individual family orders. The second section attempts to follow those identified lines with observations and supporting pedigrees (sectioned off by line in Appendix A). There are some duplications that the author feels are unavoidable given the breeding programs and specimen selections made by Red Star, Moscow, and Leningrad/St. Petersburg City Clubs and private breeders. Examinations of these lines and families in visual comparisons with available photographs demonstrates the wisdom of selections in the successes achieved.

Not all family lines and family branches have been identified and followed. This is primarily due to the enormity of this study, to translation challenges, and to the fact that data were compiled by a single individual.

Readers will also note that a number of Moscow Waterdogs and Moscow Waterdog Hybrids; e.g., Ledi, were privately owned, which again begs questions pertaining to the stated extinction of that breed.

There are a number of pedigree entries that show no physical housing location(s) for some dogs due to unavailability of data.

A few spellings of the names of dogs originating in Russia and Germany are inter-changeable so confusing; this is due to translations by computers which do not have the capability to interpret meaning.

Ownership of recorded breeding specimens shown in pedigrees in this volume are entered as: Red Star, Moscow, other city name, privately owned, or a combination denoting shared ownership: Red Star/Moscow, Red Star/St. Petersburg, Red Star/Saratov, Red Star/Privately Owned, et al. As stated above, actual names of private owners are not included in pedigrees.

Contents

The family of man and dog
No closer bond exists between divergent species
Of one mind in mutual respect and trust
The dog in repose with children at the hearth
Stands as Centurion at the gate
Unfailing in his duty 'til death takes him
Loyalty is eternal
Donald B. Anderson

Introduction

DURING THE DEVELOPMENT OF A new breed of dog, the question arises as to what constitutes a "Family". Readers have already been introduced to the Russian plan for creating a new breed through the establishment of what their experts referred to as "Groups". The first step in creating initial groups was in a number of crossbreeding experiments. To advance within the program, new specimens had to present in a specific physical format, meet identified stable temperament attributes/traits, etc., and fulfil environmental coat requirements. The next phases included breeding back to a parent, then additional crosses and mixed crosses within the original single crosses. These collective processes contributed over time to the evolution of the new Family.

Successfully developed breed-specific Groups were quickly refined and further blended. For example:

- **Karabashka Group**: Caucasian Ovcharka + Newfoundland and East European Shepherd evolving into Moscow Waterdog Group. [Refer to Vol. 2 of *The Creation of the Black Russian Terrier*.]
- **Moscow Waterdog Group**: This short lived Group played a major role in the advancement of the "Black Terrier" for which the Newfoundland Dog has been given primary credit. To this Group were added the genes of the Giant Schnauzer, the Rottweiler and the Airedale Terrier. [Refer to Vol. 2 of *The Creation of the Black Russian Terrier*.]
- **Moscow Dog Group**: Great Dane/East European Shepherd/ Rottweiler was a Group development that quickly faded and became extinct(?) reportedly because of unreliable temperament. However, this Group *was* incorporated into the growing "Black Terrier" Family with the addition of Giant Schnauzer genes. [Refer to Vol. 2 of *The Creation of the Black Russian Terrier*.]

- **Teffi Group**: From the Airedale Terrier was developed a Group by blending the Airedale's specific attributes judiciously with the Giant Schnauzer followed with the addition of Rottweiler. [Refer to Vol. 3 of *The Creation of the Black Russian Terrier*]
- **Birma Group**: Rottweiler genes were extensively blended into the construction of the "Black Terrier" in amounts pretty much equal to those of the Giant Schnauzer and contributing stable temperament, muscle bulk, strength and overall size. [Refer to Vol. 4 of *The Creation of the Black Russian Terrier*.]

Other breed inclusions involved small amounts of both Central Asian and South Russian Ovcharka plus the Russian Spotted Hound. These other breeds were added into the mix in the early development stages of the "Black Terrier" at Red Star Kennel.

Of special note in passing is that the Moscow Waterdog was originally meant to be developed as its own specific breed but failed in accomplishing that goal. More important was the major role specimens from that Group played in the creation of the "Black Terrier" Group.

Additionally, the Moscow Dog Group initially being designed as a special molosser type breed also failed and quickly faded away, but not before making serious early contributions to the "Black Terrier" Group.

These breeding Groups — each developed along specific pathways — came about primarily by matching selected specimens with the Giant Schnauzer, the end goal being the development of a relatively large number of hybrids that would be refined by breeding selectively within the members of that "Black Terrier" breeding group.

In following the first four volumes of this study, readers can see how subfamilies began taking shape, developed into a main Family, and how the roles played out into the final product. Presenting a quantum step forward into the twenty-first century is a photograph of Mikk (2010) for comparison with some of the early foundation breeds: Giant Schnauzer, Airedale Terrier, Rottweiler, Moscow Waterdog, and Moscow Dog (Great Dane and East European Shepherd).

Mikk
GCH Aristes Paint It Black (March 17, 2010)
Photo courtesy of Cindi Stumm Aristes Kennel

Visual Early Foundation Structural Components

Haytar, 1952 (Giant Schnauzer, Roy × Airedale Terrier, Sotta)

Chelkash, 1953 (Giant Schnauzer, Roy × Rottweiler, Una)

Cholka, 1953 (Giant Schnauzer, Roy × Moscow Waterdog, Tina)

Grum, 1954 (Moscow Waterdog, Fakt × Moscow Waterdog, Ufa)

Ginta, 1956 (Crossbreed, Azot × Moscow Waterdog, Hanka)

Hybrid, Chuk, 1956 (Giant Schnauzer, Roy × Moscow Dog, Chili)

Note: The breeding of Giant Schnauzer Roy to Moscow Dog Chili (Rottweiler, Beniamino × Moscow Waterdog,Toddi (Great Dane, Ralf × East European Shepherd, Pretti)) moved the pathway from the Molosser Moscow Dog type into the "Black Terrier" Group. Moscow Waterdog lines and Moscow Dog lines are covered in detail in Vol. 2.

Russia ca. 1960. (Map source unavailable.)

Growth of the Family

Groups within Groups

NOTWITHSTANDING THE NUMBER OF THE same canines [repeats] it is possible for readers to follow the multiple construction processes that were employed in building the myriad of lines (some large and some small) that were blended to create the majestic structure that was becoming the Black Russian Terrier.

With the arrival of the mid 1950s, Red Star Kennels began making a number of "Group-specific" dogs available to Moscow City Club of Service Dogs (MCKCC) and Leningrad City Club of Service Dogs (LCKCC) for further development of family groups. Blending together dogs from the initial Groups — Caucasian Ovcharka/Moscow Waterdog, Airedale Terrier, Rottweiler, Moscow Dog — quickly resulted in the refinement of general type structure built on the Giant Schnauzer format and temperament. Within a short time, the original major "Groups" began to form new subgroups. This provided a strong basis for the development of Family Lines". As these "Family Lines" evolved so grew their structured genealogy. Close inbreeding/backcrossing practices of limited numbers of family line(s) members established an ever-increasing number of hybrids advancing toward the establishment of recognizable, true-breeding "black terriers". Black Russian Terrier (BRT) officially became a recognized breed in 1985.

5

Developing Moscow Family Lines and Branches: Moving into the Future

The following Family Lines (foundations) make for a fascinating portrait experience of a developing genetic evolutionary adventure that was to become the Black Russian Terrier. This is only part of the Story, (loosely described) touching on Family Lines selected by the author. It does not include all the [dogs] bred and used for breeding at Red Star Military Kennels, the Moscow and Leningrad Clubs of Service Dogs and an array of other specially selected private breeders. [Duplications appear periodically due to compactness of breeding practices and limited favourable breeding stock.]

This study represents a challenging adventure in selecting, managing and piecing together a mass of data from a myriad of sources. Although some parts of this presentation may appear to be duplications, readers will recognize that many male and female specimens were utilized in a number of selected breedings. The following material organization is presented in a chronological order by date (year) of major developing families lines that, in fact, represent the major (strongest) family units beginning with the Family Line originating with male Crossbreed Aray (1954). Readers may recognize that from Giant Schnauzer Roy; female Rottweiler Birma and her daughters Urma, Una, Uza, and Uda and males Kastor, Beniamino, Farno, and female Firma; Airedale Terrier Sotta; Caucasian Ovcharka Karabashka; Newfoundland Dogs Negus and Lord; Moscow Waterdogs; Moscow Dogs; Great Dane and East European Shepherd; and others, were created the original Crossbreeds that were blended into the hybrid magic of possibility.

Throughout the following timeframe from the selection of foundation (Rock) breeds, the creation of Crossbreeds, through the development of multiple layers of designed Hybrids, came the establishment of the Black Terrier Group progressing along the fascinating pathway to the creation of the Black Russian Terrier. Within each of the following chronologically listed Family Lines, the individual dogs are not themselves presented in a chronological sequence. Appendix A, the pedigrees, provides more complete connections.

1954 Family Lines Based on Crossbreed Aray male

(Giant Schnauzer, Roy × Rottweiler, Urma)
- Hybrid Tuman (yr?) male (Crossbreed, Aray × Crossbreed, Htora)
- Hybrid Dina (yr?) female (Hybrid, Tuman × Unknown, Fimka)
- Crossbreed Gay (yr?) male (Crossbreed, Aray × Crossbreed, Borka)
- Hybrid Dega (yr?) female (Crossbreed, Gay × Hybrid, Dina I)
- Hybrid Atta (1964) female (Crossbreed, Gay × Hybrid, Dina)
- Hybrid Aktaj (1964) male (Crossbreed, Gay × Hybrid, Dina I)

1954 Family Lines Based on Crossbreed Azart male

(Giant Schnauzer, Roy × Rottweiler, Una)
Including the Blending of Moscow Dog Hybrid Chuk (1956) with Moscow Waterdog Hybrid Volga (1956)
- Hybrid Al'Fa (yr?) female (Hybrid, Brayt × Crossbreed, Ira) There are no currently recorded offspring of Al'Fa
- Hybrid Bars [Baron] (yr?) male (Hybrid, Brayt × Crossbreed, Chonga)
- Hybrid Berta (1961) female (Hybrid, Bars × Unknown, Fimka)
- Hybrid Dzherri (1957) male (Hybrid, Brayt × Crossbreed, Charva) There are no currently recorded offspring of Dzherri
- Hybrid Azart II (1957) male (Hybrid, Brayt × Crossbreed, Charva) There are no currently recorded offspring of Azart II
- Hybrid Ara (1957) female (Hybrid, Brayt × Crossbreed, Charva) There are no currently recorded offspring of Ara
- Hybrid Bara (1957) female (Hybrid, Brayt × Hybrid, Appa)
- Hybrid Foka (1960) male (Crossbreed, Vah × Hybrid, Bara)
- Hybrid Viy (1960) male (Crossbreed, Vah × Hybrid, Bara)
- Hybrid Agat (1957) male (Hybrid, Brayt × Crossbreed, Ahta) There are no currently recorded offspring of Agat
- Hybrid Azur (1957) male (Hybrid, Brayt × Crossbreed, Ahta) There are no currently recorded offspring of Azur
- Hybrid Brajta [Brayta] (1958) female (Hybrid, Brayt × Crossbreed, Basta) There are no currently recorded offspring of Brajta [Brayta]

- Hybrid Shrek (1958) male (Hybrid, Brayt × Crossbreed, Binta) There are no currently recorded offspring of Shrek
- Hybrid Graf (1959) male (Hybrid, Brayt × Crossbreed, Basta)There are no currently recorded offspring of Graf
- Hybrid Agat (1959) male (Hybrid, Brayt × Crossbreed, Basta) There are no currently recorded offspring of Agat
- Hybrid Nelli (1960) female (Hybrid, Brayt × Unknown, Zarna) There are no currently recorded offspring of Nelli
- Hybrid Nayda (1961) female (Hybrid, Brayt × Hybrid, Nelma)
- Hybrid Ata (yr?) female (Hybrid, Topaz × Hybrid, Nayda)
- Hybrid Ayda (yr?) female (Hybrid, Topaz × Hybrid, Nayda)
- Hybrid Fors (1964) male (Hybrid, Foka × Hybrid, Nayda)
- Hybrid Dina I (1964) male (Hybrid, Foka × Hybrid, Nayda)
- Hybrid Karat (1964) male (Hybrid, Foka × Hybrid, Nayda)
- Hybrid Ayman (1964) male (Hybrid, Foka × Hybrid, Nayda)
- Hybrid Fang (1964) male (Hybrid, Foka × Hybrid, Nayda)
- Hybrid Irda (1962) female (Hybrid, Brayt × Crossbreed, Ira) There are no currently recorded offspring of Irda
- Hybrid Chani (1962) male (Hybrid, Brayt × Crossbreed, Ira)
- Hybrid Shrek (1966) male (Hybrid, Chani × Hybrid, Alfa)
- Hybrid Nora (1966) female (Hybrid, Chani × Hybrid, Alfa)
- Hybrid Uran (1966) male (Hybrid, Chani × Crossbreed, Ohta)
- Hybrid Nelli (1966) female (Hybrid, Chani × Crossbreed, Ohta)
- Hybrid Chap (1967) male (Hybrid, Chani × Hybrid, Alfa)
- Hybrid Karat (1967) male (Hybrid, Chani × Hybrid, Alfa)
- Hybrid Varta (1967) female (Hybrid, Chani × Hybrid, Alfa)
- Hybrid Top (1968) male (Hybrid, Chani × Crossbreed, Teya)
- Hybrid Nord (1962) male (Hybrid, Brayt × Crossbreed, Ira)
- Hybrid Agat (1964) male (Hybrid, Nord × Hybrid, Alfa)
- Hybrid Lada (1964) female (Hybrid, Nord × Hybrid, Alfa)
- Hybrid Alfa (1964) female (Hybrid, Nord × Hybrid, Alfa)
- Hybrid Torri (1968) male (Hybrid, Nord × Hybrid, Nelli)
- Hybrid Lada (1968) female (Hybrid, Nord × Hybrid, Nelli)
- Hybrid Nord (1968) male (Hybrid, Nord × Hybrid, Nayda)
- Hybrid Chep (1968) male (Hybrid, Nord × Hybrid, Nayda)
- Hybrid Prints [Prince] (1968) male (Hybrid, Nord × Hybrid, Nayda)

- 1955 Moscow Dog Chili female (Rottweiler, Beniamino × Moscow Dog, Toddi)
- Hybrid Beno (1955) male (Crossbreed, Chelkash × Moscow Dog, Chili) There are no currently recorded offspring by Beno
- Moscow Dog Hybrid Chuk (1956) male (Giant Schnauzer, Roy × Moscow Dog, Chili)
- Hybrid Mirta (1960) female (Moscow Dog Hybrid, Chuk × Moscow Waterdog Hybrid, Volga)
- Hybrid Yaga (yr?) (Hybrid, Demon × Hybrid, Mirta)
- Hybrid Dega (1963) (Giant Schnauzer, Ditter f. Drahenshljuht × Hybrid, Mirta)
- Hybrid Alfa (1961) female (Moscow Dog Hybrid, Chuk × Moscow Waterdog Hybrid, Volga
- Hybrid Roy (yr?) male (Hybrid, Dan Zhan × Hybrid, Alfa)
- Hybrid Demon (yr?) male (Hybrid, Dzhaga × Hybrid, Alfa)
- Hybrid Alfa (yr?) female (Hybrid, Uran × Hybrid, Alfa)
- Hybrid Agat (1964) male (Hybrid, Nord × Hybrid, Alfa)
- Hybrid Lada (1964) female (Hybrid, Nord × Hybrid, Alfa)
- Hybrid Alfa (1964) female (Hybrid, Nord × Hybrid, Alfa)
- Hybrid Shrek (1966) male (Hybrid, Chani × Hybrid, Alfa)
- Hybrid Nora (1966 female (Hybrid, Chani × Hybrid, Alfa)
- Hybrid Chap (1967) male (Hybrid Chani × Hybrid, Alfa)
- Hybrid Karat (1967) male (Hybrid, Chani × Hybrid, Alfa)
- Hybrid Varta (1967) (Hybrid, Chani × Hybrid, Alfa)

1956 Family Lines Based on Moscow Waterdog Hybrids Volga, Brayt, Vityaz, Vishnya, Vesna, Basta, Velta
(Crossbreed, Azart × Moscow Waterdog, Hanka). Refer to 1954 Family Lines Based on Crossbreed Azart

1957 Family Lines Based on Hybrid Demon male
(Hybrid, Arras × Crossbreed, Chomga)
- Hybrid Negus (yr?) male (Hybrid, Demon × Unknown)
- Hybrid, Galka (yr?) female (Hybrid, Negus × Hybrid, Yaga)
- Hybrid Dega (1962) female (Hybrid, Demon × Hybrid, Galka)

- Hybrid Rams I (1966) male (Hybrid, Foka × Hybrid, Dega)
- Hybrid Charli 1 (yr?) male (Hybrid, Rams I × Hybrid, Chada)
- Hybrid Bush (yr?) male (Hybrid, Rams I × Hybrid, Alba)
- Hybrid Greits (yr?) male (Hybrid, Rams I × Hybrid, Nim Alma)
- Hybrid Shaman (yr?) male (Hybrid, Rams I × Hybrid, Nim Eva)
- Hybrid Al'Princ (1971) male (Hybrid, Rams I × Hybrid, Alba)
- Hybrid Artosha (1971) male (Hybrid, Rams I × Hybrid, Alba)
- Hybrid Rammi (1971) male (Hybrid, Rams I × Hybrid, Nim Alma)
- Hybrid Ereyg (1972) male (Hybrid, Rams I × Hybrid, Nim Alma)
- Hybrid Erna (1972) male (Hybrid, Rams I × Hybrid, Nim Alma)
- Hybrid Shagane (1972) female (Hybrid, Rams I × Hybrid,Varya)
- Hybrid Yulva Zhers (1973) male (Hybrid, Rams I × Hybrid, Dan-Zhenni)
- Hybrid Nochka Yulva Zhuzha (1973) female (Hybrid, Rams I × Hybrid, Dan-Zhenni)
- Hybrid Yulva Zheni (1973) female (Hybrid, Rams I × Hybrid, Dan-Zhenni)
- Hybrid Ort-Zaur (1974) male (Hybrid, Rams I × Hybrid, Dan-Orta)
- Hybrid Orri (1974) male (Hybrid, Rams I × Hybrid, Dan-Orta)
- Hybrid Tuman (1967) male (Hybrid, Tom × Hybrid, Dega)
- Hybrid Chagi (yr?) female (Hybrid, Tuman × Unknown)
- Hybrid Kras-Boss (yr?) male (Hybrid, Tuman × Hybrid, Ulma)
- Hybrid Karina-Un (yr?) female (Hybrid, Tuman × Hybrid, Ulma)
- Hybrid Maur (yr?) male (Hybrid, Tuman × Hybrid, Sekki)
- Hybrid Timur (yr?) male (Hybrid, Tuman × Hybrid, Panta)
- Hybrid Dina (yr?) female (Hybrid, Tuman × Hybrid, Panta)
- Hybrid Feya (yr?) female (Hybrid, Tuman × Unknown, Meri)
- Hybrid Yuna (yr?) female (Hybrid, Tuman × Hybrid, Yuta [Yutta])
- Hybrid Gayda (yr?) female (Hybrid, Tuman × Unknown, Chana)
- Hybrid Karem (yr?) male (Hybrid, Tuman × Hybrid, Nim Eva)
- Hybrid Inessa (yr?) female (Hybrid, Tuman × Unknown, Vanda)
- Hybrid Arto (yr?) male (Hybrid, Tuman × Unknown, Al'Fa)
- Hybrid Yarcha (1970) female (Hybrid, Tuman × Unknown, Chapa)
- Hybrid Lada (1970) female (Hybrid, Tuman × Crossbreed, Panta)
- Hybrid Rema-Greza (1970) female (Hybrid, Tuman × Hybrid, Rynda)
- Hybrid Rayma (1970) female (Hybrid, Tuman × Hybrid, Rynda)

- Hybrid Raffi (1970) female (Hybrid, Tuman × Hybrid, Rynda)
- Hybrid Ranika (1970) female (Hybrid, Tuman × Hybrid, Rynda)
- Hybrid Zhurd (1970) male (Hybrid, Tuman × Hybrid, Raksha)
- Hybrid Zhuk (1970) male (Hybrid, Tuman × Hybrid, Raksha)
- Hybrid Zhulya (1970) female (Hybrid, Tuman × Hybrid, Raksha)
- Hybrid Zhaklin (1970) female (Hybrid, Tuman × Hybrid, Raksha)
- Hybrid Yard (1970) male (Hybrid, Tuman × Unknown)
- Hybrid Yanga (1970) female (Hybrid, Tuman × Unknown)
- Hybrid Zherika (1971) female (Hybrid, Tuman × Hybrid, Nayda)
- Hybrid Lera (1972) female (Hybrid, Tuman × Hybrid, Nayda)
- Hybrid Chara (1972) female (Hybrid, Tuman × Hybrid, Nayda)
- Hybrid Kora (1972) female (Hybrid, Tuman × Hybrid, Nayda)
- Hybrid Dzhulja (1972) female (Hybrid, Tuman × Hybrid, Nayda)
- Hybrid Dor-Dintay (1973) male (Hybrid, Tuman × Hybrid, Dan-Dingo)
- Hybrid Dor-Ditta (1973) female (Hybrid, Tuman × Hybrid, Dan-Dingo)
- Hybrid Dor-Deri (1973) female (Hybrid, Tuman × Hybrid, Dan-Dingo)
- Hybrid Jermak (1967) male (Hybrid, Tom × Hybrid, Dega) There are no currently recorded offspring of Jermak
- Hybrid Dzhoya (1967) female (Hybrid, Tom × Hybrid, Dega)
- Hybrid Dan Daros (1969) male (Hybrid, Viy × Hybrid, Dzhoya)
- Hybrid Dan Darsi (1969) female (Hybrid, Viy × Hybrid, Dzhoya)
- Hybrid Dan Dingo (1969) female (Hybrid, Viy × Hybrid, Dzhoya)
- Hybrid Dan Dzhoya (1969) female (Hybrid, Viy × Hybrid, Dzhoya)
- Hybrid Dan Daza (1969) female (Hybrid, Viy × Hybrid, Dzhoya)
- Hybrid Dan Zhan (1970) male (Hybrid, Dzhim × Hybrid, Dzhoya)
- Hybrid Dan Zhuan (1970) male (Hybrid, Dzhim × Hybrid, Dzhoya)
- Hybrid Dan Zhak (1979) male (Hybrid, Dzhim × Hybrid, Dzhoya)
- Hybrid Dan Zhenni (1970) female (Hybrid, Dzhim × Hybrid, Dzhoya)
- Hybrid Dan Zhaklin (1970) female (Hybrid, Dzhim × Hybrid, Dzhoya)
- Hybrid Dan Olchigem (1972) male (Hybrid, Ayaks × Hybrid, Dzhoya)
- Hybrid Dan Oskar (1972) male (Hybrid, Ayaks × Hybrid, Dzhoya)

- Hybrid Dan Orta (1972) female (Hybrid, Ayaks × Hybrid, Dzhoya)
- Hybrid Dan Odzhina (1972) female (Hybrid, Ayaks × Hybrid, Dzhoya)
- Hybrid Dan Yaza (1974) female (Hybrid, Anchar × Hybrid, Dzhoya)
- Hybrid Dan Yamika (1974) female (Hybrid, Anchar × Hybrid, Dzhoya)
- Hybrid Dan Jana [Dan Janka] (1974) female (Hybrid, Anchar × Hybrid, Dzhoya)
- Hybrid Dan Grey (1975) male (Hybrid, Gil Devi × Hybrid, Dzhoya)
- Hybrid Dan Gloriya (1975) female (Hybrid, Gil Devi × Hybrid, Dzhoya)
- Hybrid Kara (yr?) female (Hybrid, Demon × Unknown)
- Hybrid Shaytan (yr?) male (Hybrid, Deyv × Hybrid, Kara)
- Hybrid Rika (1973) female (Hybrid, Shaytan × Hybrid, Cherri)
- Hybrid Dzherri (1979) female (Hybrid, Char-Tuman × Hybrid, Rika)
- Hybrid Dzhe-Aygar (1983) male (Hybrid, Atos × Hybrid, Dzherri)
- Hybrid Dzhe-Ahilles (1983) male (Hybrid, Atos × Hybrid, Dzherri)
- Hybrid Terri (1984) male (Hybrid, Atos × Hybrid, Dzherri)
- Hybrid Tegri Bays (1984) female (Hybrid, Atos × Hybrid, Dzherri)
- BRT Dzhe Tarhan Zhan (1985) male (Hybrid, Atos × Hybrid, Dzherri)
- BRT Dzhekson (1985) male (Hybrid, Atos × Hybrid, Dzherri)
- BRT Dzhe Sharon (1987) male (Hybrid, Lin Sharman × Hybrid, Dzherri)
- BRT Dzhe Shani (1987) male (Hybrid, Lin Sharman × Hybrid, Dzherri)
- BRT Dzhe Shelli (1987) male (Hybrid, Lin Sharman × Hybrid, Dzherri)
- Hybrid Naura (1979) female (Hybrid, Char-Tuman × Hybrid, Rika)
- Hybrid Niksa-Nuch (1984) female (Unknown, Starlayt × Hybrid, Naura)
- Hybrid Bagira (yr?) female (Hybrid, Deyv × Hybrid, Kara)
- Hybrid Kuchum (yr?) male (Hybrid, Deyv, Hybrid, Bagira)
- Hybrid Dzhu Dzherri (yr?) female (Hybrid, Kuchum × Unknown)
- Hybrid Gayde (yr?) female (Hybrid, Kuchum × Giant Schnauzer, Anni f. Raakzeje)
- Hybrid Tishka (yr?) female (Hybrid, Kuchum × Giant Schnauzer,

Anni f. Raakzeje)
- Hybrid Agat (yr?) male (Hybrid, Deyv × Hybrid, Bagira) There are no currently recorded offspring of Agat
- Hybrid Chert (yr?) male (Hybrid, Dym Varyag × Hybrid, Kara)
- Hybrid Diana (yr?) female (Hybrid, Chert × Hybrid, Lada)
- Hybrid Dessi (yr?) female (Hybrid, Atos × Hybrid, Diana)
- Hybrid Marta (yr?) female (Hybrid, Atos × Hybrid, Diana)
- Hybrid Dora (1981) female (Hybrid, Atos × Hybrid, Diana)
- Hybrid Verchert (yr?) male (Hybrid, Chert × Hybrid, Lada)
- BRT Kraft (1985) male (Hybrid, Verchert × Hybrid, Virta)
- Hybrid Viking (1980) male (Hybrid, Chert × Hybrid, Lada) There are no currently recorded offspring of Viking
- Hybrid Vil'Da (yr?) female (Hybrid, Dim Varyag × Hybrid, Kara)
- Hybrid Vega (1974) female (Hybrid, Maur × Hybrid, Vil'Da) There are no currently recorded offspring of Agat
- Hybrid Deyv (yr?) male (Hybrid, Demon × Crossbreed, Cholka)
- Hybrid Farlaf (yr?) male (Hybrid, Deyv × Crossbreed, Changa)
- Hybrid Yukon (1976) male (Hybrid, Farlaf × Hybrid, Vega)
- Hybrid Blek (1981) male (Hybrid, Yukon × Hybrid, Gamma)
- BRT Venta (1985) male Hybrid, Blek × Hybrid, Orli)
- BRT Sharl (1985) male Hybrid, Blek × Hybrid, Orli)
- BRT Zhakila Sheyla (1985) female Hybrid, Blek × Hybrid, Orli)
- BRT Zhalila Sherri (1985) female Hybrid, Blek × Hybrid, Orli)
- BRT Sh-Dana (1985) female Hybrid, Blek × Hybrid, Orli)
- BRT Elis (1986) female (Hybrid, Blek × Hybrid, Gressi)
- Hybrid Grog (1984) male (Hybrid, Yukon × Hybrid, Ferri)
- Hybrid Baks (yr?) male (Hybrid, Baks × Hybrid, Aysi Amikus Veris)
- Hybrid Nagir (1984) male (Hybrid, Grog × Hybrid, Virta)
- Hybrid Nord (1984) male (Hybrid, Grog × Hybrid, Virta)
- BRT Nera (1985) female (Hybrid, Grog × Hybrid, Virta)
- BRT Oliver (1986) male (Hybrid, Grog × Hybrid, Linda)
- BRT Oskar (1986) male (Hybrid, Grog × Hybrid, Linda)
- BRT Orel (1986) female (Hybrid, Grog × Hybrid, Linda)
- BRT Olda (1986) female (Hybrid, Grog × Hybrid, Linda)
- BRT Naura Ness (1988) (Hybrid, Grog × BRT, Nika)
- BRT Nora Ness (1988) (Hybrid, Grog × BRT, Nika)
- BRT Makler (1988) male (Hybrid, Grog, × BRT, Meggi)

- BRT Margeyt Foks Linda (1988) female (Hybrid, Grog × BRT, Meggi)
- BRT Chigis (1988) male (Hybrid, Grog × BRT, Bikichi)
- BRT Cezar (1988) male (Hybrid, Grog × BRT, Bikichi)
- BRT Chara Linda (1988) female (Hybrid, Grog × BRT, Bikichi)
- BRT Olva (1989 (female (Hybrid, Grog × Hybrid, Inara)
- BRT Okris (1989) female (Hybrid, Grog × Hybrid, Inara)
- BRT Odelfiya (1989) female (Hybrid, Grog × Hybrid, Inara)
- BRT Sheyla (1989) female (Hybrid, Grog × BRT, Dzhe Shani)
- BRT Sha Gretta (1989) female (Hybrid, Grog × BRT, Dzhe Shani)
- BRT Ketrin (1990) female (Hybrid, Grog × Hybrid, Linda Bek)
- BRT Shagretta Vayus (1990) female (Hybrid, Grog × Hybrid, Vagris Dors)
- BRT Irokez (1990) male (Hybrid, Grog × BRT, Perri)
- BRT Irka (1990) female (Hybrid, Grog × BRT, Perri)
- BRT Kwadra (1990) female (Hybrid, Grog × Hybrid, Lin Ditta)
- BRT Klara (1990) female (Hybrid, Grog × Hybrid, Lin Ditta)
- Hybrid Izon (1984) male (Hybrid, Yukon × Hybrid, Virdzhiniya Vasilina Asker) There are no currently recorded offspring of Agat
- Hybrid Inara (1984) female (Hybrid, Yukon × Hybrid, Virdzhiniya Vasilina Asker)
- BRT Bardi (1986?) male (Hybrid, Dzhe Aygar × Hybrid, Inara)
- BRT Olva (1989) female (Hybrid, Grog × Hybrid, Inara)
- BRT OKRIS (1989) female (Hybrid, Grog × Hybrid, Inara)
- BRT Odelfiya (1989) female (Hybrid, Grog × Hybrid, Inara)
- BRT Ralf (1989) male (Hybrid, Terri × Hybrid, Inara)
- Hybrid Irika (1984) female (Hybrid, Yukon × Hybrid, Virdzhiniya Vasilina Asker)
- BRT Zhak Lin (1986?) male (BRT, Rich Rey × Hybrid, Irika)
- BRT Paul (1986) male (Hybrid, Konsul × Hybrid, Irika)
- BRT Pepilotta (1986) female (Hybrid, Konsul × Hybrid, Irika)
- BRT Hort (1987) male (Hybrid, Lin Sharman × Hybrid, Irika)
- BRT Heppi (1987) female (Hybrid, Lin Sharman × Hybrid, Irika)
- BRT Hetti (1987) female (Hybrid, Lin Sharman × Hybrid, Irika)
- Hybrid Ivika (1984) female (Hybrid, Yukon × Hybrid, Virdzhiniya Vasilina Asker)
- BRT Terri (1986?) female (Hybrid, Zeman × Hybrid, Ivika) [Note:

sire of Zeman was [new] Giant Schnauzer Jaguar (1982) see
p. 184.]
- Hybrid Kuchum (yr?) male (Hybrid, Deyv × Hybrid, Bagira)
- Hybrid Dzhu Dzherri (yr?) female (Hybrid, Kuchum × Unknown)
- Hybrid Bagira (yr?) female (Hybrid, Martin × Hybrid, Dzhu Dzherri)
- Hybrid Al Berta (1981) female (Hybrid, Karat × Hybrid, Bagira)
- Hybrid Gayde (1975?) female (Hybrid, Gayde × Giant Schnauzer,
  Anni f. Raakzeje)
- Hybrid Bes (1979) male (Hybrid, Bars × Hybrid, Gayde)
- Hybrid Sherri Bek (1982) male (Hybrid, Bes × Hybrid, Ped Shanel)
- Hybrid Sholom (1982) male (Hybrid, Bes × Hybrid, Ped Shanel)
- Hybrid Shella (1982) male (Hybrid, Bes × Hybrid, Ped Shanel)
- BRT Naira (1985) female (Hybrid, Bes × Hybrid, Dolli Bek)
- BRT Nord (1985) male (Hybrid, Bes × Hybrid, Dolli Bek)
- BRT Nika (1985) female (Hybrid, Bes × Hybrid, Dolli Bek)
- BRT Tom-Tifrina (1987) female (Hybrid, Bes × Sherri-Torri)
- Hybrid Tishka (1975) female (Hybrid, Gayde × Giant Schnauzer,
  Anni f. Raakzeje) There are no currently recorded offspring of
  Tishka
- Hybrid Agat (yr?) male (Hybrid, Deyv × Hybrid, Bagira) There are
  no currently recorded offspring of Agat
- Hybrid Mezon (yr?) male (Hybrid, Deyv × Unknown, Vesta)
- Hybrid Hilda (yr?) female (Hybrid, Mezon × Hybrid, Zeyda)
- Hybrid Oks Hort Hilda (1976) male (Hybrid, Oksay × Hybrid, Hilda)
- BRT Vilma (1985) female (Hybrid, Oks Hort Hilda × Hybrid,
  Tsimmi)
- Hybrid Oks Hristina Hilda (1976) female (Hybrid, Oksay × Hybrid,
  Hilda)
- Hybrid Hanzurit (1982) male (Hybrid, Dey Devi × Hybrid, Oks
  Hristina)
- Hybrid Helcher (1982) female (Hybrid, Dey Devi × Hybrid, Oks
  Hristina)
- Hybrid Oks Hanta Hilda (1976) female (Hybrid, Oksay × Hybrid,
  Hilda)
- Hybrid Bagrat-1 (1979) male (Hybrid, Brut Roy Engri × Hybrid, Oks
  Hanta)
- Hybrid Brut Hilda (1979) (Hybrid, Brut Roy Engri × Hybrid, Oks

Hanta)
- Hybrid Shaytan (yr?) male (Hybrid, Deyv × Hybrid, Kara)
- Hybrid Rika (1973) male (Hybrid, Shaytan × Hybrid, Cherri)
- Hybrid Dzherri (1979) female (Hybrid, Char-Tuman × Hybrid, Rika)
- Hybrid Dzhe Aygar (1983) male (Hybrid, Atos × Hybrid, Dzherri)
- Hybrid Dzhe Ahilles 1983 male (Hybrid, Atos × Hybrid, Dzherri)
- Hybrid Terri (1984) male (Hybrid, Atos × Hybrid Dzherri)
- Hybrid, Tegri Bays (1984) female (Hybrid,, Atos × Hybrid, Dzherri)
- BRT Dzhe Tarhan Zhan (1985) male (Hybrid,, Atos × Hybrid, Dzherri)
- BRT Dzhekson (1985) male (Hybrid,, Atos × Hybrid, Dzherri)
- BRT Dzhe-Sharon (1987) male (Hybrid, Lin Sharman × Hybrid, Dzherri)
- BRT Dzhe Shani (1987) female (Hybrid, Lin Sharman × Hybrid, Dzherri)
- BRT Dzhe Shelli (1987) female (Hybrid, Lin Sharman × Hybrid, Dzherri)
- Hybrid Naura (1979) female (Hybrid, Char-Tuman × Hybrid, Rika)
- Hybrid Niksa-Nuch (1984) female (Hybrid, Starlayt × Hybrid, Naura) (Sire and dam of Starlayt are of unknown ancestry)
- Hybrid Bagira (yr?) female (Hybrid, Deyv × Hybrid, Kara)
- Hybrid Kuchum (yr?) male (Hybrid, Deyv × Hybrid, Bagira)
- Hybrid Agat (yr?) male (Hybrid, Deyv × Hybrid, Bagira) (See Bagira offspring data under Hybrids Kuchum and Agat above)
- Hybrid Chvang (1969) male (Hybrid, Deyv × Unknown, Vesta) There are no currently recorded offspring of Chvang
- Hybrid Changa (1969) female (Hybrid, Deyv × Unknown, Vesta)
- Hybrid Oksa (1969) female (Hybrid, Skif × Hybrid, Changa)
- Hybrid Kora (1973) female (Hybrid, Chap × Hybrid, Oksa)
- Hybrid Nemfred (1976) male (Hybrid, Urchan × Hybrid, Kora)
- Hybrid Chika (1969) female (Hybrid, Deyv × Unknown) There are no currently recorded offspring of Chika
- Hybrid Chayka (1969) female (Hybrid, Deyv × Unknown) There are no currently recorded offspring of Chayka
- Hybrid Terri (1970) male (Hybrid, Deyv × Unknown)
- Hybrid Arkas (1975) male (Hybrid, Terri × Hybrid, Donya Nevka)
- Hybrid Tay Markiz (1978) male (Hybrid, Arkas × Hybrid, Tayna-

Mikki)
- Hybrid Neron (1982) male (Hybrid, Tay Markiz × Hybrid, Sandra)
- Hybrid Nora (1982) female (Hybrid, Tay Markiz × Hybrid, Sandra)
- Hybrid Akbar-Bel (1982) male (Hybrid, Tay Markiz × Hybrid, Van Lada)
- Hybrid Arina-Bel (1982) female (Hybrid, Tay Markiz × Hybrid, Van Lada)
- Hybrid Alba-Bel (1982) female (Hybrid, Tay Markiz × Hybrid, Van Lada)
- Hybrid Ayna-Bel (1982) female (Hybrid, Tay Markiz × Hybrid, Van Lada)
- Hybrid Ada (1982) female (Hybrid, Tay Markiz × Hybrid, Van Lada)
- Hybrid Aza-Bel (1982) female (Hybrid, Tay Markiz × Hybrid, Van Lada)
- Hybrid Aya Gans (1984) female (Hybrid, Tay Markiz × Hybrid, Ganna-Fil)
- BRT Ladushka (1987) female (Hybrid, Tay Markiz × Hybrid, Linda)
- Hybrid Yaga (yr?) female (Hybrid, Demon × Hybrid, Mirta)
- Hybrid Galka (yr?) female (Hybrid, Negus × Hybrid, Yaga)
- Hybrid Dega (1962) female (Hybrid, Demon × Hybrid, Galka)
- Hybrid Rams I (1966) male (Hybrid, Foka × Hybrid, Dega)
- Hybrid Charli 1 (yr?) male (Hybrid, Rams I × Hybrid, Chara)
- Hybrid Bush (yr?) male (Hybrid, Rams I × Hybrid, Alba)
- Hybrid Greits (yr?) male (Hybrid, Rams I × Hybrid, Nim Alma)
- Hybrid Shaman (yr?) male (Hybrid, Rams I × Hybrid, Nim Eva)
- Hybrid Al'Princ (1971) male (Hybrid, Rams I × Hybrid, Alba)
- Hybrid Artosha (1971) male (Hybrid, Rams I × Hybrid, Alba)
- Hybrid Rammi (1971) male (Hybrid, Rams I × Hybrid, Nim Alma)
- Hybrid Ereyg (1972) male (Hybrid, Rams I × Hybrid, Nim Alma)
- Hybrid Erna (1972) male (Hybrid, Rams I × Hybrid, Nim Alma)
- Hybrid Shagane (1972) female (Hybrid, Rams I × Hybrid, Varya)
- Hybrid Yulva Zhers (1973) male (Hybrid, Rams I × Hybrid, Dan-Zherri)
- Hybrid Nochka Yulva Zhuzha (1973) female (Hybrid, Rams I × Hybrid, Dan-Zherri)
- Hybrid Yulva Zheni (1973) female (Hybrid, Rams I × Hybrid, Dan-Zherri)

- Hybrid Ort-Zaur (1974) male (Hybrid, Rams I × Hybrid, Dan Orta)
- Hybrid Orri (1974) male (Hybrid, Rams I × Hybrid, Dan Orta)
- Hybrid Tuman (1967) male (Hybrid, Tom × Hybrid, Dega) See Tuman listing starting on p. 32
- Hybrid Jermak (1967) male (Hybrid, Tom × Hybrid, Dega) There are no currently recorded offspring of Jermak
- Hybrid Dzhoya (1967) female (Hybrid, Tom × Hybrid, Dega)
- Hybrid Ayshe (1961) female (Hybrid, Demon × Hybrid, Ledi)
- Hybrid Dzhin (1964) male (Hybrid, Dik × Hybrid, Ayshe) There are no currently recorded offspring of Dzhin
- Hybrid Agat (1964) male (Hybrid, Dik × Hybrid, Ayshe) There are no currently recorded offspring of Agat
- Hybrid Aydina (1964) female (Hybrid, Dik × Hybrid, Ayshe)
- Hybrid Atos (1969) male (Hybrid, Lord × Hybrid, Aydina)
- Hybrid Zeyda (yr?) female (Hybrid, Atos × Hybrid, Dar Karmen)
- Hybrid Hilda (yr?) female (Hybrid, Mezon × Hybrid, Zeyda)
- Hybrid Heppi Er Sherli (yr?) female (Hybrid, Atos × Hybrid, Kheppi)
- Hybrid Sher Buka (yr?) (Hybrid, Gil Devi × Heppi Er Sherli)
- Hybrid Kana (1972) female (Hybrid, Atos × Hybrid, Lera)
- Hybrid Tsuri (1979) female (Hybrid, Tsorn × Hybrid, Kana)
- Hybrid Tayna-Mikki (1973) female (Hybrid, Atos × Hybrid, Raffi)
- Hybrid Tay Markiz (1978) male (Hybrid,Araks × Hybrid, Tayna-Mikki)
- Hybrid Baron (1983) male (Hybrid, Dor Dintay × Hybrid, Tayna-Mikki)
- Hybrid Damir (1970) male (Hybrid, Dzhim × Hybrid, Aydina)
- Hybrid Ahill (1976) male (Hybrid, Damir × Hybrid, Dan-Yaza)
- Hybrid Adasza (yr?) female (Hybrid, Ahill × Hybrid, Pedi)
- Hybrid Vanda (1981) female (Hybrid, Ahill × Unknown)
- Hybrid Bir-Ayshe (1981) female (Hybrid, Ahill × Hybrid, Shel Biruta)
- Hybrid Grimmi Shem (1981) male (Hybrid, Ahill × Hybrid, Shemmi)
- Hybrid Greb Shem (1981) male (Hybrid, Ahill × Hybrid, Shemmi)
- Hybrid Gretta Shem (1981) female (Hybrid, Ahill × Hybrid, Shemmi)
- Hybrid Doris (1981) female (Hybrid, Ahill × Hybrid, Moya Mariya)
- Hybrid Ars (1981) female (Hybrid, Ahill × Hybrid, Vilma)

- Hybrid Vagir-Mak (1982) male (Hybrid, Ahill × Hybrid, Chada)
- Hybrid Vanda Mak (1982) female (Hybrid, Ahill × Hybrid, Chada)
- Hybrid Oktar Asher (1983) male (Hybrid, Ahill × Hybrid, Sherli)
- Hybrid Oskar Asher (1983) male (Hybrid, Ahill × Hybrid, Sherli)
- Hybrid Oris Asher (1983) male (Hybrid, Ahill × Hybrid, Sherli)
- Hybrid Olori Asher (1983) female (Hybrid, Ahill × Hybrid, Sherli)
- Hybrid Ordi Asher (1983) female (Hybrid, Ahill × Hybrid, Sherli)
- Hybrid Ava Almar (1985) female (Hybrid, Ahill, × Hybrid,Alisa)
- Hybrid Asshon [Ralf] (1976) male (Hybrid, Damir × Hybrid, Dan-Yaza)
- Hybrid Tsen Chuk (1979) male (Hybrid, Asshon (Ralf) × Hybrid, Gerta)
- Hybrid Tsaya (1979) female (Hybrid, Asshon (Ralf) × Hybrid, Gerta)
- Hybrid Astor (1976) male (Hybrid, Damir × Hybrid, Dan-Yaza) There are no currently recorded offspring of Dzhin
- Hybrid Adana (1976) female (Hybrid, Damir × Hybrid, Dan-Yaza)
- Hybrid Demon Adan (1981) male (Hybrid, Ted Tulat × Hybrid, Adana)
- Hybrid Darti Adan (1981) male (Hybrid, Asshon (Ralf) × Hybrid, Gerta)
- Hybrid Ledi Adan (1981) female (Hybrid, Asshon (Ralf) × Hybrid, Gerta)
- Hybrid Dan (1970) male (Hybrid, Dzhim × Hybrid, Aydina)
- Hybrid Fer-Ayshe (1974) female (Hybrid, Dan × Hybrid, Ata)
- Hybrid Van Lada (1978) female (Hybrid,Dor Dintay × Hybrid, Fer Ayshe)
- Hybrid Nikta (1974) female (Hybrid, Dan × Hybrid, Ranika)
- Hybrid Dzherik (1976) male (Hybrid, Sedis Sedzh × Hybrid, Nikta)
- Hybrid Lyana (1976) female (Hybrid, Sedis Sedzh × Hybrid, Nikta)
- Hybrid Lasta (1974) female (Hybrid, Dan × Hybrid, Ata) There are no currently recorded offspring of Lasta
- Hybrid Blek-Topaz (1977) male (Hybrid, Dan × Hybrid, Gem Galka)
- Hybrid Taj Ga Dzsuli (yr?) female (Hybrid, Blek Topaz × Hybrid, Ul'Tori)
- Hybrid Beking-Fil (1984) male (Hybrid, Blek-Topaz × Hybrid,

Beata)
- Hybrid Berta-Fil (1984) female (Hybrid, Blek-Topaz × Hybrid, Beata)
- Hybrid Be Aza Fil (1984) female (Hybrid, Blek-Topaz × Hybrid, Beata)
- Hybrid Filipp I (1977) male (Hybrid, Dan × Hybrid, Charodeyka)
- Hybrid Glora Fil (1980) female (Hybrid, Filipp I × Hybrid, Gabi)
- Hybrid Ganna-Fil (1980) female (Hybrid, Filipp I × Hybrid, Gabi)
- Hybrid Deli (1978) female (Hybrid, Dan × Unknown)
- Hybrid Dajna (1982) female (Unknown × Hybrid, Deli)
- Hybrid Topaz (1978) male (Hybrid, Dan × Hybrid, Setti)
- Hybrid Tobbi (1984) male (Hybrid, Topaz × Hybrid, Dzhina)
- Hybrid Teddi (1984) male (Hybrid, Topaz × Hybrid, Dzhina)
- Hybrid Til (1984) male (Hybrid, Topaz × Hybrid, Dzhina)
- Hybrid Kraft (1985) male (Hybrid, Topaz × Hybrid, Ketti Kar)
- Hybrid Katrin (1985) female (Hybrid, Topaz × Hybrid, Ketti Kar)
- Hybrid Karina [Korina] (1985) female (Hybrid, Topaz × Hybrid, Ketti Kar)
- Hybrid Kara (1985) female (Hybrid, Topaz × Hybrid, Ketti Kar)
- Hybrid Terri (1978) female (Hybrid, Dan × Hybrid, Setti)
- Hybrid Noy Boy (1981) male (Hybrid, Ted Tulat × Hybrid, Terri)
- Hybrid Adzhi-Shahra (1964) female (Hybrid, Dik × Hybrid, Ayshe)
- Hybrid Barhan-Zhan (1969) male (Hybrid, Bechel × Adzhi-Shahra)
- Hybrid Sabina-Diana (1973) female (Hybrid, Barhan-Zhan × Hybrid, Rema Greza)
- Hybrid Setti (1973) female (Hybrid, Barhan-Zhan × Hybrid, Rema Greza)
- Hybrid Seggi (1973) female (Hybrid, Barhan-Zhan × Hybrid, Rema Greza)
- Hybrid Rin-Dzhaga (1974) male (Hybrid, Barhan-Zhan × Hybrid, Dor-Ditta)
- Hybrid Rin-Deza (1974) female (Hybrid, Barhan-Zhan × Hybrid, Dor-Ditta)
- Hybrid Tim Ilza (1975) female (Hybrid, Barhan-Zhan × Hybrid, Radzh-Mira)
- Hybrid Bahor Boss (1969) male (Hybrid, Bechel × Adzhi-Shahra)
  There are no currently recorded offspring by Hybrid Bahor Boss

- Hybrid Burkhan (1969) male (Hybrid, Bechel × Adzhi-Shahra)
  There are no currently recorded offspring by Hybrid Burkhan
- Hybrid Bella (1969) female (Hybrid, Bechel × Adzhi-Shahra)
- Hybrid Nerhan (1973) male (Hybrid, Nord × Hybrid, Bella)
- Hybrid Basma (1969) female (Hybrid, Bechel × Adzhi-Shahra)
  There are no currently recorded offspring by Hybrid Basma
- Hybrid Ayda (1964) female (Hybrid, Dik × Hybrid, Ayshe)
- Hybrid Chari (1969) female (Hybrid, Bechel × Hybrid, Ayda)
- Hybrid Poldi Char (1972) female (Hybrid, Dzhim × Hybrid, Chari)
  There are no currently recorded offspring by Hybrid Poldi Char
- Hybrid Men (1969) male (Hybrid, Bechel × Hybrid, Ayda) There
  are no currently recorded offspring by Hybrid Men
- Hybrid Adi (1964) female (Hybrid, Dik × Hybrid, Ayshe)
- Hybrid Zitta (yr?) female (Hybrid, Karat × Hybrid,Adi)
- Hybrid Osman (1967) male (Hybrid, Tom × Hybrid, Adi)
- Hybrid Dinka (1967) female (Hybrid, Tom × Hybrid, Adi)
- Hybrid For-Zhanna (1969) female (Hybrid, Topaz × Hybrid, Adi)
- Hybrid Tana (1969) female (Hybrid, Topaz × Hybrid, Adi)
- Hybrid Tapa (1969) female (Hybrid, Topaz × Hybrid, Adi)
- Hybrid Aida (1964) female (Hybrid, Dik × Hybrid, Ayshe)
- Hybrid Alma (1966) female (Giant Schnauzer, Dasso f.
  Drahenshljuht × Hybrid, Aida)
- Hybrid Lira (1966) female (Giant Schnauzer, Dasso f.
  Drahenshljuht × Hybrid, Aida)
- Hybrid Terri (1966) female (Giant Schnauzer, Dasso f.
  Drahenshljuht × Hybrid, Aida)
- Hybrid Dzhan (1964) female (Hybrid, Dik × Hybrid, Ayshe)
- Hybrid Diva (yr?) female (Hybrid, Viy × Hybrid, Dzhan)
- Hybrid Sekki (1962) female (Hybrid, Demon × Hybrid, Arsa)
- Hybrid Maur (yr?) male (Hybrid, Tuman × Hybrid, Sekki)
- Hybrid Lada (yr?) female (Hybrid, Maur × Unknown, Vlasta
- Hybrid Vega (1974) female (Hybrid, Maur × Hybrid, Vil'da)
- Hybrid Kitri (1967) female (Hybrid, Karat × Hybrid, Sekki)
- Hybrid Zevs (1970) male (Hybrid, Skif × Hybrid,Kitri)
- Hybrid Din (1968) male (Hybrid, Karat × Hybrid, Sekki) There are
  no currently recorded offspring by Hybrid Din
- Hybrid Chada (1968) female (Hybrid, Karat × Hybrid, Sekki)

- Hybrid Charli I (yr?) male (Hybrid, Rams I × Hybrid, Chada)
- Hybrid Lada (yr?) female (Hybrid, Agat × Hybrid, Chada)
- Hybrid Vayda (yr?) female (Hybrid, Vays × Hybrid, Chada)
- Hybrid Eva (yr?) female (Hybrid, Vays × Hybrid, Chada)
- Hybrid Blek-Veda (1968) female (Hybrid, Karat × Hybrid, Sekki)
- Hybrid Argo (1971) male (Hybrid,Alf × Hybrid, Blek-Veda)
- Hybrid Bara (1968) female (Hybrid, Karat × Hybrid, Sekki) There are no currently recorded offspring by Hybrid Bara
- Hybrid Kapitan Flint (1969) male (Hybrid, Topaz × Hybrid, Sekki)
- Hybrid Grey (yr?) male (Hybrid, Kapitan Flint × Hybrid, Dezi)
- Hybrid Gerda (yr?) female (Hybrid, Kapitan Flint × Hybrid, Dezi)
- Hybrid Gertruda (yr?) female (Hybrid, Kapitan Flint × Hybrid, Dezi)
- Hybrid Sello Un (1973) male (Hybrid, Kapitan Flint × Hybrid Ulma)
- Hybrid Sunika Un (1973) female (Hybrid, Kapitan Flint × Hybrid, Ulma)
- Hybrid Santa Un (1973) female (Hybrid, Kapitan Flint × Hybrid, Ulma)
- Hybrid Dzhina (1973) female (Hybrid, Kapitan Flint × Hybrid, Dzhudi)
- Hybrid Din (1973) male (Hybrid, Kapitan Flint × Hybrid, Diva)
- Hybrid Changa (1975) female (Hybrid, Kapitan Flint × Hybrid, Deya)
- Hybrid Dodzh (1976) male (Hybrid, Kapitan Flint × Unknown)
- Hybrid Zhan Grey (1976) male (Hybrid, Kapitan Flint × Hybrid, Chara)
- Hybrid Dega (1962) female (Hybrid, Demon × Hybrid, Galka)
- Hybrid Rams I (1966) male (Hybrid, Foka × Hybrid, Dega)
- Hybrid Charli 1 (yr?) male (Hybrid, Rams I × Hybrid, Chara)
- Hybrid Bush (yr?) male (Hybrid, Rams I × Hybrid, Alba)
- Hybrid Greits (yr?) male (Hybrid, Rams I × Hybrid, Nim Alma)
- Hybrid Shaman (yr?) male (Hybrid, Rams I × Hybrid, Nim Eva)
- Hybrid Al'Princ (1971) male (Hybrid, Rams I × Hybrid, Alba)
- Hybrid Artosha (1971) male (Hybrid, Rams I × Hybrid, Alba)
- Hybrid Rammi (1971) male (Hybrid, Rams I × Hybrid, Nim Alma)
- Hybrid Ereyg (1972) male (Hybrid, Rams I × Hybrid, Nim Alma)
- Hybrid Erna (1972) male (Hybrid, Rams I × Hybrid, Nim Alma)
- Hybrid Shagane (1972) female (Hybrid, Rams I × Hybrid, Varya)

- Hybrid Yulva Zhers (1973) male (Hybrid, Rams I × Hybrid, Dan-Zherri)
- Hybrid Nochka Yulva Zhuzha (1973) female (Hybrid, Rams I × Hybrid, Dan-Zherri)
- Hybrid Yulva Zheni (1973) female (Hybrid, Rams I × Hybrid, Dan-Zherri)
- Hybrid Ort-Zaur (1974) male (Hybrid, Rams I × Hybrid, Dan Orta)
- Hybrid Orri (1974) male (Hybrid, Rams I × Hybrid, Dan Orta)
- Hybrid Tuman (1967) male (Hybrid, Tom × Hybrid, Dega) See Tuman listing starting below on p. 32
- Hybrid Jermak (1967) male (Hybrid, Tom × Hybrid, Dega) There are no currently recorded offspring by Hybrid Jermak
- Hybrid Dzhoya (1967) female (Hybrid, Tom × Hybrid, Dega)
- Hybrid Dan Daros (1969) male (Hybrid, Viy × Hybrid, Dzhoya)
- Hybrid Dan-Darsi (1969) female (Hybrid, Viy × Hybrid, Dzhoya)
- Hybrid Dan-Dingo (1969) female (Hybrid, Viy × Hybrid, Dzhoya)
- Hybrid Dan-Dzhoya (1969) female (Hybrid, Viy × Hybrid, Dzhoya)
- Hybrid Dan-Daza (1969) female (Hybrid, Viy × Hybrid, Dzhoya)
- Hybrid Dan-Zhan (1970) male (Hybrid, Dzhim × Hybrid, Dzhoya)
- Hybrid Dan-Zhuan (1970) male (Hybrid, Dzhim × Hybrid, Dzhoya)
- Hybrid Dan-Zhak (1970) male (Hybrid, Dzhim × Hybrid, Dzhoya)
- Hybrid Dan-Zhenni (1970) female (Hybrid, Dzhim × Hybrid, Dzhoya)
- Hybrid Dan-Zhaklin (1970) female (Hybrid, Dzhim × Hybrid, Dzhoya)
- Hybrid Dan-Olchigem (1972) male (Hybrid, Ayaks [Ajaks] × Hybrid, Dzhoya)
- Hybrid Dan Oskar (1972) male (Hybrid, Ayaks [Ajaks] × Hybrid, Dzhoya)
- Hybrid Dan-Orta (1972) female (Hybrid, Ayaks [Ajaks] × Hybrid, Dzhoya)
- Hybrid Dan-Odzhina (1972) female (Hybrid, Ayaks [Ajaks] × Hybrid, Dzhoya)
- Hybrid Dan-Yaza (1974) female (Hybrid, Anchar × Hybrid, Dzhoya)
- Hybrid Dan-Yamika (1974) female (Hybrid, Anchar × Hybrid, Dzhoya)

- Hybrid Dan-Jana (Dan-Janka) (1974) female (Hybrid, Anchar × Hybrid, Dzhoya)
- Hybrid Dan Grey (1975) male (Hybrid, Gil Devi × Hybrid, Dzhoya)
- Hybrid Dzhessi (1963) female (Hybrid, Demon × Hybrid, Ledi)
- Hybrid Arma (yr?) female (Hybrid, Tom × Hybrid, Dzhessi) There are no currently recorded offspring by Hybrid Arma
- Hybrid Roza (1963) female (Giant Schnauzer, Dasso f. Drahenshljuht × Hybrid, Dzhessi)
- Hybrid Nord (1969) male (Hybrid, Uran × Hybrid, Roza) There are no currently recorded offspring by Hybrid Nord
- Hybrid Robin (1966) male (Hybrid, Viy × Hybrid, Dzhessi) There are no currently recorded offspring by Hybrid Robin
- Hybrid Sarra [Sara] (1966) female (Hybrid, Viy × Hybrid, Dzhessi)
- Hybrid Re-Byuti (1968) female (Hybrid, Dik × Hybrid, Sarra [Sara])
- Hybrid Re-Dzhon (1968) female (Hybrid, Dik × Hybrid, Sarra [Sara])
- Hybrid Re-Dik-Sar (1968) female (Hybrid, Dik × Hybrid, Sarra [Sara])
- Hybrid Blek (1964) male (Hybrid, Demon × Unknown, Sekki) There are no currently recorded offspring by Hybrid Blek

1958 Family Lines Based on Hybrid Dik male

(Crossbreed, Haytar × Hybrid, Vishnya)
- Hybrid Re-Dzhek (yr?) male (Hybrid, Dik × Unknown) There are no currently recorded offspring of Re-Dzhek
- Hybrid Re-Byuti (yr?) female (Hybrid, Dik × Hybrid, Sarra [Sara]) There are no currently recorded offspring of Re-Byuti
- Hybrid Dzhin (1964) male (Hybrid, Dik × Hybrid, Ayshe) There are no currently recorded offspring of Dzhin
- Hybrid Agat (1964) male (Hybrid, Dik × Hybrid, Ayshe) There are no currently recorded offspring of Agat
- Hybrid Aydina (1964) female (Hybrid, Dik × Hybrid, Ayshe)
- Hybrid Atos (1969) male (Hybrid, Lord × Hybrid, Aydina)
- Hybrid Damir (1970) male (Hybrid, Azhim × Hybrid, Aydina)
- Hybrid Dan (1970) male (Hybrid, Azhim × Hybrid, Aydina)
- Hybrid Adzhi-Shahra (1964) female (Hybrid, Dik × Hybrid, Ayshe)
- Hybrid Barhan-Zhan (1969) male (Hybrid, Bechel × Hybrid,

Adzhi-Shahra)
- Hybrid Bhor Boss (1969) male (Hybrid, Bechel × Hybrid, Adzhi-Shahra)
- Hybrid Burkhan (1969) male (Hybrid, Bechel × Hybrid, Adzhi-Shahra)
- Hybrid Bella (1969) female (Hybrid, Bechel × Hybrid, Adzhi-Shahra)
- Hybrid Basma (1969) female (Hybrid, Bechel × Hybrid, Adzhi-Shahra)
- Hybrid Ayda (1964) female (Hybrid, Dik × Hybrid, Ayshe)
- Hybrid Men (1969) male (Hybrid, Bechel × Hybrid, Ayda)
- Hybrid Chari (1969) female (Hybrid, Bechel × Hybrid, Ayda)
- Hybrid Adi (1964) female (Hybrid, Dik × Hybrid, Ayshe)
- Hybrid Zitta (yr?) female (Hybrid, Karat × Hybrid, Adi)
- Hybrid Osman (1967) male (Hybrid, Tom × Hybrid, Adi)
- Hybrid Dinka (1967) female (Hybrid, Tom × Hybrid, Adi)
- Hybrid For-Zhanna (1969) female (Hybrid, Topaz × Hybrid, Adi)
- Hybrid Tana (1969) female (Hybrid, Topaz × Hybrid, Adi)
- Hybrid Tapa (1969) female (Hybrid, Topaz × Hybrid, Adi)
- Hybrid Aida (1964) female (Hybrid, Dik × Hybrid, Ayshe)
- Hybrid Terri (1966) male (Giant Schnauzer, Dasso f. Drahenshljuht × Hybrid, Aida)
- Hybrid Alma (1966) female (Giant Schnauzer, Dasso f. Drahenshljuht × Hybrid, Aida)
- Hybrid Lira (1966) female (Giant Schnauzer, Dasso f. Drahenshljuht × Hybrid, Aida)
- Hybrid Dzhan (1964) female (Hybrid, Dik × Hybrid, Ayshe)
- Hybrid Diva (yr?) female (Hybrid, Viy × Hybrid, Dzhan)
- Hybrid Dzhema (1964) female (Hybrid, Dik × Unknown, Lada)
  There are no currently recorded offspring of Dzhema
- Hybrid Pirat-Anchar (1964) female (Hybrid, Dik × Unknown, Lada)
  There are no currently recorded offspring of Pirat-Anchar
- Hybrid Skif (1965) male (Hybrid, Dik × Hybrid, Nastya)
- Hybrid Zevs (1970) male (Hybrid, Skif × Hybrid, Kitri)
- Hybrid Lusha (1971) female (Hybrid, Skif × Hybrid, Dar Ritsa)
- Hybrid Layma (1971) female (Hybrid, Skif × Hybrid, Dar Ritsa)
- Hybrid Lapa (1971) female (Hybrid, Skif × Hybrid, Dar Ritsa)

- Hybrid Oksa (1971) female (Hybrid, Skif × Hybrid, Changa)
- Hybrid Saks (1965) male (Hybrid, Dik × Hybrid, Nastya) There are no currently recorded offspring of Saks
- Hybrid Smok (1965) male (Hybrid, Dik × Hybrid, Nastya) There are no currently recorded offspring of Smok
- Hybrid Stesha (1965) female (Hybrid, Dik × Hybrid, Nastya)
- Hybrid Ayaks (Ajaks) (1967) male (Hybrid, Karat × Hybrid, Stesha)
- Hybrid Antey (1967) male (Hybrid, Karat × Hybrid, Stesha)
- Hybrid Ayna (1967) female (Hybrid, Karat × Hybrid, Stesha)
- Hybrid Arni (1967) female (Hybrid, Karat × Hybrid, Stesha)
- Hybrid Arisha (1967) female (Hybrid, Karat × Hybrid, Stesha)
- Hybrid Ada (1967) female (Hybrid, Karat × Hybrid, Stesha)
- Hybrid Atika (1967) female (Hybrid, Karat × Hybrid, Stesha)
- Hybrid Arta (1967) female (Hybrid, Karat × Hybrid, Stesha)
- Hybrid Ryzhiy (1966) male (Hybrid, Dik × Hybrid, Nastya) There are no currently recorded offspring of Ryzhiy
- Hybrid Roksa (1966) female (Hybrid, Dik × Hybrid, Nastya)
- Hybrid Vays (1969) male (Hybrid, Lord × Hybrid, Roksa)
- Hybrid Viking (1969) male (Hybrid, Lord × Hybrid, Roksa)
- Hybrid Vard (1969) male (Hybrid, Lord × Hybrid, Roksa)
- Hybrid Venta (1969) female (Hybrid, Lord × Hybrid, Roksa)
- Hybrid Varya (1969) female (Hybrid, Lord × Hybrid, Roksa)
- Hybrid Tseron (1972) male (Hybrid, Lord × Hybrid, Roksa)
- Hybrid Tsatsa (1972) female (Hybrid, Lord × Hybrid, Roksa)
- Hybrid Tseyla (1972) female (Hybrid, Lord × Hybrid, Roksa)
- Hybrid Ruza (1966) female (Hybrid, Dik × Hybrid, Nastya)
- Hybrid Jolka (1969) female (Hybrid, Fang × Hybrid, Ruza)
- Hybrid Radda (1966) female (Hybrid, Dik × Hybrid, Nastya)
- Hybrid Dym Varyag (1969) male (Hybrid, Oskar × Hybrid, Radda)
- Hybrid Dzhafar (1969) male (Hybrid, Oskar × Hybrid, Radda)
- Hybrid Donya Nevka (1969) female (Hybrid, Oskar × Hybrid, Radda)
- Hybrid Dara (1969) female (Hybrid, Oskar × Hybrid, Radda)
- Hybrid Dasha (1969) female (Hybrid, Oskar × Hybrid, Radda)
- Hybrid Rufa (1966) female (Hybrid, Dik × Hybrid, Nastya) There are no currently recorded offspring of Rufa
- Hybrid Vud (1967) male (Hybrid, Dik × Hybrid, Velta)

- Hybrid Kerri (yr?) female (Hybrid, Vud × Hybrid, Chara)
- Hybrid Dzhilda (yr?) female (Hybrid, Vud × Hybrid, Chara)
- Hybrid Leda (yr?) female (Hybrid, Vud × Hybrid, Chara)
- Hybrid Dinga (yr?) female (Hybrid, Vud × Hybrid, Dzhulja)
- Hybrid Rams 2 (yr?) female (Hybrid, Vud × Hybrid, Diva)
- Hybrid Devi (yr?) female (Hybrid, Vud × Hybrid, Diva)
- Hybrid Kleopatra (1971) female (Hybrid, Vud × Hybrid, Miledi)
- Hybrid Dzhudi (1971) female (Hybrid, Vud × Hybrid, Miledi)
- Hybrid Chapa (1967) female (Hybrid, Dik × Hybrid, Velta) There are no currently recorded offspring of Chapa
- Hybrid Chana (1967) female (Hybrid, Dik × Hybrid, Velta) There are no currently recorded offspring of Chana
- Hybrid Tishka (1967) male (Hybrid, Dik × Hybrid, Nora)
- Hybrid Atos (yr?) male (Hybrid, Tishka × Hybrid, Chara)
- Hybrid Nik-Din (1972) male (Hybrid, Tishka × Hybrid, Lada)
- Hybrid Neda (1972) male (Hybrid, Tishka × Hybrid, Lada)
- Hybrid Dvin (1967) male (Hybrid, Dik × Hybrid, Velta) There are no currently recorded offspring of Dvin
- Hybrid Devel-Blek (1967) male (Hybrid, Dik × Hybrid, Velta) There are no currently recorded offspring of Devel-Blek
- Hybrid Dzhenni-Vega (1967) female (Hybrid, Dik × Hybrid, Velta) There are no currently recorded offspring of Dzhenni
- Hybrid Re-Dzhon (1968) male (Hybrid, Dik × Hybrid, Sarra [Sara] There are no currently recorded offspring of Re-Dzhon
- Hybrid Re-Dik-Sar (1968) male (Hybrid, Dik × Hybrid, Sarra [Sara] There are no currently recorded offspring of Re-Dik-Sar
- Hybrid Vik (1968) male (Hybrid, Dik × Hybrid, Velta) There are no currently recorded offspring of Vik

1958 Family Lines Based on Hybrid Shaytan male
(Hybrid, Dik × Crossbreed, Ahta)
- Hybrid Nayt (1964) male (Hybrid, Shaytan × Crossbreed, Teya) For offspring by Nayt see his entry at p. 28
- Hybrid Chap (1964) male (Hybrid, Shaytan × Crossbreed, Teya) There are no currently recorded offspring by Hybrid Chap

1959 Family Lines Based on Hybrid Ledi female
(Moscow Waterdog, Grum × Hybrid, Ginta)
- Hybrid Ayshe (1961) female (Hybrid, Demon × Hybrid, Ledi) See listing under Hybrid Demon (1957)
- Hybrid Dzhessi (1963) female (Hybrid, Demon × Hybrid, Ledi) See listing under Hybrid Demon (1957)

1960 Family Lines Based on Giant Schnauzer Dasso f. Drahenshljuht male
(Giant Schnauzer, Ajax vom Kliatal × Giant Schnauzer, Azra f. Notr-Dam)
- Hybrid Lera (yr?) female (Giant Schnauzer, Dasso f. Drahenshljuht × Hybrid, Ila)
- Hybrid Darli (1970) male (Hybrid, Nayt × Hybrid, Lera)
- Hybrid, Dega (1970) female (Hybrid, Nayt × Hybrid, Lera)
- Hybrid Kana (1972) female (Hybrid, Atos × Hybrid, Lera)
- Hybrid Reks (yr?) male (Giant Schnauzer, Dasso f. Drahenshljuht × Hybrid, Gloriya)
- Hybrid Dezi (1971) female (Hybrid, Reks × Hybrid, Lada)
- Crossbreed Changa (1962) female (Giant Schnauzer, Dasso f. Drahenshljuht × Crossbreed, Teya)
- Hybrid Farlaf (yr?) male (Hybrid, Deyv × Crossbreed, Changa)
- Hybrid Agat (1969) male (Hybrid, Topaz × Crossbreed, Changa)
- Hybrid Alba (1969) female (Hybrid, Topaz × Crossbreed, Changa)
- Hybrid Deya (1971) female (Hybrid, Agat × Crossbreed, Changa)
- Hybrid Aza (1973) female (Hybrid, Chuk × Crossbreed, Changa)
- Hybrid Algredi (1973) female (Hybrid, Chuk × Crossbreed, Changa)
- Hybrid Roza (1963) female (Giant Schnauzer, Dasso f. Drahenshljuht × Hybrid, Dzhessi)
- Hybrid Nord (1969) male (Hybrid, Uran × Hybrid, Roza)
- Hybrid Ditta (1964) female (Giant Schnauzer, Dasso f. Drahenshljuht × Hybrid, Vanda)
- Hybrid Karay (1967) male (Hybrid, Nayt × Hybrid, Ditta)
- Hybrid Jar (1967) male (Hybrid, Nayt × Hybrid, Ditta)

- Hybrid Dina II (1967) female (Hybrid, Nayt × Hybrid, Ditta)
- Hybrid Dar-Ditta (1967) female (Hybrid, Nayt × Hybrid, Ditta)
- Hybrid Dzhun (1967) female (Hybrid, Nayt × Hybrid, Ditta)
- Hybrid Denas (1968) male (Hybrid, Nayt × Hybrid, Ditta)
- Hybrid Darli (1968) male (Hybrid, Nayt × Hybrid, Ditta)
- Hybrid Dinar (1968) male (Hybrid, Nayt × Hybrid, Ditta)
- Hybrid Dar-Ditsa (1968) male (Hybrid, Nayt × Hybrid, Ditta)
- Hybrid Danchar (1972) male (Hybrid, Dzhaga × Hybrid, Ditta)
- Hybrid Dzhaga (1965) male (Giant Schnauzer, Dasso f. Drahenshljuht × Hybrid, Berta)
- Hybrid Dzhin (yr?) male (Hybrid, Dzhaga × Unknown)
- Hybrid Kora (yr?) female (Hybrid, Dzhaga × Hybrid, Nayda)
- Hybrid Demon (yr?) male (Hybrid, Dzhaga × Hybrid, Alfa)
- Hybrid Darti (yr?) male (Hybrid, Dzhaga × Hybrid, Yuta [Yutta])
- Hybrid Unga (1970) female (Hybrid, Dzhaga × Hybrid, Yuta [Yutta])
- Hybrid Urchan (1970) male (Hybrid, Dzhaga × Hybrid, Yuta [Yutta])
- Hybrid Zhela (1971) female (Hybrid, Dzhaga × Hybrid, Ata)
- Hybrid Urs (1971) male (Hybrid, Dzhaga × Hybrid, Karmen)
- Hybrid Radzh Muk (1971) male (Hybrid, Dzhaga × Hybrid, Raksha)
- Hybrid Radzh-Mira (1971) female (Hybrid, Dzhaga × Hybrid, Raksha)
- Hybrid Radzh-Mymra (1971) female (Hybrid, Dzhaga × Hybrid, Raksha)
- Hybrid Radzh-Mayra (1971) female (Hybrid, Dzhaga × Hybrid, Raksha)
- Hybrid Danchar (1972) male (Hybrid, Dzhaga × Hybrid, Ditta)
- Hybrid Vesta (1973) female (Hybrid, Dzhaga × Hybrid,Yuna)
- Hybrid Lassi (1965) female (Giant Schnauzer, Dasso f. Drahenshljuht × Hybrid, Berta) There are no currently recorded offspring of Lassi
- Hybrid Dzhina (1965) female (Giant Schnauzer, Dasso f. Drahenshljuht × Hybrid, Ila) There are no currently recorded offspring of Dzhina

- Crossbreed Tsezar (1966) male (Giant Schnauzer, Dasso f. Drahenshljuht × Crossbreed, Teya)
- Hybrid Dezi (yr?) female (Crossbreed, Tzezar × Hybrid, Dina I)
- Hybrid Roj (Roy) (yr?) male (Crossbreed, Tzezar × Hybrid, Dina I)
- Hybrid Kassij (yr?) male (Crossbreed, Tzezar × Hybrid, Dina I)
- Hybrid Bakhram (yr?) male (Crossbreed, Tzezar × Hybrid, Dina I)
- Hybrid Yudzhin (yr?) male (Crossbreed, Tzezar × Hybrid, Dina I)
- Hybrid Alma (1966) female (Giant Schnauzer, Dasso f. Drahenshljuht × Hybrid, Aida)
- Hybrid Karu (1970) male (Hybrid, Dzhek × Hybrid, Alma)
- Hybrid Karolina (1970) female (Hybrid, Dzhek × Hybrid, Alma)
- Hybrid Kristi (1970) female (Hybrid, Dzhek × Hybrid, Alma)
- Hybrid Kassi (1970) female (Hybrid, Dzhek × Hybrid, Alma)
- Hybrid Lira (1966) female (Giant Schnauzer, Dasso f. Drahenshljuht × Hybrid, Aida)
- Hybrid Ljuter (Luther?) (1969) male (Hybrid, Lord × Hybrid, Lira)
- Hybrid Loli (1969) female (Hybrid, Lord × Hybrid, Lira)
- Hybrid Terri (1966) male (Giant Schnauzer, Dasso f. Drahenshljuht × Hybrid, Aida) There are no currently recorded offspring of Terri

1960 Family Lines Based on Giant Schnauzer Ditter f. Drahenshljuht male

(Giant Schnauzer, Ajax vom Kliatal × Giant Schnauzer, Azra f. Notr-Dam) (Ditter's pepper and salt coat would have had a profound genetic effect through his substantial breedings)

- Hybrid Gajda [Gayda] (yr?) female Giant Schnauzer, Ditter f. Drahenshljuht, × Unknown) There are no currently recorded offspring of Gajda [Gayda]
- Hybrid Meggi (1961) female (Giant Schnauzer, Ditter f. Drahenshljuht × Hybrid, Gayda)
- Hybrid Oskar (1964) male (Crossbreed, Vah × Hybrid, Meggi)
- Hybrid Velta (1964) female (Crossbreed, Vah × Hybrid, Meggi)
- Hybrid Darling (1964) female (Crossbreed, Vah × Hybrid, Meggi)
- Hybrid Vilma (1962) female (Giant Schnauzer, Ditter f. Drahenshljuht × Hybrid, Vanda)

- Hybrid Arstan (1966) male (Hybrid, Daks × Hybrid, Vilma)
- Hybrid Gaj [Gay] (1966) male (Hybrid, Daks × Hybrid, Vilma)
- Hybrid Richard (1966) male (Hybrid, Daks × Hybrid, Vilma)
- Hybrid Estera-Rokka (1966) female (Hybrid, Daks × Hybrid, Vilma)
- Hybrid Veda (1962) female (Giant Schnauzer, Ditter f. Drahenshljuht × Hybrid, Vanda)
- Hybrid Alf (1966) male (Hybrid, Daks × Hybrid, Veda)
- Hybrid Antej [Antey] (1966) male (Hybrid, Daks × Hybrid, Veda)
- Hybrid Blek-Boj [Blek-Boy] (1966) male (Hybrid, Daks × Hybrid, Veda)
- Hybrid Mukhtar (1966) male (Hybrid, Daks × Hybrid, Veda)
- Hybrid Rynda (1966) female (Hybrid, Daks × Hybrid, Veda)
- Hybrid Nora (1962) female (Giant Schnauzer, Ditter f. Drahenshljuht × Hybrid, Vanda)
- Hybrid Darling (1965) male (Hybrid, Daks × Hybrid, Nora)
- Hybrid Inga (1965) female (Hybrid, Daks × Hybrid, Nora)
- Hybrid Dzhina (1965) female (Hybrid, Daks × Hybrid, Nora)
- Hybrid Til'Da (1965) female (Hybrid, Daks × Hybrid, Nora)
- Hybrid Tishka (1967) male (Hybrid, Dik × Hybrid, Nora)
- Hybrid Dega (1963) female (Giant Schnauzer, Ditter f. Drahenshljuht × Hybrid, Mirta)
- Hybrid Zhanna (1965) female (Hybrid, Viy × Hybrid, Dega)
- Hybrid Girey (1967) male (Hybrid, Nayt × Hybrid, Dega)
- Hybrid Gosha (1967) male (Hybrid, Nayt × Hybrid, Dega)
- Hybrid Grayt (1967) male (Hybrid, Nayt × Hybrid, Dega)
- Hybrid Gana (1967) female (Hybrid, Nayt × Hybrid, Dega)
- Hybrid Borey (1969) male (Hybrid, Nayt × Hybrid, Dega)
- Hybrid Beta (1969) female (Hybrid, Nayt × Hybrid, Dega)
- Hybrid Nur (1971) male (Hybrid, Torri × Hybrid, Dega)

1961 Family Lines Based on Hybrid Ayshe female
(Hybrid, Demon × Hybrid, Ledi) See listing under Hybrid Demon (1957)

1963 Family Lines Based on Hybrid Dzhessi female
(Hybrid, Demon × Hybrid, Ledi) See listing under Hybrid Demon (1957)

1964 Family Lines Based on Hybrid Nayt male

(Hybrid, Shaytan × Crossbreed, Teya)

- Hybrid Miledi (date) female (Hybrid, Nayt × Hybrid, Dzhina)
- Hybrid Yarayt (yr?) male (Hybrid, Darli × Hybrid, Miledi)
- Hybrid Kleopatra (1971) female (Hybrid, Vud × Hybrid, Miledi)
- Hybrid Karay (1967) male (Hybrid, Nayt × Hybrid, Ditta)
- Hybrid Potap (yr?) male (Hybrid, Karay × Unknown)
- Hybrid Irokez (yr?) male (Hybrid, Karay × Unknown)
- Hybrid Irbis (1970) male (Hybrid, Karay × Hybrid, Ayna)
- Hybrid Ildar (1970) male (Hybrid, Karay × Hybrid, Ayna)
- Hybrid Irgiz (1970) male (Hybrid, Karay × Hybrid, Ayna)
- Hybrid Irisha (1970) female (Hybrid, Karay × Hybrid, Ayna)
- Hybrid Inza (1970) female (Hybrid, Karay × Hybrid, Ayna)
- Hybrid Set (1971) male (Hybrid, Karay × Hybrid, Arni)
- Hybrid Irtish (1976) male (Hybrid, Karay × Hybrid, Irisha)
- Hybrid Irvish (1976) male (Hybrid, Karay × Hybrid, Irisha)
- Hybrid Ivan-SF (1976) male (Hybrid, Karay × Hybrid, Irisha)
- Hybrid Jar (1967) male (Hybrid, Nayt × Hybrid, Ditta) There are no currently recorded offspring of Jar
- Hybrid Dina II (1967) female (Hybrid, Nayt × Hybrid, Ditta)
- Hybrid Ulma (1969) female (Hybrid, Topaz × Hybrid, Dina II)
- Hybrid Todi (1969) male (Hybrid, Topaz × Hybrid, Dina II)
- Hybrid Agat (1969) male (Hybrid, Topaz × Hybrid, Dina II)
- Hybrid Dar-Ditta (1967) female (Hybrid, Nayt × Hybrid, Ditta) There are no currently recorded offspring of Dar-Ditta)
- Hybrid Dzhun (1967) female (Hybrid, Nayt × Hybrid, Ditta) There are no currently recorded offspring of Dzhun
- Hybrid Girey (1967) male (Hybrid, Nayt × Hybrid, Dega) There are no currently recorded offspring of Terri
- Hybrid Gosha (1967) male (Hybrid, Nayt × Hybrid, Dega) There are no currently recorded offspring of Gosha
- Hybrid Grayt (1967) male (Hybrid, Nayt × Hybrid, Dega) There are no currently recorded offspring of Grayt
- Hybrid Gana (1967) male (Hybrid, Nayt × Hybrid, Dega) There are no currently recorded offspring of Gana
- Hybrid Denas (1968) male (Hybrid, Nayt × Hybrid, Dega) There are no currently recorded offspring of Gana

- Hybrid Darli (1968) male (Hybrid, Nayt × Hybrid, Dega) There are no currently recorded offspring of Darli
- Hybrid Dinar (1968) male (Hybrid, Nayt × Hybrid, Dega) There are no currently recorded offspring of Dinar
- Hybrid Dar Ritsa (1968) male (Hybrid, Nayt × Hybrid, Dega)
- Hybrid Lusha (1971) female (Hybrid, Skif × Hybrid, Dar Ritsa)
- Hybrid Layma (1971) female (Hybrid, Skif × Hybrid, Dar Ritsa)
- Hybrid Lapa (1971) female (Hybrid, Skif × Hybrid, Dar Ritsa)
- Hybrid Vaksa (1973) female (Hybrid, Karu × Hybrid, Dar Ritsa)
- Hybrid Hippi (1968) male (Hybrid, Nayt × Hybrid, Dzhina) There are no currently recorded offspring of Hippi
- Hybrid Borey (1969) male (Hybrid, Nayt × Hybrid, Dega) There are no currently recorded offspring of Borey
- Hybrid Beta (1969) female (Hybrid, Nayt × Hybrid, Dega)
- Hybrid Martin (yr?) male (Hybrid, Ayaks [Ajaks] × Hybrid, Beta)
- Hybrid Muza (yr?) female (Hybrid, Ayaks [Ajaks] × Hybrid, Beta)
- Hybrid Molloh (1971) male (Hybrid, Lord × Hybrid, Beta)
- Hybrid Misha (1971) male (Hybrid, Lord × Hybrid, Beta)
- Hybrid Mavr (1971) male (Hybrid, Lord × Hybrid, Beta)
- Hybrid Mars (1971) male (Hybrid, Lord × Hybrid, Beta)
- Hybrid Masha (1971) female (Hybrid, Lord × Hybrid, Beta)
- Hybrid Malva (1971) female (Hybrid, Lord × Hybrid, Beta)
- Hybrid Malta (1971) female (Hybrid, Lord × Hybrid, Beta)
- Hybrid Mika (1971) female (Hybrid, Lord × Hybrid, Beta)
- Hybrid Darli (1970) male (Hybrid, Nayt × Hybrid, Lera)
- Hybrid Yarayt (yr?) male (Hybrid, Darli × Hybrid, Miledi)
- Hybrid Dega (1970) female (Hybrid, Nayt × Hybrid, Lera) There are no currently recorded offspring of Dega

1964 Family Lines Based on Hybrid Tom male
(Crossbreed, Gay × Hybrid, Dina)
- Hybrid Dzhim (yr?) male (Hybrid Tom × Crossbreed, Panta)
- Hybrid Cherri (yr?) female (Hybrid, Tom × Hybrid, Dzhina)
- Hybrid Arma (yr?) female (Hybrid, Tom × Hybrid, Dzhessi)
- Hybrid Nora (1966) female (Hybrid, Tom × Hybrid, Irda)
- Hybrid Lord (1966) male (Hybrid, Tom × Hybrid, Dina I)
- Hybrid Osman (1967) male (Hybrid, Tom × Hybrid, Adi)

- Hybrid Dinka (1967) female (Hybrid, Tom × Hybrid, Adi)
- Hybrid Dzhim (1967) male (Hybrid, Tom × Hybrid, Dzhina)
- Hybrid Nensi (1967) female (Hybrid, Tom × Hybrid, Dzhina)
- Hybrid Topaz (1967) male (Hybrid, Tom × Hybrid, Lada)
- Hybrid Tuman (1967) male (Hybrid, Tom × Hybrid, Dega) See Tuman listing starting on p. 32
- Hybrid Jermak (1967) male (Hybrid, Tom × Hybrid, Dega)
- Hybrid Dzhoya (1967) female (Hybrid, Tom × Hybrid, Dega) See Dzhoya listing under Hybrid Dega above
- Hybrid Yuta [Yutta] (1968) female (Hybrid, Tom × Hybrid, Rokki)

1964 Family Lines Based on Hybrid Karat male
(Hybrid, Foka × Hybrid, Nayda)
- Hybrid Raksha (yr?) female (Hybrid, Karat × Hybrid, Irda)
- Hybrid Rokki (yr?) female (Hybrid, Karat × Crossbreed, Dila)
- Hybrid Zitta (yr?) female (Hybrid, Karat × Hybrid, Adi)
- Hybrid Dzhek (1966) male (Hybrid, Karat × Hybrid, Ata)
- Hybrid Bechel (1966) male (Hybrid, Karat × Crossbreed, Ila)
- Hybrid Dzhim (1966) male (Hybrid, Karat × Crossbreed, Teya)
- Hybrid Nayda (1966) female (Hybrid, Karat × Crossbreed, Teya)
- Hybrid Chanita (1966) female (Hybrid, Karat × Crossbreed, Teya)
- Hybrid Vita (1966) female (Hybrid, Karat × Crossbreed, Teya)
- Hybrid Lada (1967) female (Hybrid, Karat × Hybrid, Irda)
- Hybrid Irda (1967) female (Hybrid, Karat × Hybrid, Irda)
- Hybrid Kitri (1967) female (Hybrid, Karat × Hybrid, Sekki)
- Hybrid Ayaks [Ajaks] (1967) male (Hybrid, Karat × Hybrid, Stesha)
- Hybrid Antey (1967) male (Hybrid, Karat × Hybrid, Stesha)
- Hybrid Ayna (1967) female (Hybrid, Karat × Hybrid, Stesha)
- Hybrid Arni (1967) female (Hybrid, Karat × Hybrid, Stesha)
- Hybrid Arisha (1967) female (Hybrid, Karat × Hybrid, Stesha)
- Hybrid Ada (1967) female (Hybrid, Karat × Hybrid, Stesha)
- Hybrid Atika (1967) female (Hybrid, Karat × Hybrid, Stesha)
- Hybrid Arta (1967) female (Hybrid, Karat × Hybrid, Stesha)
- Hybrid Dzhim (1968) male (Hybrid, Karat × Hybrid, Nora)
- Hybrid Din (1968) male (Hybrid, Karat × Hybrid, Sekki)
- Hybrid Chada (1968) female (Hybrid, Karat × Hybrid, Sekki)
- Hybrid Blek-Veda (1968) female (Hybrid, Karat × Hybrid, Sekki)

- Hybrid Bara (1968) female (Hybrid, Karat × Hybrid, Sekki)
- (Hybrid Chuk (1968) male (Hybrid, Karat × Hybrid, Irda)
- (Hybrid Chara (1968) female (Hybrid, Karat × Hybrid, Irda)
- (Hybrid Chuta (1968) female (Hybrid, Karat × Hybrid, Irda)
- (Hybrid Chili (1968) female (Hybrid, Karat × Hybrid, Irda)
- (Hybrid Chana (1968) female (Hybrid, Karat × Hybrid, Irda)

1967 Family Lines Based on Hybrid Vud male
(Hybrid, Dik × Hybrid, Velta)

- Hybrid Kerri (yr?) female (Hybrid, Vud × Hybrid, Chara)
- Hybrid Dzhilda (yr?) female (Hybrid, Vud × Hybrid, Chara)
- Hybrid Leda (yr?) female (Hybrid, Vud × Hybrid, Chara)
- Hybrid Dinga (yr?) female (Hybrid, Vud × Hybrid, Dzhula) There are no currently recorded offspring of Dinga
- Hybrid Rams 2 (yr?) male (Hybrid, Vud × Hybrid, Diva)
- Hybrid Eva (yr?) female (Hybrid, Rams 2 × Hybrid, Chuta)
- Hybrid Charodeyka (yr?) female (Hybrid, Rams 2 × Hybrid, Chuta)
- Hybrid Devi (yr?) male (Hybrid, Vud × Hybrid, Diva) There are no currently recorded offspring of Devi
- Hybrid Kleopatra (1971) female (Hybrid, Vud × Hybrid, Miledi)
- Hybrid Len Klaus (1974) male (Hybrid, Artosha × Hybrid, Kleopatra)
- Hybrid Dzhudi (1971) female (Hybrid, Vud × Hybrid, Diva)
- Hybrid Dzhina (1973) female (Hybrid, Kapitan Flint × Hybrid, Dzhudi)

1967 Family Lines Based on Hybrid Tuman male
(Hybrid, Tom × Hybrid, Dega)

- Hybrid Chagi (yr?) female (Hybrid, Tuman × Unknown)
- Hybrid Rald Chang (1975) (Hybrid Bim I × Hybrid, Chagi)
- Hybrid Kras-Boss (yr?) male (Hybrid, Tuman × Hybrid, Ulma) There are no currently recorded offspring of Kras-Boss
- Hybrid Karina-Un (yr?) female (Hybrid, Tuman × Hybrid, Ulma) There are no currently recorded offspring of Karina-Un
- Hybrid Maur (yr?) male (Hybrid, Tuman × Hybrid, Sekki)
- Hybrid Lada (yr?) female (Hybrid, Maur × Unknown, Vlasta)
- Hybrid Vega (1974) female (Hybrid, Maur × Hybrid, Vil'Da

- Hybrid Timur (yr?) male (Hybrid, Tuman × Crossbreed, Panta)
- Hybrid Vajs [Vays] (yr?) male (Hybrid, Timur × Hybrid, Vayda)
- Hybrid Virta (yr?) female (Hybrid, Timur × Hybrid, Vayda)
- Hybrid Verda (yr?) female (Hybrid, Timur × Hybrid, Vayda)
- Hybrid Vietta (yr?) female (Hybrid, Timur × Hybrid, Vayda)
- Hybrid Dina (yr?) female (Hybrid, Tuman × Crossbreed, Panta)
- Hybrid Le Dani Mir (yr?) female (Hybrid, Dzhin × Hybrid, Dina)
- Hybrid Feya (yr?) female (Hybrid, Tuman × Unknown, Meri)
- Hybrid Ketti (1973) female (Hybrid, Anchar × Hybrid, Feya)
- Hybrid Yuna (yr?) female (Hybrid, Tuman × Hybrid, Yuta [Yutta])
- Hybrid Vesta (1973) female (Hybrid, Dzhaga × Hybrid, Yuna)
- Hybrid Gayda (yr?) female (Hybrid, Tuman × Unknown, Chana)
- Hybrid Ertsog (yr?) female (Hybrid, King × Hybrid, Gayda)
- Hybrid Karem (yr?) male (Hybrid, Tuman × Hybrid, Nim Eva)
- Hybrid Dallar (1974) male (Hybrid, Karem × Hybrid, Gerda)
- Hybrid Darvi (1974) female (Hybrid, Karem × Hybrid, Gerda)
- Hybrid Dezi (1976) female (Hybrid, Karem × Hybrid, Gerda)
- Hybrid Inessa (yr?) female (Hybrid, Tuman × Unknown, Vanda)
There are no currently recorded offspring of Inessa
- Hybrid Arto (yr?) male (Hybrid, Tuman × Unknown, Al'Fa) There are no currently recorded offspring of Arto
- Hybrid Yarcha (1970) female (Hybrid, Tuman × Unknown, Chapa) There are no currently recorded offspring of Yarcha
- Hybrid Lada (1970) female (Hybrid, Tuman × Hybrid, Panta) There are no currently recorded offspring of Lada
- Hybrid Rema-Greza (1970) female (Hybrid, Tuman × Hybrid, Rynda)
- Hybrid Sabina-Diana (1973) female (Hybrid, Barhan-Zhan × Hybrid, Rema-Greza)
- Hybrid Setti (1973) female (Hybrid, Barhan-Zhan × Hybrid, Rema-Greza)
- Hybrid Seggi (1973) female (Hybrid, Barhan-Zhan × Hybrid, Rema-Greza)
- Hybrid Rayma (1970) female (Hybrid, Tuman × Hybrid, Rynda)
- Hybrid Lo-Rom (1973) male (Hybrid, Dan-Zhan × Hybrid, Rayma)
- Hybrid Dajmos Banga (1984) female (Hybrid, Bim II × Hybrid, Rayma)

- Hybrid Raffi (1970) female (Hybrid, Tuman × Hybrid, Rynda)
- Hybrid Tayna-Mikki (1973) female (Hybrid, Atos × Hybrid, Raffi)
- Hybrid Ranika (1970) female (Hybrid, Tuman × Hybrid, Rynda)
- Hybrid Nikta (1974) female (Hybrid, Dan × Hybrid, Ranika)
- Hybrid Zhurd (1970) male (Hybrid, Tuman × Hybrid, Raksha)
- Hybrid Aza (yr?) female (Hybrid, Zhurd × Hybrid, Astra)
- Hybrid Ingo (1973) male (Hybrid, Zhurd × Hybrid, Irisha)
- Hybrid Izhen (1973) male (Hybrid, Zhurd × Hybrid, Irisha)
- Hybrid Ilona (1973) female (Hybrid, Zhurd × Hybrid, Irisha)
- Hybrid Ista (1973) female (Hybrid, Zhurd × Hybrid, Irisha)
- Hybrid Zhuk (1970) male (Hybrid, Tuman × Hybrid, Raksha) There are no currently recorded offspring of Zhuk
- Hybrid Zhulya (1970) female (Hybrid, Tuman × Hybrid, Raksha)
- Hybrid Oksay (1973) male (Hybrid, Set × Hybrid, Zhulya)
- Hybrid Om (1973) male (Hybrid, Set × Hybrid, Zhulya)
- Hybrid Ora (1973) female (Hybrid, Set × Hybrid, Zhulya)
- Hybrid Oyta (1973) female (Hybrid, Set × Hybrid, Zhulya)
- Hybrid Olesya (1973) female (Hybrid, Set × Hybrid, Zhulya)
- Hybrid Zhaklin (1970) female (Hybrid, Tuman × Hybrid, Raksha) There are no currently recorded offspring of Zhaklin
- Hybrid Yard (1970) male (Hybrid, Tuman × Unknown) There are no currently recorded offspring of Yard
- Hybrid Yanga (1970) female (Hybrid, Tuman × Unknown) There are no currently recorded offspring of Yanga
- Hybrid Zherika (1971) female (Hybrid, Tuman × Hybrid, Nayda) There are no currently recorded offspring of Zherika
- Hybrid Lera (1972) female (Hybrid, Tuman × Hybrid, Nayda)
- Hybrid Purga (yr?) female (Hybrid, Dan Zhan × Hybrid, Lera)
- Hybrid Bjula (yr?) female (Hybrid, Bim × Hybrid, Lera)
- Hybrid Gerta (1977) female (Hybrid, Dan Zhan × Hybrid, Lera)
- Hybrid Atos (1978) male (Hybrid, Dan Zhan × Hybrid, Lera)
- Hybrid Chara (1972) female (Hybrid, Tuman × Hybrid, Nayda)
- Hybrid Zhan Gret (1976) male (Hybrid, Kapitan Flint × Hybrid, Chara)
- Hybrid Kora (1972) female (Hybrid, Tuman × Hybrid, Nayda)
- Hybrid Radin (yr?) female (Hybrid, Dzhek × Hybrid, Kora)
- Hybrid Daza (1976) female (Hybrid, Dzhek × Hybrid, Kora)

- Hybrid Dzhulja (1972) female (Hybrid, Tuman × Hybrid, Nayda)
- Hybrid Dinga (yr?) female (Hybrid, Vud × Hybrid, Dzhulja
- Hybrid Dor-Dintay (1973) male (Hybrid, Tuman × Hybrid, Dan-Dingo)
- Hybrid Van Lada (1978) female (Hybrid, Dor Dintay × Hybrid, Fer-Ayshe)
- Hybrid Baron (1983) male (Hybrid, Dor-Dintay × Hybrid, Tayna-Mikki)
- Hybrid Dor-Ditta (1973) female (Hybrid, Tuman × Hybrid, Dan-Dingo)
- Hybrid Rin-Dzhaga (1974) male (Hybrid, Barhan-Zhan × Hybrid, Dor-Ditta)
- Hybrid Rin-Deza (1974) male (Hybrid, Barhan-Zhan × Hybrid, Dor-Dittta)
- Hybrid Grand (1978) male (Hybrid, Bars × Hybrid, Dor-Ditta)
- Hybrid Dor-Deri (1973) female (Hybrid, Tuman × Hybrid, Dan-Dingo) There are no currently recorded offspring of Dor-Deri

1970 Family Lines Based on Hybrid Dan Zhan male
(Hybrid, Dzhim × Hybrid, Dzhoya)

1973 Family Lines Based on Hybrid Lo-Rom male
(Hybrid, Dan Zhan × Hybrid, Rayma)

1974 Family Lines Based on Hybrid Ped-Shvarc male
(Hybrid, Dan Zhan × Hybrid, Dezi)

1975 Family Lines Based on Hybrid Tap Arto male
(Hybrid, Chingiz Rhan × Hybrid, Tapa)

1976 Family Lines Based on Hybrid Mashka female
(Hybrid, Urban × Hybrid, Masha)

1978 Family Lines Based on Hybrid Atos male
(Hybrid, Dan Zhan × Hybrid, Lera)

1979–1982–1983 Family Lines Based on Hybrid Mashka female
(Hybrid, Urban × Hybrid, Masha)

1980 Family Lines Based on Hybrid Panta male
(Hybrid, Tsorn × Hybrid, Charda)

Addendum:
1978 Giant Schnauzer females Ledi and Anni f. Raakzeje

Giant Schnauzer Boj male littermate of Giant Schnauzer Roy

1950–56 Offspring of Giant Schnauzer Roy
To demonstrate the intensity of the involvement of [patriarch] Giant Schnauzer Roy (1947?) and the major breeds (Rocks) combined with Roy in the initial selection processes here follows a list of his 36 male and 45 female offspring currently recorded in the Database. Roy was used only at Red Star Kennels Moscow.

1. 1951? Atta Crossbreed female (Roy × Rottweiler, Una)
2. 1952? Cheka Crossbreed female (Roy × South Russian Ovcharka, Fihta)
3. 1952 Haytar Crossbreed male (Roy × Airedale Terrier, Sotta)
4. 1952 Hazar Crossbreed male (Roy × Airedale Terrier, Sotta)

5. 1952 Hizha [Hinga] Crossbreed female (Roy × Airedale Terrier, Sotta)
6. 1952 Htora Crossbreed female (Roy × Airedale Terrier, Sotta)
7. 1952 Hroma Crossbreed female (Roy × Airedale Terrier, Sotta)
8. 1952 Hiza Crossbreed female (Roy × Airedale Terrier, Sotta)
9. 1952 Harzan Crossbreed male (Roy × Airedale Terrier, Sima)
10. 1952 Hadzhi [Hodzha] Crossbreed female (Roy × Airedale Terrier, Sima)
11. 1952 Hmur Crossbreed female (Roy × Airedale Terrier, Sima)
12. 1952 Harza Crossbreed female (Roy × Airedale Terrier, Sima)
13. 1953 Chonga Crossbreed female (Roy × Airedale Terrier, Sotta)
14. 1953 Chonga Crossbreed female (Roy × Airedale Terrier, Salma)
15. 1953 Chiit Crossbreed male (Roy × Airedale Terrier, Sotta)
16. 1953 Chudniy Crossbreed male (Roy × Rottweiler, Uda)
17. 1953 Chibris Crossbreed male (Roy × Rottweiler, Uda)
18. 1953 Chalita Crossbreed female (Roy × Rottweiler, Uda)
19. 1953 Chirok Crossbreed male (Roy × Rottweiler, Una)
20. 1953 Chelkash Crossbreed male (Roy × Rottweiler, Una)
21. 1953 Churek Crossbreed male (Roy × Rottweiler, Una)
22. 1953 Charva Crossbreed female (Roy × Rottweiler, Una)
23. 1953 Chelka Crossbreed female (Roy × Rottweiler, Una)
24. 1953 Chadra Crossbreed female (Roy × Rottweiler, Una)
25. 1953 Top Crossbreed male (Roy × Airedale Terrier, Salma)
26. 1953 Chinga Crossbreed female (Roy × Airedale Terrier, Salma)
27. 1953 Cherri Crossbreed female (Roy × Airedale Terrier, Salma)
28. 1953 Chernushka Crossbreed female (Roy × Airedale Terrier, Salma)
29. 1953 Chalyj Crossbreed male (Roy × Moscow Waterdog, Tina)
30. 1953 Char Crossbreed male (Roy × Moscow Waterdog, Tina)
31. 1953 Chaj Crossbreed male (Roy × Moscow Waterdog, Tina)
32. 1953 Chad Crossbreed male (Roy × Moscow Waterdog, Tina)
33. 1953 Cholka Crossbreed male (Roy × Moscow Waterdog, Tina)
34. 1953 Chub Crossbreed male (Roy × Moscow Waterdog, Tiza)
35. 1953 Mukha Crossbreed female (Roy × Moscow Waterdog, Tiza)
36. 1953 Chubek Crossbreed male (Roy × South Russian Ovcharka, Fihta)
37. 1953 Chomga Crossbreed female (Roy × Rottweiler, Femka)

38.   1953 Chubarik Crossbreed male (Roy × Moscow Waterdog, Ufa)
39.   1953 Chiba Crossbreed female (Roy × Moscow Waterdog, Ufa)
40.   1953 Chernjavka Crossbreed female (Roy × Moscow Waterdog, Ufa)
41.   1954 Azart Crossbreed male (Roy × Rottweiler, Una)
42.   1954 Ahta Crossbreed female (Roy × Rottweiler, Una)
43.   1954 Agitka Crossbreed female (Roy × Rottweiler, Una)
44.   1954 Aray Crossbreed male (Roy × Rottweiler, Urma)
45.   1954 Afishka Crossbreed female (Roy × Unknown, Teseja)
46.   1954 Askold Crossbreed male (Roy × Moscow Waterdog, Tessi)
47.   1954 Azot Crossbreed male (Roy × Rottweiler, Firma)
48.   1954 Avaria Crossbreed female (Roy × Rottweiler, Firma)
49.   1954 Anush Crossbreed female (Roy × Rottweiler, Firma)
50.   1954 Art Crossbreed male (Roy × Moscow Waterdog, Tiza)
51.   1954 Atava Crossbreed female (Roy × Moscow Waterdog, Tiza)
52.   1954 Amfibija Crossbreed female (Roy × Moscow Waterdog, Tiza)
53.   1954 Arioza Crossbreed female (Roy × Moscow Waterdog, Tiza)
54.   1954 Aorta Crossbreed female (Roy × Moscow Waterdog, Tiza)
55.   1954 Aul Crossbreed male (Roy × Moscow Waterdog, Ufa)
56.   1954 Arkan Crossbreed male (Roy × Moscow Waterdog, Ufa)
57.   1954 Arenda Crossbreed female (Roy × Moscow Waterdog, Ufa)
58.   1954 Ata Crossbreed female (Roy × Moscow Waterdog, Ufa)
59.   1954 Ampa Crossbreed female (Roy × Moscow Waterdog, Ufa)
60.   1954 Agat Crossbreed male (Roy × Moscow Waterdog, Tina)
61.   1954 Alan Crossbreed male (Roy × Moscow Waterdog, Tina)
62.   1954 Agor Crossbreed male (Roy × Moscow Waterdog, Tina)
63.   1954 Arbita Crossbreed female (Roy × Moscow Waterdog, Tina)
64.   1954 Chap Hybrid* male (Roy × Crossbreed, Fomka)
65.   1954 Ajur Hybrid* male (Roy × Crossbreed, Fomka)
66.   1954 Aza Hybrid* female (Roy × Crossbreed, Fomka)
67.   1954 Ajuta Hybrid* female (Roy × Crossbreed, Fomka)
68.   1954 Adra Hybrid* female (Roy × Crossbreed, Fomka)
69.   1954 Anda Hybrid* female (Roy × Crossbreed, Fomka)
70.   1955 Brig Crossbreed male (Roy × Rottweiler, Urma)
71.   1955 Bich Crossbreed male (Roy × Rottweiler, Urma)
72.   1955 Basta Crossbreed female (Roy × Rottweiler, Urma)

73. 1955 Borka Crossbreed female (Roy × Rottweiler, Urma)
74. 1955 Ralf Crossbreed male (Roy × Moscow Waterdog, Tessi)
75. 1955 Bata Hybrid* female (Roy × Hybrid, Avda)
76. 1955 Vah Crossbreed male (Roy × Rottweiler, Una)
77. 1955 Dzhena Crossbreed female (Roy × Rottweiler, Una)
78. 1956 Chuk Hybrid* male (Roy × Crossbreed, Chili)
79. 1956 Tarzan Hybrid* male (Roy × Crossbreed, Arsa)
80. 1956 Bul Hybrid* male (Roy × Hybrid, Aza)
81. 1956 Karsa Hybrid* female (Roy × Hybrid, Aza)

_____

These Hybrids sired by Giant Schnauzer Roy are a combination of two or more of Moscow Waterdog, Rottweiler, or Airedale Terrier. In the case of No. 78, Chuk, his dam, Chili, was a Cross of Rottweiler, Beniamino × Moscow Waterdog Toddi.

Family Lines

1954: Based on Crossbreed Aray (Male) (Giant Schnauzer, Roy × Rottweiler, Urma)

ARAY CAME FROM AN ORIGINAL crossing of Giant Schnauzer Roy and Rottweiler Urma in 1954. No other offspring from that litter are currently recorded in the Database. For further information and interest, in 1955 Roy and Urma produced a litter containing males Brig and Bich and females Basta and Borka.

Family Pillars of Aray

Crossbreed, Aray, 1954.

These included the males Tuman (Aray × Htora) and Gay (Aray × Borka) possibly born in or around 1956 given Aray's birth year as mid 1954. The remarkable aspects of these two males is that Tuman is a hybrid mixture of Giant Schnauzer, Rottweiler, and Airedale Terrier, while Gay is a crossbreed of Giant Schnauzer and Rottweiler. In both cases the Giant Schnauzer is Roy and the Rottweiler, Urma. It will be noted that Gay is inbred on Roy and Urma.

Hybrid Tuman (1956?) male
(Crossbred, Aray × Crossbreed, Htora)
Tuman was the sire of female Dina (Tuman × Fimka). Of additional future note a second Hybrid Tuman (1967) male (Hybrid, Tom × Hybrid, Dega)

would present eleven years later. His paternal grandsire and grand dam were Tuman (1956) × Unknown, Fimka, through hybrids Dina and Tom. Hybrid Tuman (1967) has 9 male and 23 female recorded offspring tracing back to Crossbreed Aray (1954).

It is interesting to note that Dina's paternal blending is of Giant Schnauzer Roy, Rottweiler Urma, and Airedale Terrier Sotta, three of the original breeds, and that

Hybrid, Tom, 1964.

Dina's dam, Fimka, is of unknown ancestry. It never fails to excite me when examining the early breeding combinations, and the fact that Red Star cynologists and geneticists conducted risk management experiments in selecting dogs, based primarily on visual assessment, that may or may not have been purebred. Did Fimka resemble Giant Schnauzer, Rottweiler, Airedale Terrier, or something else? Unfortunately again, there is no photograph of Fimka. However, when viewing photographs of other specimens of similar ancestry, the format of Giant Schnauzer Roy always predominates.

And get this, Hybrid Dina was the dam of Hybrid female Ata and male Tom (Crossbreed, Gay × Hybrid Dina). These two Hybrids had Crossbreed Aray on both sides of their lineage. Note also that Crossbreed Borka was also by Giant Schnauzer Roy and Rottweiler Urma. Gay was a crossbreed of Giant Schnauzer and Rottweiler from Aray (1954) and Borka (1955) who were siblings from litters one year apart. See Appendix A, beginning on p. 187, Aray Section.

Crossbreed Gay also sired Hybrid female Dega female and male Aktaj (Gay × Hybrid, Dina I) who currently have no recorded offspring, although derived from well-developed early lineage. Examining this Dega and Aktaj's maternal great grandparents, we can trace Vah back to Roy × Una; Bara through Brayt to Roy × Una and Roy × Sotta; Brayt through Azart to Roy × Una; and Nelma through Haytar to Roy × Sotta. Nayda, through both her sire Brayt and dam Nelma, is closely bred on Giant Schnauzer Roy and Moscow Waterdog Hanka. This pedigree profile presents a well-planned, closely bred, impressive line. One would suspect they might have been used in further breeding. Note that Dega and Aktaj's dam is Dina I (Hybrid, Foka × Hybrid, Nayda) and not Dina. See pedigree of Hybrid Tom in Appendix A, Aray Section. Aktaj's Database pedigree shows both him and his dam, Hybrid Dina I, to be born in 1964. Dina I was probably born in 1962–63 given that her dam, Hybrid Nayda, was born in mid 1961. With Aktaj currently showing no recorded offspring, this further verification is not currently available.

Family Lines

1954: Based on Crossbreed Azart (Male) (Giant Schnauzer, Roy × Rottweiler, Una)

FAMILY LINES BASED ON CROSSBREED Azart included the blending of Moscow Dog Hybrid Chuk (1956) with Moscow Waterdog Hybrid Volga (1956) producing female Hybrid Alfa

Note that Crossbreed Aray (1954) (Giant Schnauzer, Roy × Rottweiler, Urma, and Crossbreed Azart (1954) (Giant Schnauzer, Roy × Rottweiler, Una) were half siblings. See pedigree of Vishnya *et al.*, for lineage of Azart in Appendix A, Azart Section.

Azart was the product of the union of Giant Schnauzer Roy and Rottweiler Una. He was one of three recorded offspring from a litter born in 1954, the other two being females Ahta and Agitka. Azart was definitely a balanced combination of Giant Schnauzer and Rottweiler, tending to appear much like a Giant Schnauzer but heavier and stronger in format. It is reported that he stood 67 cm (26.5 in) at the shoulder with a weight of 42 kg (92.5 lb). Azart was a prolific breeder siring exceptional offspring that played major roles in the future development of the Black Terrier Group of the early years. Azart currently shows 4 male and 8 female offspring by difference females, recorded in the Database.

It is truly unfortunate that a more complete photo collage could not be assembled at this time.

The offspring of Azart (Giant Schnauzer, Roy × Rottweiler, Una) were pillars of the "Black Terrier Group". Following these offspring of Azart, combining his genes with those of the Airedale Terrier, Moscow Waterdog (Newfoundland × Caucasian Ovcharka), Moscow Dog, and South Russian Ovcharka, readers can easily and quickly come to appreciate how quickly and efficiently the building blocks found their fit in the developing mosaic if they examine closely the "flow" in combining the pedigrees of Volga, Azart, and Lada. [Appendix A, Azart Section.]

The pairing of Crossbreed Azart with Moscow Waterdog Hanka in 1956 produced Moscow Waterdog Hybrids Volga, Brayt, Vishnya, Vesna, Vityaz, Basta, and Velta. So began an evolution of family lines that would contribute immensely to the coming breed. Throughout the 1950s and early in the 1960s, Azart was was bred to different females, expanding the value of his genetic combination.

Moscow Waterdog Hybrid Volga was bred to Moscow Dog Hybrid

Moscow Waterdog Hybrid Volga, 1956   *Moscow Dog Chuk, 1956*   *Moscow Waterdog Hybrid Brayt, 1956*

Crossbreed Azart, 1954   *Moscow Waterdog Hanka, 1952*

Rottweiler Una, 1950   *Giant Schnauzer, Roy, 1947?*

Chuk (probably in 1958), to produce Mirta and Alfa, and and thus bring in new main players toward developing the "Black Terrier" into a superb genetic mix. Records [questionably] indicate that Chuk was used for breeding only this one time.

Alfa has 4 male and 2 female offspring recorded in the Database. Alfa was bred to Nord (Brayt × Ira) to produce female Lada and male Agat. Brayt and Volga were littermates, contributing an inbreeding base on Crossbreed Azart and Moscow Waterdog Hanka. Lada was bred to Tom and produced the incomparable male Topaz (1967). In 1969, bred to Hybrid Changa, Topaz sired female Hybrid Alba who in turn produced 3 male offspring in 1971 with male Hybrid Rams I in Bush, Al'Princ, and Artosha.

Within this Line eventually came male Hybrid Lin Sharman (1984) (Hybrid, Shvarts 2 × Hybrid, Linda Bek). Hybrid Lin Sharman sired 12 male and 40 female offspring with a number of females from 1986 through 1992. Here, readers can appreciate the growing breeding base that had by this point pretty much spread to a world-wide status. Looking into the pedigree of Hybrid Lin Sharman (1984), one extends:

Paternal lineage:
- Hybrid Rams I (Hybrid, Foka × Hybrid, Dega) (Rams I was also the sire of Hybrid Artosha)

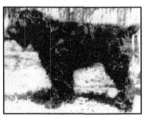

Hybrid, Topaz, 1967

Hybrid, Tom, 1964

Hybrid, Alba, 1969

Hybrid, Bush, 1971

Hybrid, Artosha, 1971

Hybrid, Lin Sharman, male, 1984
(Hybrid, Shvarts 2 × Hybrid, Linda Bek)

Hybrid, Shvarts 2, male, 1977

Hybrid, Linda Bek, female, 1980

- Hybrid Chada (1968) (Hybrid, Karat × Hybrid, Sekki)
- Hybrid Vud (1967) (Hybrid, Dik × Hybrid, Velta)
- Hybrid Chara (1968) (Hybrid, Karat × Hybrid, Irda)

Hybrid, Dzhe-Sharon, 1987

Maternal lineage:
- Hybrid Ort-Zaur (1974) (Hybrid, Rams I × Hybrid,Dan-Orta)
- Hybrid Layna (1973) (Hybrid,Dzhek × Hybrid, Zhela)
- Hybrid Artosha (1971) (Hybrid, Rams I × Hybrid, Alba)
- Hybrid Dzherri (1974) (Hybrid, Vays × Hybrid, Zitta)

One can easily witness the "growth of family" lines (as breed development moved through the 1980s with the simple example of Hybrid Dzhe-Sharon (1987) male (Hybrid, Lin Sharman × Hybrid, Dzherri [no photo]) who sired 22 male and 26 female offspring. Of interest is also the locale spread of dogs used: Dzhe-Sharon (Novosibirsk); Lin Sharman (Moscow); Dizherri (Ekaterinburg); Svharts 2 (Red Star); Linda Bek (Moscow); Char-Tuman (Ekaterinburg); Rika (locale?).

As an aside, it is quite interesting to note the format similarities in

Crossbreed Azart, 1954   *Moscow Waterdog Hybrid*   *Moscow Dog Chuk,*
                              Volga, 1956   *1956*

Azart (1954) and Chuk (1956) given the differences in their lineage, one might surmise coming through Giant Schnauzer Roy.

Reader reminder: Moscow Dog Hybrid Chuk (Giant Schnauzer, Roy × Moscow Dog, Chili (Rottweiler, Beniamino × Moscow Dog, Toddi (German Great Dane, Ralf × East European Shepherd, Pretti)).

Arsa (Azart × Arsa) (date of birth not recorded)

Arsa, family Azart, bred to Demon (1957), produced the female Sekki who in turn produced female Blek-Veda (Karat × Sekki); male Maur (Tuman × Sekki); female Kitri (1967) (Karat × Sekki); female Chada and male Din (1968) Karat × Sekki: Kapitan Flint (1969) (Topaz × Sekki). Of these offspring, two stand out somewhat above the rest: Chada producing 1 male and 3 females by Rams I, Agat, and Vays; and Kapitan Flint who sired 5 male and 6 female offspring that were placed with a number of owners throughout Russia and Estonia.

Of the offspring produced by Hybrid Chada, the most interesting was male Charli 1 (1970?) (Hybrid. Rams I × Hybrid, Chada). The intensity from Hybrid Foka and Hybrid Demon is evident in Charli 1's pedigree. Charli 1 sired female Hybrid Peppi from Hybrid Ped Shanel and male Hybrid Shvarts 2 from Hybrid Kerri both in 1977. He also sired male Hybrid Bim II and female Hybrid Birza out of Hybrid Sabina-Diana in 1979.

Hybrid, Chada, 1968

Hybrid, Rams I, 1966

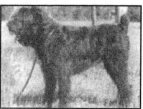

Hybrid, Karat, 1964

Hybrid, Demon, 1957

Hybrid, Foka, 1960

Crossbreed, Vah, 1956

Hybrid, Peppi, 1977, female (Hybrid, Charli 1 × Ped-Shanel)

Hybrid, Shvarts 2, 1977 (Hybrid, Charli 1 × Hybrid, Kerri)

Unfortunately, there is no photograph of Charli 1. However, his lineage does present an interesting trail culminating in photos of 2 offspring, Hybrids Peppi and Shvarts, from his two 1977 litters.

It is noted above that Hybrid Arsa was bred to Hybrid Demon and produced Hybrid Sekki, and Sekki produced Hybrid Maur. In the pedigree of Hybrid Maur, one notes his inbreeding on Hybrid Demon. By extension, Maur's paternal great grand dam, Galka, was also inbred on Hybrid Demon.

Hybid Kitri (1967) female (Hybrid, Karat × Hybrid, Sekki)

Kitri had 1 male recorded offspring: Zevs (1970) (Skif × Kitri). Other offspring by Hybrid Karat and Hybrid Sekki included male Din and females Chada, Blek-Veda, and Bara in 1968. Kitri was well-described as a show winner of good proportions with a mildly spiteful temperament which would have been acceptably tolerated for the time. Currently she has no other recorded offspring. Hybrid Brayt was sired by Crossbreed Azart out of Moscow Waterdog Hanka.

Hybrid, Kitri, 1967, female

The photos of Hybrids Kitri (1957) and (1989) are included here merely for comparison with a 22-year period between them. They both originated from lineage with Karat on both sides. Karat genes in Hybrid, Kitri 1989 came primarily through inbreeding of his sire Hybrid Ners back through Hybrid Set paternally and Hybrid Monstr-Dzhimmi-Set maternally.

Hybrid Kapitan Flint was heavily imbedded with the genes of Crossbreed Azart on both side of his lineage with his paternal great grandsire Crossbreed Gay being double inbred on Giant Schnauzer Roy

Hybrid, Kitri, 1989, female (Hybrid, Ners × Hybrid, Kenta)

from Rottweiler Urma. Kapitan Flint's maternal great grandsire was also Crossbreed Azart. Hybrid Nord's paternal grandsire was also Crossbreed Azart and his paternal grand dam Hybrid Alfa's dam Moscow Waterdog Volga was also sired by Crossbreed Azart.

The original [genetic] intensity coming from Crossbreed Azart reflects his (omnipotent) significance within the breed's early development in setting physical format.

Hybrid Gloriya (yr?) female (Crossbreed, Azart × Crossbreed, Cholka) family Azart has 1 recorded offspring: Reks (male) (Giant

Hybrid, Sekki, 1962, female
(Hybrid, Demon × Hybrid,
Arsa)

Schnauzer, Dasso f. Drahenshljuht × Hybrid, Gloriya). In 1971 Reks sired female Dezi (Reks × Lada) and Reks was bred to Hybrid, Lada (1968) produced female Dezi with Hybrid, Lada. Hybrid, Gloriya's sire Azart was a crossbreed of Giant Schnauzer, Roy × Rottweiler, Una, while her dam Moscow Waterdog Hybrid, Cholka was by Giant Schnauzer, Roy × Moscow Waterdog, Tina.

Hybrid Dezi presents an additional interest in that her maternal line also includes, through her great grand dam Ohta, a cross of Russian Spotted Hound × Rottweiler coming from her great great grand dam Crossbreed Chuta. Hybrid Dezi produced Hybrids male Ped-Shvarc and females Ped-Shanel, Ped Shelli and Pedi by Hybrid Dan Zhan.

Hybrid, Reks yr?, male (Giant
Schnauzer, Dasso × Moscow
Waterdog Hybrid)

Hybrid, Lada, 1968, female
(Hybrid, Nord × Hybrid, Nelli)

Vishnya (1956) female (Crossbreed, Azart × Moscow Waterdog Hanka), family Azart

At this point we have a blending of 25% Giant Schnauzer and 25% Rottweiler with 50% Moscow Waterdog, again highlighting the role played

Hanka, 1952   *Azart, 1954*

by the Moscow Waterdog in the early breeding processes and shown in the photos of Vishnya, Volga and Basta below. From this litter in 1956 came some fabulous early Black Terrier prototypes. This was an exceptional litter. Although hybrids by definition, for all intents and purposes, this was a litter of Moscow Waterdog Hybrids, adding somewhat to the nomenclature confusion, with both terms used interchangeably.

Readers will recognize that these dogs were whelped in 1956, a mere six years since breeding programs began in earnest at Red Star Military Kennel. Examination of these photographs shows the incredible progress in reaching a measurable format type notwithstanding other breeds that would come into the mix.

Vishnya produced male Hybrid, Dik (1958) (Crossbreed, Haytar × Moscow Waterdog Hybrid, Vishnya).

Hybrid Dik was an exceptional produced siring 15 male and 16 female recorded offspring. The Azart family line contribution coming through Hybrid Dik, his offspring and their offspring, throughout the 1960s and 1970s was impressive. Dik shows on both sides of many hybrid Black Terrier pedigree records in Moscow, Leningrad and other locations in Russia. Photographs and pedigree of Hybrid, Rams 2 follows to show the contribution from Hybrid, Dik on both side of his lineage, and by extension crossbreeds Haytar and Azart. Rams 2 currently records only 2 female female offspring Eva and Charodeyka in Database. Eva records 1 female offspring and Charodeyka 3 male and 3 female offspring in 1966 and 1977.

Vishnya, 1956, female   *Volga, 1956, female*

Moscow Waterdog Hybrid,
littermates by (Crossbreed, Azart
(1954) × Moscow Waterdog, Hanka
(1952))

Basta, 1956, male

Velta, 1956   *Brayt, 1956*

Moscow Waterdog Hybrid Volga (1956) (Azart × Hanka), family Azart

Moscow Waterdog Hybrid, Volga was a member of an exceptional early litter that was a combination of Giant Schnauzer, Rottweiler, and through Moscow Waterdogs Hanka and Tiza, the combined genes of Newfoundland Dog and Caucasian Ovcharka. Breeding Volga with Moscow Dog Chuk Hybrid was a stroke of genius, producing female Hybrids Mirta and Alfa.

Crossbreed, Haytar, 1952

Hybrid, Dik, 1958

Hybrid Mirta produced females Hybrids Yaga (1962?) (Hybrid, Demon × Mirta) and Dega (1963) (Giant Schnauzer, Ditter f. Drahenshljuht × Mirta). See earlier Mirta (1958) (Crossbreed, Azart × Crossbreed, Binta) at p. 60.

Hybrid, Rams 2 1969? (Hybrid, Vud (1967) × Hybrid, Diva (1966?))

Hybrid Yaga (1962?) currently shows only 1 recorded offspring in Hybrid Galka sired by Hybrid Negus. Of note is that both Yaga and Negus were sired by Hybrid Demon. Hybrid Galka records only 1 offspring in Hybrid Dega (1962) female (Hybrid, Demon × Hybrid, Galka) inbred on Hybrid Demon. Dega (1962) was bred to Hybrid Foka in 1966 and produced the exceptional male Hybrid Rams I who sired 12 male and 13 female recorded offspring. Bred to Hybrid Tom in 1967, Dega (1962) produced males Tuman and Jermak and female Dzhoya. Hybrid Tuman sired 9 male and 23 female offspring. Hybrid Dzhoya was the dam of 7 male and 12 female recorded offspring. Dzhoya was bred to the exceptional Hybrid males Viy, Dzhim, Ayaks [Ajaks], Anchar and Gil Devi from 1969 through 1975. Detailed information on these specimens is located in their more appropriate location within this volume.

Hybrid Dega (1963) currently records 5 male and 3 female offspring sired by Viy in 1965, Nayt in 1967 and 1969, and with Torri in 1971. Hybrid Dega (1963) was born at Red Star but was sent to St. Petersburg. The locations of her offspring are not currently recorded with the exception

Hybrid Beta (1969) female (Hybrid, Nayt × Hybrid, Dega) in St. Petersburg. Hybrid Beta currently records 5 male and 5 female offspring. These specimens are covered in more detail in Volume 6 *Leningrad Families*. City names Leningrad/St. Petersburg are used interchangeably.

Hybrid Alfa produced 6 male and 5 female recorded offspring with a number of exceptional males in the mid 1960s. Readers can see from the pedigree(s) of Mirta and Alfa (in Appendix A, Azart Section) a possibility of confusion regarding the birth dates of these two specimens. The dates could be a simple Database entry error or Chuk and Volga were bred a second time approximately 1 year apart. It appears that all of Alfa's offspring were located at Red Star, but may have been used for breeding at Moscow City Club.

To understand the following, readers need to see that there are two females (mother and daughter) named Alfa. The mother, Alfa (Moscow Dog Hybrid, Chuk 1956 × Moscow Waterdog Hybrid, Volga 1956), and daughter, Alfa (Uran × Alfa). See pedigree of Bim I.

Alfa (Chuk × Volga) produced 4 male and 2 female offspring: female Lada and male Agat (Nord × Alfa); male Demon (Dzhaga × Alfa); female Alfa (Uran × Alfa); male Chap (Chani × Alfa).

Hybrid Bim I (1969–70?) male (Hybrid, Ayman × Hybrid, Alfa (Uran × Alfa)) — note again that the two Alfa's are mother and daughter — presents an interesting study in that he sired a number of offspring throughout the 1970s that continued the breed development progression with the genes of Giant Schnauzer × Rottweiler crossbreed Azart coming through Alfa and Volga. Readers will also appreciate the infusion of Moscow Dog Hybrid Chuk coming through Alfa in combination with Volga. Also that the second Alfa through her sire Uran, through Ohta, brings the genes of Russian Spotted Hound Uteshay (Uteshay × Rottweiler, Uza). See pedigrees of Bim I and Alfa. The dam of Bim I — the second Alfa (Uran × Alfa) — does not have any other recorded offspring. Note: Hybrid Bim I may have been born in 1969–70 given his maternal grandsire Uran 1966 and his dam possibly in 1968. Hybrid Bim I comes from an inbreeding base of Giant Schnauzer Roy, Crossbreed Azart, Moscow Waterdog Hanka, and Hybrid Brayt.

Of further interest in Bim I is that his sire Hybrid Ayman, carried the "huge" black terrier format into the mix that created him. It is quite obvious that the Moscow Dog and Russian Spotted Hound, coming from his maternal side, had no style/format influence. However, although Volga had pretty much faded by this point, she would have complemented and bolstered the paternal side of Bim I with her coat and size. As witnessed in the photographs that follow of Bim I, Ayman, Foka, Chani, Brayt, Vah, Chuk and Volga, readers can view the progressive development over the period 1956 to possibly 1966–68 or somewhat later. Although we have no date of birth for Bim I, he sired offspring from 1972–73 through 1977.

Bim I, 1969–70?   *Ayman, 1964*

Foka, 1960   *Chani, 1962*

Brayt, 1956   *Vah, 1956*

Chuk, 1956   *Volga, 1956*

Hybrid Chani, a maternal great grandsire of Bim I, was a son of Brayt. Brayt was a paternal great grandsire of Bim I. These two males contribute size and coat from Giant Schnauzer and Moscow Waterdog. Brayt was also the sire of Bara (Brayt × Appa) (Rottweiler × Airedale Terrier). Nelma was a combination of Giant Schnauzer, Airedale Terrier, Moscow Waterdog, with a touch of Rottweiler.

Hybrid Chani (1962) sired male Uran and female Nelli (Chani × Ohta); male Chap (1967) (Chani × Alfa); male Top (1968) (Chani × Teya). Nord sired 5 male and 2 females offspring: female Lada and male Agat (Nord × Alfa); female Lada and male Torri (1968) (Nord × Nelli); males Nord, Chep, Prints (1968) (Nord × Nayda).

Of note is ***Moscow Waterdog Hybrid Brayt (1956)*** being instrumental in the Black Terrier development and identified at this juncture for his foundation role in reaching Hybrid Chani (1962). Again readers witness the simplicity in the complicated journey of the early development of the "base breeds". Complicated? Yes. Interesting, oh yes!

***Hybrid Bars'*s** dam Chonga was a first crossbreeding of Giant Schnauzer Roy × Airedale Terrier Salma. Records indicate that Chonga was 60 cm (23.5 in) tall, weighed 25 kg (55 lb), and presented in the style of the Airedale Terrier. Bars's sire, Brayt, on the other hand, came from a combination of the big players: Giant Schnauzer, Rottweiler, Newfoundland, and Moscow Waterdog. Bars sired Hybrid Berta (1961) female (Hybrid, Bars × Fimka) with Fimka being of unknown ancestry. Hybrid Berta produced male Dzhaga and female Lassi (1965) (Giant Schnauzer, Dasso f. Drahenshljuht × Berta). Hybrid Dzhaga (1965) was also a premium sire with 7 male and 7 female recorded offspring from 1967 through 1973 with females Yutta, Ata, Karmen, Raksha, Ditta and Vesta. Hybrid Brayt contributed to the Azart line by siring 10 male and 7 female offspring.

Hybrid Lada Tag (1959) and Hybrid Dzhoy (1957), family Azart

Readers note that Hybrid Dzhoy sired female Lada Tag (1959) (Hybrid, Dzhoy × Crossbreed, Dzhena) and that Lada Tag's paternal great grand dam Hadzhi [Hodzha] was a cross of Giant Schnauzer Roy × Airedale Terrier Sima (Airedale Terrier, Bil (fon) Askania × Airedale Terrier, Teffi).

Lada Tag produced male Rom (Tyapa × Lada Tag); female Nastya, males Daks and Rem (1962) (Foka × Lada Tag); female Lynda, male Shamil (1964) (Foka × Lada Tag). Linda had no recorded offspring. Shamil sired 3 male and 1 female offspring. Nastya is a female of considerable interest in the development of the Black Terrier Group, having produced female Stesha and males Skif, Saks, Smok (1965) (Dik × Nastya); females Roksa, Ruza, Radda, Rufa and male Ryzhiy (1966) (Dik × Nastya). All of Nastya's offspring played significant roles in the breed development, mostly at Leningrad. Hybrid Nastya and her litter from Hybrid Dik in 1966 is of special note for the impact from them in the breed development in Leningrad. They are covered in detail in Volume 6, *Leningrad Families.*

Mirta (1958) (Azart × Binta), family Azart

This Mirta (Azart × Binta) was a different Mirta than the one shown on p. 56 (Moscow Dog Hybrid, Chuk × Moscow Waterdog Hybrid, Volga) whose paternal grandsire was also Azart. Note this Mirta's pedigree in Appendix A, Azart Section, showing her to have been a very tightly blended cross of Giant Schnauzer and Rottweiler. Mirta (1960) and Alfa (1961) were Hybrids.

Although there are currently no photographs of this Mirta, those of her sire Azart and maternal great grand dam Charva, may well be representative of just how she would have looked. She presently shows no recorded offspring in the Database. Again we note the Giant Schnauzer coat type presented by Azart and Charva who were born one year apart.

Azart sired 4 male and 9 female offspring, and Charva produced 4 male and 6 female offspring

It is interesting to note that Mirta's dam Binta also produced female Irda (Bul × Binta) and male Shrek (1958) (Brayt × Binta). Although with Irda, breeding moved away from Azart, it is important to follow the progression, keeping in mind the (early) years and limited gene base. [There are three other Irdas listed in the Database: Irda (Unknown × Unknown); Irda (1962) (Hybrid, Brayt × Hybrid, Ira) ; and Irda (1967) (Hybrid, Karat × Hybrid, Irda) whose dam was Hybrid Irda (1962) below.

Crossbreed, Azart, 1954 (Giant Schnauzer, Roy × Rottweiler, Una)

Hybrid Irda (1962) presents an interesting contribution through her sire Bul (Giant Schnauzer, Roy × Moscow Waterdog Hybrid, Aza). Readers will recall that this author has created the designations *Moscow Waterdog Hybrid* and *Moscow Dog Hybrid* to better describe [in his opinion] a specific genetic advancement utilizing the Moscow Waterdog (Breed) and Moscow Dog (Breed), with the infusion of the Giant Schnauzer, primarily Roy,

Crossbreed, Charva, 1953 (Giant Schnauzer, Roy × Rottweiler, Una)

which "set" the format of the Giant Schnauzer type. Readers will also note the heavy involvement of Giant Schnauzer Roy on both sides of Irda's lineage. She produced a number of important recorded offspring in 1 male and 9 females during the period 1964 through 1975 with males Karat, Tom, and Akbar f. Raakzeje [Raakze]. In 1975, Irda, bred to Akbar, produced female Chezetta. In 1978, Chezetta with male Lo-Rom, produced Hybrid male Volf-Gross and female Vaksa.

Although ***Hybrid Shrek*** (1958) currently has no recorded offspring in the Database, he is an interesting mixture of Giant Schnauzer, Rottweiler and Moscow Waterdog. Shrek (1958) was sired by Hybrid Brayt (1956) (Crossbreed, Azart (Giant Schnauzer, Roy × Rottweiler, Una) × Moscow Waterdog, Hanka).

Note: A second Hybrid Shrek presents in 1966 at Red Star Kennel

(Hybrid, Chani × Hybrid, Alfa). See pedigree in Appendix A, Azart Section. This male has great grandsire Crossbreed Azart and Moscow Waterdog, Hanka on both side of his lineage. The Airedale Terrier Meri appears as a paternal great grand dam with Moscow Dog Hybrid Chuk and Moscow Waterdog Hybrid Volga appearing maternally. Hybrid Shrek (1966) has a powerful lineage of "large" dog specimens. Unfortunately, no photograph could be located. This Hybrid Shrek (1966) sired males Tsebus and Chek, and female Tsu-Franta (Crossbreed, Vah × Crossbreed Teya. These offspring currently show no recorded offspring.

Azor (1961) (Azart × Bayta), family Azart
Hybrid Azor shows no recorded offspring, littermates, or full siblings in the Database. A major interest in him comes through his dam Bayta and maternal great grand dam Fihta who was a South Russian Ovcharka.

In the face-on photograph of Azor it appears that he might present with a rather large patch of white hair in the centre of his chest. However, it is more likely to be jacket material of the handler. If it were the case, it would probably have come through his great grand dam South Russian Ovcharka Fihta. South Russian Ovcharkas are primarily pure white. Although without a photo of Fihta, there is no proof that she, in fact, was white. But if not, she would have been cream or cream and beige colour, and would have carried the white coat gene.

Azor, 1961

Azor, 1961

Although the quality of the photograph of Chudniy (Giant Schnauzer, Roy × Rottweiler, Uda) is a bit grainy, it is presented to demonstrate the coat of Giant Schnauzer Roy and bulk of Rottweiler. Chudniy is the maternal grandsire of Azor. What is also interesting here is that Azor does not present the bulk of Chudniy but appears to have been somewhat refined through his sire Azart.

Azor, 1961

Crossbreed, Azart, 1954. Sire of Azor

Hybrid, Chudniy, 1953. Maternal Grandsire of Azor

Family Lines

1955: Based on Rottweiler Geyni (Male) (Rottweiler, Armin f. Tize × Rottweiler, Kora f. Schneidenplatz)

GEYNI (1955) WAS AN EARLY Rottweiler contributor whose parents were, by their names, probably of direct German descent. Geyni's date of birth was not recorded and neither were those of his sire and dam.

He has 1 male and 3 female offspring recorded, whose birth dates are also not recorded. However, his first listed litter records 2 females, Ila and Ilma (Geyni × Crossbreed, Dila), also with no recorded date of birth. Dila (Rottweiler, Farno × Crossbreed, Chuta) is interesting in that Chuta was one of the few Russian Spotted Hound × Rottweiler contributions at an early stage in the cross-breeding experiments. Chuta was by Russian Spotted Hound, Uteshay × Rottweiler, Uza.

Family Pillars of Geyni

Crossbreed Ila was bred to Hybrid Karat (Foka × Nayda) and produced male Bechel who, in turn with different females, produced a number of

Hybrid, Bechel, male

offspring in the late 1960s and early 1970s. From a rather dark photograph it appears that Bechel (no date of birth) was a solidly built male with a thick neck, large head and substantial body mass. Bechel has an abundance of Rottweiler in his extended lineage, with a reasonable content of Moscow Waterdog and a spattering of Airedale Terrier, with Giant

Crossbreed, Ila, female   *Crossbreed, Dila, female*

Schnauzer Roy present throughout his paternal side. Although Bechel had a quality heavy coat, it appears from his photograph that he was light on facial furnishings. Bechel comes from a blending of Geyni and Karat lines. His maternal great grand dam Chuta contributed the genes of Russian Spotted Hound Uteshay.

Crossbreed Ila also produced female Lera (Giant Schnauzer, Dasso f. Drahenshljuht × Ila) bringing an intensification of Giant Schnauzer genes into the Geyni family, again demonstrating the practice of breeding back to the Giant Schnauzer. Lera records male Darli and female Dega (1970) by Nayt and female Kana (1972) by Atos. Kana records female Tsuri (1979) (Tsorn × Kana).

Crossbreed Ilma, littermate to Ila, has only one offspring listed, the female Panta (1965) (Karen I × Ilma) also with no recorded date of birth. Panta is interesting indeed in that she is inbred on Dila, making her an exciting combination of Rottweiler and Russian Spotted Hound, through Chuta. Although the Russian Spotted Hound may not have played a significant role in the Black Russian Terrier, its intensity here, in Panta, is quite impressive in relation to body format. A close look at photographs of Dila and her female offspring Ila (above) is genetically revealing in two aspects. First, mating Chuta with Farno expresses a streamlining change in the Rottweiler format in Dila. Secondly, when breeding Dila back to the Rottweiler (Geyni), the body format returns to Rottweiler, masking the strengths of the Russian Spotted Hound. Note that Dila was also was bred to Rottweiler Linch producing Crossbreed Karen 1 sire of Panta. A great interest would be in examining photographs of Crossbreeds Karen 1 and

Ilma to see if there was a format return, of any degree, to that exhibited in Crossbreed Dila.

Although there is no available photograph of Crossbreed Panta, her contribution to the developing breed was also impressive through her off-spring male Dzhim (Tom × Panta), male Timur and females Dina and Lada (Tuman × Panta). The only photograph located of her offspring was that of male Hybrid Dzhim who was sired by Hybrid Tom (1964). Tom was a combination of Giant Schnauzer, Rottweiler and Airedale Terrier. Hybrid Tom delivered the dominance of Giant Schnauzer format concealing any physical relationship to Crossbreed Dila.

Hybrid, Dzhim, male (Hybrid, Tom × Crossbreed, Panta)

Hybrid Tuman (Hybrid, Tom × Hybrid, Dega) was bred to Panta, to add significantly to the mix combining the Geyni and Tom families, ending the continued progression of the Geyni family with Hybrids Dina and Timur. Tuman in his own right was a very good producer of fine specimens with 8 male and 22 female recorded offspring.

From the combination of Hybrid Tuman × Crossbreed Panta (1970?) came female Hybrid Dina who was reported as being of medium size with fairly strong bone and of square format. She had a large well-defined correct head, with a strong correct bite. [Pedigree in Appendix A, Azart Section.] Her disadvantages were an arched back and short legs. Her coat was short and hard combining black and grey hair. Dina currently records only 1 offspring from Dzhim, female Hybrid Le Dani Mr (yr?) who, with Hybrid Nerhan, produced female Hybrid Dani-Nandi (1981). Also from her breeding to Hybrid Tuman, Panta produced male Timur and female Lada. Timur sired 1 male and 3 females with Hybrid Vayda (yr?). Hybrid Lada currently records no offspring. The point here again is that the Russian Spotted Hound × Rottweiler combination is now nowhere to be seen.

In Hybrid Dina's pedigree, readers will note paternal great grandsire Demon (1957) and great grand dam Galka. It is also worth noting that Galka's paternal and maternal grandsire was Demon (1957). At this point, the Giant Schnauzer format has again imprinted its genetic dominance.

Readers will note that this Dana has a paternal grand dam named

Dina who was owned privately in Moscow. This Dina (probably around 1955–60) was sired by another Tuman (Crossbreed, Aray (Giant Schnauzer, Roy × Rottweiler, Urma)) × Crossbreed, Htora (Giant Schnauzer, Roy × Airedale, Terrier, Sotta)). WOW! One truly needs patience to carefully follow the curves thrown by same-names/like-names through the generations. Missing dates of birth also challenge one's resolve in attempting to sort out and keep the record straight. I again express my admiration for Mr. Yuri Semenov and his team for a Yeoman's job in developing the Virtual Breed Database.

Red Star Military Black Russian Terriers at work.

Red Star Military Kennel main gate entrance.

Family Lines

1956: Based on Moscow Dog Hybrid Chuk (Male) (Giant Schnauzer, Roy × Moscow Dog, Chili)

FAMILY PILLARS OF CHUK (1956) were extremely limited in that Chuk in fact did not form a successful line. Although there must have been some relatively extensive experimental breeding with Chuk, he has only two recorded female offspring in Mirta and Alfa (Chuk × Volga). When we take into consideration the breeds used in creating Chuk, we can easily see and appreciate the powerful effect coming from Giant Schnauzer Roy in establishing the desired format type of dog, minus the heavy facial hair furnishings. Chuk presents as a perfect "working" type for military and guarding duties.

Moscow Dog Hybrid, Chuk, 1956 (Giant Schnauzer, Roy × Moscow Dog, Chili)

Chuk was a solidly built, heavy boned and tightly muscled dog of sufficient substance to be an effective man-stopper. Consider his lineage with every member breed (Giant Schnauzer, Rottweiler, German Great Dane and East European Shepherd/German Shepherd) having a long history of guarding work. It is reported that the Moscow Dog came with an uncontrollable viciousness which — like the Moscow Waterdog — was the reason for its not being further developed for military duties, and that (almost) all specimens were destroyed by order of the Russian Military hierarchy. We do know however, that was not entirely true in that specimens (with manageable temperaments) were around in the mid to late 1960s or longer.

[As an author/researcher of stories canine, I have a fascination for what may have been or what in fact has become of the Moscow Dog. I also doubt that the Moscow Dog and Moscow Waterdog became extinct and do not exist in 2016 in some improved form from the 1950s. I am certain these two breeds were too important in canine evolution for private Russian breeders to have ignored them.]

Arguably, one could make the point that the Moscow Dog influence was minimal (and probably was). However the fact cannot be dismissed genetically that overall format and temperament was affected by this Hybrid anomaly. The foundation structure comprised German Great Dane and East European Shepherd to which was added the Rottweiler, creating the Moscow Dog, Chili. To Moscow Dog Chili was added the genetic predominance of Giant Schnauzer Roy, so perfectly presented in male Moscow Dog Hybrid Chuk. It is obvious to interested readers that a new planned pathway was created at Red Star Kennel with the introduction to the Moscow Dog of the genes of Giant Schnauzer Roy.

What piques my interest is in the question of what happened to the development pathway emanating from the creation of the Moscow Dog and Moscow Waterdog as separate purebred entities. I raise this question because of the contributions of these two breeds toward the creation of the Black Terrier/Black Russian Terrier. Both the Moscow Dog and Moscow Waterdog are reported as being extinct. However, I feel strongly that they both must still exist in some modified format.

The great interest here is that Hybrid Mirta (1960) (Chuk × Volga) was a combination of Moscow Dog + Moscow Waterdog + Rottweiler + Giant Schnauzer and included Great Dane, Newfoundland Dog, and East European Shepherd. The hybridization of Moscow Dog through Chuk was carried forward into the developing "Black Terrier Groups" by way of female Hybrids Mirta (1960) and Alfa (1961) with the equal fortification of genes from the Moscow Waterdog. As witnessed throughout this study, the Moscow Waterdog was a major contributor to the format and temperament of the Black Terrier Group and into the creation of the Black Russian Terrier.

Mirta and Alfa are perfect examples of "wonderment" over why so few offspring are recorded from them. This is especially intriguing when their recorded offspring played such important roles in the breed development. Mirta, in particular, with only two recorded female offspring, was a jackpot contributor with Yaga (Demon × Mirta), date of birth not recorded, and Dega 1963 (Ditter f. Drahenshljuht × Mirta). The earlier burning question again arises regarding the probable effect of the pepper and salt coat colour related to Giant Schnauzer Ditter.

Hybrid Yaga produced 1 recorded female offspring Galka. Galka produced the female Dega (Demon × Galka).

Hybrid Dega (1962) produced male Rams I (1966) (Foka × Dega) and female Dzhoya (1967) (Tom × Dega) and male Tuman (1967) (Tom × Dega). It is at this point that readers will note that Moscow Dog Hybrid Chuk, sire of Mirta and Moscow Waterdog Hybrid Volga, dam of Mirta, are no longer in the picture.

Moscow Waterdog Hybrid, Brayt, 1956

Hybrid Alfa, on the other hand, has 4 male and 2 female recorded offspring: male Roy (Dan Zhan × Alfa); male Agat and female Lada (Nord × Alfa); male Demon (Dzhaga × Alfa); female Alfa (Uran × Alfa); male Chap 1967 (Chani × Alfa). Only Chap has a recorded birth date.

Moscow Waterdog Hanka, 1952

Crossbreed, Azart, 1954

Hybrid Chap (1967), offspring of Alfa, is interesting in that he sired female Kora 1973 (Hybrid, Chap × Oksa) and Kora was the dam of Nemfred 1976 (Urchan × Kora). Nemfred was the sire of Hybrid Sid 1979 (Hybrid, Nemfred × Hybrid, Charita), Sid being a big producer in Moscow

and Leningrad; Hybrid males Erofey and Ezur 1981 (Hybrid, Nemfred ×
Hybrid, Unita). Throughout the 1980s Hybrid Ezur recorded 5 male and 11
female offspring. Another point of interest is Ira, a cross of Rottweiler and
Airedale Terrier.

Crossbreed Ira with Moscow Waterdog Hybrid Brayt also produced
Hybrid females Al'Fa and Irda and male Nord in 1962. As shown elsewhere, male Hybrids Chani and Nord each sired 5 male and 3 female
recorded offspring through 1962 to 1968.

Hybrid Kora's maternal lineage is rather sketchy and as such one
could assume that she may have been born in St. Petersburg or was sent
there from Red Star. Readers can see in Nemfred's pedigree (Appendix
A, Chuk Section) that Chuk as well as Volga, sire and dam of Hybrid Alfa,
have now faded from the pedigree picture.

Moscow Waterdog Hybrid, Basta

Moscow Waterdog Hybrid, Velta

*Moscow Waterdog Hybrid,
Vishnya*

*Moscow Waterdog Hybrid,
Volga*

*Photographs of female 1956 littermates of Moscow Waterdog Hybrid, Brayt
(Crossbreed, Azart × Moscow Waterdog, Hanka)*

Family Lines

1956: Based on Moscow Waterdog Hybrid Brayt (Male) (Crossbreed, Azart × Moscow Waterdog, Hanka)

MOSCOW WATERDOG HYBRID BRAYT WAS a strong influence on the developing "Black Terrier" from the early beginnings. His photograph demonstrates the blending of a number of ingredients, similar to the way an artist mixes and blends the paint colours on his pallet as he works to portray the depth of his painting on canvas.

Hybrid Brayt was a masterpiece of Giant Schnauzer, Rottweiler, Moscow Water Dog (Newfoundland × Caucasian Ovcharka.). The only missing colours on this pallet were the Airedale Terrier and Moscow Dog (Great Dane × East European Shepherd). A study of Brayt's photograph (and those of his 1956 female littermates Volga, Vishnya, Basta, and Velta) show a remarkable consistency coming from a mix of Crossbreed Azart (Giant Schnauzer × Rottweiler) with Moscow Waterdog Hanka (Newfoundland × Caucasian Ovcharka)

Hybrid Brayt was also an exceptional stud dog, reproducing his image with a number of very fine breed-representative females. He sired 10 male and 7 female recorded Hybrid offspring:

- Al'Fa (yr?) female (Brayt × Crossbreed, Ira)
- Bars (yr?) male (Brayt × Hybrid, Chonga)
- Dzherri (1957) male (Brayt × Crossbreed, Charva)
- Azart II (1957) male (Brayt × Crossbreed, Charva)
- Ara (1957) female (Brayt × Crossbreed, Charva)
- Bara (1957) female (Brayt × Hybrid, Appa)
- Agat (1957) male (Brayt × Crossbreed, Ahta)
- Azur (1957) male (Brayt × Crossbreed, Ahta)

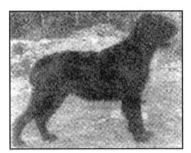

Hybrid, Chani, 1962, male *Hybrid, Al'Fa, yr?, female*

- Brajta (1958) female (Brayt × Crossbreed, Basta)
- Shrek ((1958) (male) (Brayt × Crossbreed, Binta)
- Graf (1959) males (Brayt × Crossbreed, Basta)
- Agat (1959) males (Brayt × Crossbreed, Basta)
- Nelli (1960) female (Brayt × Unknown, Zarna)
- Nayda (1961) female) (Brayt × Hybrid, Nelma):

Hybrid, Foka, 1960, male *Hybrid, Viy, 1960, male*

Hybrid, Dan-Darsi, 1969, female *Hybrid, Dzhoya, 1967, female*

- Irda (1962) female (Brayt × Crossbreed, Ira)
- Nord (1962) male (Brayt × Crossbreed, Ira)
- Chani (1962) male (Brayt × Crossbreed, Ira)

Unfortunately there is a great deal of missing information on the progeny of Hybrid Brayt.

[Again, to clarify a contradiction in terms/classification, Brayt and his littermates, male Vityaz and females Vishnya, Volga, Vesna, Basta, and Velta (1956) (Crossbreed, Azart × Moscow Waterdog, Hanka) were, by definition, according to this author, Moscow Waterdog Hybrids. This is relative to this study of the creation of the Black Russian Terrier. The hypothesis of this author is that once Giant Schnauzer Roy was introduced into the hybrid mix, the offspring moved from the (Group) of Moscow Waterdog into that of the Black Terrier. Readers are encouraged to make their own assessment.]

Family Pillars of Brayt

- Hybrid Chani (1962) (Hybrid, Brayt × Crossbreed, Ira) 3 male and 2 female recorded offspring. Chani was a good sire with females Ohta, Alfa, and Teya
- Hybrid Bars [Baron] (Brayt × Chonga) 1 recorded female offspring: Berta (Hybrid, Bars × Unknown Fimka).
- Hybrid Ara, female (1957) (Brayt × Crossbreed, Charva); no recorded offspring

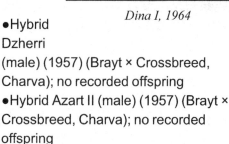

Dina I, 1964

- Hybrid Dzherri (male) (1957) (Brayt × Crossbreed, Charva); no recorded offspring
- Hybrid Azart II (male) (1957) (Brayt × Crossbreed, Charva); no recorded offspring

Karat, 1964

Ayman, 1964

Bim I

Hybrid Bara (1957) female (Hybrid, Brayt × Hybrid, Appa) 2 male recorded offspring. Bara was another important early brood bitch, producing 2 exceptional male offspring in littermates Foka and Viy 1960 (Vah × Bara). These two brothers were very different in coat and format. Their photographs are repeated hereunder for easy comparison, demonstrating the extreme difference in coat possibilities within the same litter. By examining the pedigrees (Appendix A, Brayt Section), readers can see that the "Roy coat factor" is being somewhat diminished (with Viy) through the infusions of heavy doses of Rottweiler. However the "Roy" format remains strong and true with Foka.

Unfortunately, the only available photograph of Viy's nine recorded offspring is that of Hybrid Dan-Darsi (1969) (Viy × Dzhoya), and she presents in the "typical" sought-after harsh coat. Although Brayt is somewhat out of the picture at this point, he is, however, Dan-Darsi's paternal great grandsire. It can also been seen through the pedigree and photograph of Dan-Darsi how the new breed is well along the road to type/format stabilization.

Hybrid Nayda (1961) female (Hybrid, Brayt × Hybrid, Nelma) 3 male and 3 female recorded offspring. Nayda (1961) should not be confused with Nayda (1966) (Karat × Teya). Nayda well demonstrates the intense use of Moscow Waterdog with Giant Schnauzer Roy along with the blending in of Rottweiler through Una and from Azot (Giant Schnauzer, Roy × Rottweiler Firma) plus a touch of Airedale Terrier through Sotta.

Ata (female) (Topaz × Nayda) 4 recorded female offspring.

Ayda (female) (Topaz × Nayda) no recorded offspring.

Hybrid Dina I (1964) female (Hybrid, Foka × Hybrid, Nayda) 2 male and 2 female recorded offspring.

Dina I's date of birth is March 19, 1964 and the following 3 males (Karat, Ayman, and Fang) are recorded as September 28, 1964. If this is accurate, it would mean that Dina I was was bred to Foka twice in one year, which would present a rather unusual practice as historically seen in the records available.

Karat (1964) male (Foka × Nayda) 8 male and 19 recorded offspring. See Karat under his own family line.

Ayman (1964) male (Foka × Nayda) 1 recorded male offspring: Bim I (Ayman × Alfa). Bim I recorded 4 male and 1 female offspring with 5 different females in 1974, 1975 and 1977.

Hybrid Fang (1964) male (Foka × Nayda) 1 female recorded offspring: Jolka (1969) (Fang × Ruza). Jolka became very important to the breed when she went to Finland where she established her own line, in particular with the male Max (Dzhim × Inga) (Karat × Teya and Daks ×

Nora). Jolka and Max produced, among others, females Anastasia, Alicjezebel, (1972) Jolkas Check and males Ctsecu and Carrie (1964). The Jolkas family line produced many excellent breed representatives that spread into much of Western Europe.

Hybrid, Demon, 1957

Hybrid, Arras, 1954

Family Lines

1957: Based on Hybrid Demon (Male) (Hybrid, Arras × Crossbreed, Chomga)

IT IS REPORTED THAT A group of stud dogs based on Demon was founded in Chelyabinsk, a city located in central-west Russia on the eastern foothills of the Ural Mountains on the Miass River, 1490 km (928 mi.) east of Moscow, illustrating the early widespread breeding program in Russia.

Even a cursory examination of Demon's pedigree (Appendix A, Demon Section) and photograph demonstrates just how quickly a desired type and format was achieved utilizing a rather masterful combination of Giant Schnauzer, Rottweiler, and Airedale Terrier. This in itself is most amazing in that the success came from two crossbreeds: Arras × Chomga.

Used extensively at Moscow's Red Star Kennel, Demon (Arras × Chomga) was reported to be a large strong male with a rough constitution, good bone, a well muscled body, and a (regular) bite. On the down side, his head was excessively wide, and although he was slightly cow-hocked, his movement was free and frictionless. In examining the pedigree and photographs of Demon and Arras, one notes the influence of coat colour and texture coming from Giant Schnauzer Roy. Hybrid Demon was born at Red Star kennel then privately owned by one (G.A. Esilevskaa) in the Russian port city of Saratov located on the Volga River approximately 860 km southeast of Moscow.

Hybrid Demon was said to have been "a large representative of [pureblood] breeding, showy, massive and powerful, with a rough coat of long wavy hair". Demon 1957 derived from the early blending of Giant Schnauzer, Rottweiler, and Airedale Terrier.

Recorded offspring of Hybrid Demon:

- Hybrid Negus (yr?) male (Hybrid, Demon × Unknown) 1 female offspring
- Hybrid Kara (yr?) female (Hybrid, Demon × Unknown) 2 male 2 female offspring
- Hybrid Deyv (yr?) male (Hybrid, Demon × Hybrid, Cholka) 7 male 4 female offspring
- Hybrid Yaga (yr?) female (Hybrid, Demon × Hybrid, Mirta) 1 female offspring
- Hybrid Ayshe (1961) female (Hybrid, Demon × Hybrid, Ledi) 2 male 6 female offspring
- Hybrid Sekki (1962) female (Hybrid, Demon × Hybrid, Arsa) 3 male 4 female offspring
- Hybrid Dega (1962) female (Hybrid, Demon × Hybrid, Galka) 3 male 1 female offspring
- Hybrid Dzhessi (1963) female (Hybrid, Demon × Hybrid, Ledi) 1 male 3 female offspring
- Hybrid Blek (1964) male (Hybrid, Demon × Hybrid, Sekki) No recorded offspring

Two important female Hybrids in the Demon Line were Ayshe (1961) and Dzhessi (1963) (Hybrid, Demon × Hybrid, Ledi). Ayshe produced 2 male and 6 female recorded offspring and Dzhessi has recorded 1 male and 3 female offspring. As we know, Hybrid

Hybrid, Demon, 1957, male. Photo from a second book by Gerasimova (undated) (1959–60?.
This is a second photo of Demon giving another perspective of his size and bulk.)

Moscow Waterdog Grum, 1954, male

Demon was inbred on Giant Schnauzer Roy through Crossbreeds Arras and Chomga.

Offspring from **Hybrid Ayshe** all come from 1 recorded litter in 1964 sired by Hybrid Dik (1958) (Crossbreed, Haytar × Hybrid, Vishnya). An interesting observation in this litter is that Dik's dam, Vishnya, was by Crossbreed, Azart × Moscow Waterdog, Hanka. Readers will further note that Ayshe's maternal great grandsire was Crossbreed, Azot (1954) (Giant Schnauzer, Roy × Rottweiler, Firma). Again, like-name confusion (Crossbreed Azart 1954 and Crossbreed Azot 1954).

The arrival of female Hybrids Ayshe and Dzhessi is one of those many [crossover] points that justifies repeating some pertinent information in maintaining the flow of Family development. In this case, I have included the combined pedigrees (Appendix A) of Ayshe and Dzhessi in introducing their separate trailway lines. I headlined each of these Hybrid females separately because, although they have the same sire and dam, they were born in separate litters two years apart. This section will point out the serious over-crossing and separation of lines as they developed.

Hybrid, Aydina, 1964, female

Moscow Waterdog Grum × Hybrid Ledi presented a fascinating combination of Moscow Waterdogs with a touch of Giant Schnauzer and Rottweiler bringing readers to female Hybrids Ayshe and Dzhessi. Moscow Waterdog Grum's sire, Fakt, was paternally from Newfoundland Lord × Moscow Waterdog, Tina and his dam, Ufa, was by Newfoundland Negus f. Mangeym × East European Shepherd, Rina.

Ledi's maternal grandsire was Crossbreed Azot (Giant Schnauzer, Roy a Rottweiler, Firma) and her grand dam was Moscow Waterdog Hanka (Newfoundland, Lord × Moscow Waterdog, Tiza).

Readers will see the magnificent result from this combination in the photograph of Grum. A close examination of his photograph [the only one discovered] would suggest a near-perfect streamlined version of the Newfoundland Dog.

Hybrid, Adzhi-Shahra, 1964, female

Recent videos (2014) viewed on the Internet would suggest that this [type] breed is alive and well at Red Star Military Kennel. Such a "breed" might not have met the military requirement for "water rescue" work, but may very well have been discovered valuable for other military uses. It could also be that some Moscow Waterdogs survived the "destroy all" order (maybe in the hands of private breeders) and evolved into an exceptional "special services" breed. A visit to Red Star by those able to make the journey might prove very productive in finding answers to the questions: Does a modified Moscow Waterdog exist at Krasnaya Zvezka (Red Star Military Kennel)? and if so, What [new] ingredients went into the evolution of the breed? Or was the breed modified purely through selection for desired traits?

The following offspring of Hybrid Ayshe apply equally to the pedigree of Aydina in Appendix A:

- Hybrid Aydina (1964) female;   3 male recorded offspring
- Hybrid Dzhin (1964) male;   no recorded offspring
- Hybrid Agat (1964) male;   no recorded offspring
- Hybrid Adzhi-Shahra (1964) female - 3 male 4 female offspring
- Hybrid Ayda (1964) female;   1 male 1 female recorded offspring
- Hybrid Adi (1964) female;   1 male 5 female recorded offspring
- Hybrid Aida (1964) female 1 male 2 female recorded offspring
- Hybrid Dzhan (1964);   1 female recorded offspring

Readers will note that all offspring in the same litter do not necessarily have names beginning with the same letter, as noted above. If no photographs appear for any given specimen, none could be found.

Hybrid Dzhessi was bred with 3 different males Hybrid Tom (1964) (Crossbreed,Gay × Hybrid, Dina) producing female Hybrid Arma (1966?); Giant Schnauzer, Dasso f. Drahenshljuht (1960) producing female Hybrid Roza (1963); Hybrid Viy (1960) producing Hybrids male Robin and female Sarra [Sara] in 1966. None of these offspring were exceptional producers relative to current records, with Sarra [Sara] producing males Re-Dzhon, Re-Dik-Sar and female Re-Byuti with Hybrid Dik in 1968.

Of interest is that Hybrids Appa and Arras (Rottweiler, Beniamino × Crossbreed, Hizha [Hinga] (Giant Schnauzer, Roy × Airedale Terrier, Sotta)) bring Airedale Terrier genes into the mix, noting as well that Hybrid Arras was the sire of Hybrid Demon.

Family Lines

1958: Based on Hybrid Dik (Male) (Crossbreed, Haytar × Hybrid, Vishnya)

AS A MATTER OF INTEREST to readers there were two earlier male Hybrids named Dik both born at Red Star in 1956. One was by Crossbreed, Chubarik × Crossbreed, Chadra. Chubarik was by Giant Schnauzer, Roy × Moscow Waterdog Ufa. Chadra was by Giant Schnauzer, Roy × Rottweiler, Una). The other was by Crossbreed, Chelkash × Crossbreed, Atava. Chelkash was by Giant Schnauzer, Roy × Rottweiler, Una. Atava was by Giant Schnauzer, Roy × Moscow Waterdog, Tiza. The first Hybrid Dik, sired by Chubarik, records 2 male offspring, Shaytan and Sambo, out of Crossbreed Ahta. The second, sired by Chelkash, currently shows no recorded offspring.

Hybrid Dik (1958) (Crossbreed, Haytar × Hybrid, Vishnya) was a prolific breeding male, having a profound influence on the development of the breed within the time frame of 1960 through 1968, as recorded in the Black Russian Terrier Database. It is quite conceivable that a great deal more information on Dik — and his influence — will come to light in the

future as more people become involved in recording the history of the Black Russian Terrier. Dik currently has 10 male and 15 female offspring recorded in the Database. These numbers are small in relation to the two to three hundred offspring being recorded by some twenty-first century stud dogs. Readers will recognize that Dik and a number of early crossbreeds/hybrids of the "Black Terrier Group" were the foundation pillars

Dik, 1958

Haytar, 1952   *Vishnya, 1956*

on which the modern Black Russian Terrier was built.

Hybrid Dik was the product of the original foundation breeds. His sire, Haytar, was an original crossbreed of Giant Schnauzer Roy × Airedale Terrier Sotta. His dam, Vishnya, was also an original hybrid that combined the genes of Crossbreed Azart and Moscow Waterdog Hanka. Azart was by Giant Schnauzer Roy × Rottweiler Una and Hanka came by way of the blending of the original Newfoundland Dog Lord with the Moscow Waterdog Tiza, who was by Newfoundland Dog Negus f. Mangeym and Caucasian Ovcharka Karabashka.

Crossbreed, Chubarik, 1953   *Hybrid, Sambo, 1958*

Family Pillars of Dik

Hybrid Aydina (female) (1964) (Hybrid, Dik × Hybrid, Ayshe) appears from a photograph (next page) as having been fairly large and heavy set with a somewhat wooly-coat appearance. She was born in 1964 and owned privately in Moscow. In 1969, she is recorded as having produced male Hybrid Atos (Hybrid, Lord (1966) × Hybrid, Dina I (1964). Hybrid Atos (photo next page) appears physically very much like his dam Aydina.

Hybrid, Aydina, 1964   *Hybrid, Atos, 1969*

(See pedigree of Aydina in Appendix A, Dik Section.)

Hybrid Adzhi-Shahra (female) (1964) (Dik × Ayshe) 2 male and 2 female recorded offspring. Bred at Moscow with Hybrid Bechel in 1969 she produced Hybrid males Barhan-Zhan, Bahor Boss, and Burkhan and females Bella and Basma. From this litter, Barhan-Zhan records 3 female offspring in 1973 with Hybrid Rema Greza and 1 male and 1 female offspring in 1974 with Hybrid Dor-Ditta. Hybrid Bella produced 1 recorded male offspring sired by Hybrid Nord in 1973.

Hybrid Ayda female (1964) (Hybrid, Dik × Hybrid, Ayshe) produced 1 male (Men) and 1 female (Chari) 1969 (Hybrid, Bechel × Hybrid, Ayda).

Hybrid Adi female (1964) (Hybrid, Dik × Hybrid, Ayshe) 1 male and 5 recorded female offspring: Hybrid Zitta (yr?) female (Hybrid, Karat × Hybrid, Adi); Hybrids male Osman, female Dinka (1967) (Hybrid, Tom × Hybrid, Adi; Hybrid females For-Ahanna, Tana, and Tapa (1969) (Hybrid, Topaz × Hybrid, Adi). Of this group, only Hybrid Zitta currently has recorded offspring in Hybrid female Tan Irza (Hybrid, Chingiz Rhan × Hybrid, Zitta).

Hybrid Aida female (1964) (Hybrid, Dik × Hybrid, Ayshe) 1 male and 1 female recorded offspring. Aida currently records 3 offspring in 1966 sired by Giant Schnauzer, Dasso f. Drahenshljuht: Hybrids male Terri and females Alma and Lira. Hybrids Terri and Lira remained at Red Star. Hybrid Alma went into the breeding program at St. Petersburg. When bred with Hybrid Dzhek, she produced male Karu and females Karolina, Kristi, and Kassi in 1970.

Hybrid Dzhan female (1964) (Hybrid, Dik × Hybrid, Ayshe) currently records 1 female offspring in Diva (yr?) who appears to have been privately owned at Moscow. Hybrid Diva records 1 female, Dzhudi, and 2 male offspring, Rams 2 and Devi (1971) (Hybrid, Vud × Hybrid, Diva). These offspring appear to have been privately owned at Moscow.

Hybrid, Adzhi-Shahra

Hybrid, Bechel

Hybrid, Barhan-Zhan

Hybrid, Burkhan

Hybrid, Rams 2

Hybrid, Devi

Hybrid Dzhi (male) (1964) (Dik × Ayshe) shows no recorded offspring.

Hybrid Re-Dzhek (male) (Dik × Unknown) shows no recorded offspring.

Hybrid Re-Byuti (female) (Dik × Sarra) shows no recorded offspring.

Hybrid Stesha (1965) female (Hybrid, Dik × Hybrid, Nastya) produced 2 male and 6 female offspring in 1967 sired by Hybrid Karat (1964). Stesha's dam, Nastya, was born at Red Star but at some point went on to St. Petersburg where she was was bred to Hybrid Dik in 1965. Stesha was rated as of excellent quality and granted the great Golden Medal at the Leningrad Show of 1969. Both Hybrids Stesha and Nastya will be featured in detail in Volume 6, *Leningrad Families*.

Other offspring sired by Hybrid Dik that are detailed in Volume 6, *Leningrad Families* include those from Hybrid Nastya in 1965 (males Skif, Saks, and Smok and female Stesha); and in 1966 (male Ryzhiy and females Roksa, Ruza, Radda, and Rufa).

- Hybrid Dzhema (1964) female (Hybrid, Dik × Hybrid, Lada) shows no recorded offspring.
- Hybrid Pirat-Anchar (1964) male (Hybrid, Dik × Hybrid, Lada) shows no recorded offspring.
- Hybrid Vud (1967) male (Hybrid, Dik × Hybrid, Velta) records 2 male and 6 female offspring
- Hybrid Chapa (1967) female (Hybrid, Dik × Hybrid, Velta) shows no recorded offspring.
- Hybrid, Chana (1967) female (Hybrid, Dik × Hybrid, Velta) shows no recorded offspring.
- Hybrid Dvin (1967) male (Hybrid, Dik × Hybrid, Velta) shows no recorded offspring.
- Hybrid Devel-Blek (1967) male (Hybrid, Dik × Hybrid, Velta) shows no recorded offspring.
- Hybrid Dzhenni-Vega (1967) female (Hybrid, Dik × Hybrid, Velta) shows no recorded offspring.

Hybrid Tishka (1967) male (Hybrid, Dik × Hybrid, Nora) records 3 offspring in male Hybrid Atos (yr?) (Hybrid, Tishka × Hybrid, Chara); Hybrids Nik-Din (male) and Neda (female) (1972) (Hybrid, Tishka ×

Hybrid, Lada). Located at Red Star Kennel, Atos sired male Lord, females Aza-1 and Ekka-Elsi out of Hybrid Virta in 1977; male Hybrid Larsen also in 1997 out of Hybrid Dan-Yamika; and in 1983 female Hybrid Dzhimmi out of Hybrid Virta. In 1987, Dizhimmi was bred to male Hybrid Erop producing male Hybrid Werevolf. Erop's sire was Hybrid Zorro (Hybrid, Irtish × Hybrid Kroshka) and his dam Gloriya came from (Hybrid, Monstr-Dzhimmi-Set × Hybrid, Ilona). With such an incredible lineage, Werevolf records only one offspring in Meri Krista (1990) [Irkutsk, Russia] female (Hybrid, Werevolf × Hybrid, Shelli Urs). Meri Krista traces back solidly to Hybrid Dik paternally and maternally through her great grandsire Hybrid Ahill.

Hybrid Re-Dzhon (1968) male (Hybrid, Dik × Hybrid Sarra [Sara] shows no recorded offspring.

Hybrid Re-Dik-Sar (1968) male (Hybrid, Dik × Hybrid, Sarra [Sara] shows no recorded offspring.

Hybrid Vik (1968) male (Hybrid, Dik × Hybrid, Velta) shows no recorded offspring.

Family Lines

1958: Based on Hybrid Shaytan (Male) (Hybrid, Dik × Crossbred, Ahta)

FAMILY PILLARS OF SHAYTAN INFORMATION in Database recorded offspring — and other sources — is currently very limited in that he shows only 2 recorded offspring in male Hybrids Nayt and Chap (1964) (Hybrid, Shaytan × Crossbreed, Teya). Hybrid Shaytan and his male littermate, Sambo, are recorded as having been born in 1958, and two male half siblings Agat and Azur (Hybrid, Brayt × Crossbreed, Ahta) were born in 1957.

I know I raise this observation often but it is important to witness the limited number of early dogs and breeds used in accomplishing greatness. Note the inbreeding on Giant Schnauzer Roy and Rottweiler Una blended with a dash of Roy × Moscow Waterdog Ufa (Newfoundland, Negus Mangeym × East European Shepherd, Rina). Again also note the role of the East European Shepherd, which by now readers know was/is a [Russian] German Shepherd with a tad of Caucasian Ovcharka steroids [plus other genes] and first choice of the KGB as a policing partner.

Hybrid Chap (1964) currently shows no recorded offspring in the Database.

Hybrid Nayt was a somewhat different story with currently (2016) showing 19 recorded offspring with 11 males and 8 females with a number of exceptional females who fully met the identified [new] breed requirements for further breeding from 1966 through 1970.

As stated throughout this study, the development of the Black Russian Terrier Virtual Database is an ongoing work of invaluable breed

Crossbreed, Chubaric, 1953

Crossbreed, Ahta, 1954

Hybrid, Nayt, 1964

information with new data being added on a continuing basis. Hopefully Shaytan's valuable contribution to the development of the Black Terrier vis-à-vis Black Russian Terrier will soon come to light.

Family Lines

1959: Based on Hybrid Ledi (Moscow Waterdog, Grum × Moscow Waterdog Hybrid, Ginta)

LEDI WAS A REINFORCED "KARABASHKA dog", a superb breeding example of the Moscow Waterdog Hybrid — including all its major constituent parts.

The original foundation was based on two crossings of three separate breeds. The first was male Newfoundland Dog, Negus f. Mangeym with female Caucasian Ovcharka, Karabashka, producing female Moscow Waterdog, Tiza (1949). The second was crossing of male Newfoundland Dog, Negus f. Mangeym with female East European Shepherd, Rina, producing Moscow Waterdog, Ufa (1950).

Tiza was then was bred to Newfoundland Dog, Lord, producing male Moscow Waterdog, Fakt (1951). From the mating of Moscow Waterdogs, Fakt and Ufa, was born male Moscow Waterdog, Grum [date of birth not recorded but probably in the time frame of 1953-54].

In spite of a diverse format in the descendants of Ledi within the first three generations, it is recorded that there was sufficient common exterior features about them to justly identify them as a "Moscow Waterdog" family group, by distinguishing pedigree, good [typical] physical development, and well structured acceptable bites. Coats were reported to be black and of a stiff or rough consistency, although not consistently well developed. Frequent deficiencies [as in the other groups] were unstable toplines, with some excessive rear sloping, straight hocks and uncharacteristic movements of the hind limbs. In tracing Ledi's lineage the only available photographs are of Grum, Ginta, Hanka and Roy.

Hanka (Moscow Waterdog)
Dam of Ginta

Grum (Moscow Waterdog)
Sire of Ledi

To appreciate the lineage of Ledi we have to also examine the pedigrees and photographs of her parents, Moscow Waterdog, Grum and Moscow Waterdog Hybrid, Ginta.

From a separate mating of Lord × Moscow Waterdog, Tiza came the female Moscow Waterdog, Hanka (1952). Ledi's dam, Moscow Waterdog Hybrid Ginta was 50% Moscow Waterdog through Hanka, with Ginta also bringing into the mix the genes of Giant Schnauzer, Roy and Rottweiler, Firma, through Azot. Also note that Fakt and Hanka were [sibling] grandparents of Ledi.

Hybrid Ginta, 1956
Dam of Ledi

Ledi embodied the benefits of the progressive processes of combining the genes of Newfoundland and Caucasian Ovcharka with East European Shepherd, Rottweiler, and Giant Schnauzer (Roy). She was "the bedrock" of the Moscow Waterdog inclusion in formulating the developing "Black Terrier Group" in Red Star

Hybrid Demon, 1957

Military kennels at Moscow and Moscow City Club. It is most unfortunate, at this time, that none of Ledi's littermates or siblings are recorded in the database.

In view of the importance of the infusion of the Moscow Waterdog into the make-up of the "Black Terrier" breeding Group, I feel this is a good place to present a note regarding the male Moscow Waterdog Grum. This enlarged photograph of Grum depicts a dog that could be thought of as a Newfoundland Dog with some refinement from the East European Shepherd.

Knowing his genetic make-up one could understand why the Russian developers may have referred to him and his kind as the Moscow Newfoundland Dog. I have seen videos recorded recently at Red Star, displaying canines with a remarkable likeness to Grum. (Are they New-foundland Dogs or are they Moscow Newfoundland Dogs?) This tends to beg a further question. In reality is the Moscow Waterdog extinct? Can these "like" canines be a refinement or reincarnation of the earlier breed? Grum is a perfect representative of what a Moscow Waterdog should be.

Without photographs of Moscow Waterdogs Fakt and Ufa, readers have to picture for themselves what the results may have been by cross-ing — in one case the Newfoundland Dog × Caucasian Ovcharka, and in another case, the Newfoundland Dog × East European Shepherd (VEO). Readers are familiar with the Newfoundland and have seen photographs of Caucasian Ovcharka "Karabashka" and VEOs within the volumes of this study. The VEO is reminiscent of a strong, healthy German Shepherd Dog, but being a combination of early twentieth-century German Shepherd Dog, Caucasian and Central Asian Ovcharka, and Russian Laika breeds.

One's imagination does not have to be stretched to appreciate the predominance coming from the Newfoundland Dog, Grum being a perfect example, just as was Giant Schnauzer Roy, in passing on coat dominance. As we know, once Roy was introduced into the Moscow Waterdog gene pool, he impressed his coat style into the mix.

The only individual specimen description the author located within this breeding group was of Moscow Waterdog Ufa, depicting her as being a "typical" strong bitch with a good head, dry lips, and dark eyes. She was reportedly well-balanced with a good quality outer- and undercoat which would have come from both the Newfoundland Dog and the VEO. She attained an excellent rating, achieving the Lord Provost Degree I for her breed in 1956. The thing about UFA comes from her contributing a strong Moscow Waterdog influence through offspring by Moscow Waterdog Fomka, Moscow Waterdog, Fakt, and Giant Schnauzer, Roy.

Confusing Dates

With Ginta's pedigree, there again rises a spectre of confusion regarding her date of birth and sire (Azot). The Database records Ginta's birth date as [dd-mm-yr] 09-03-1956 (Azot × Hanka) and her half siblings, (Brayt, Vishnya, Volga, Vesna, Vityaz, Basta, and Velta) (Azart × Hanka) [dd-mm-yr] 28-01-1956. Note that the dam of both litters was Moscow Waterdog, Hanka. It seems probable that a data entry is incorrect; however, when searching available offspring data, I was unable to confirm the anomaly. Could it possibly be an entry confusion between the "like-names" of Crossbreeds Azot (15-07-1954) (Roy × Firma) and Azart (08-05-1954) (Roy × Una) both born in 1954?

An examination of the breeding of Demon and Ledi identifies a serious undertaking at blending the Moscow Waterdog into the foundation stock of the "Black Terrier Group". The selection of Demon × Ledi may well have been made with the expectation of obtaining offspring of size and bulk clothed in a rough, thick, relatively long-haired coat. The only breed in this lineage with a short coat was the Rottweiler which was heavily represented through Demon. However, it was well known that in dogs with significant Newfoundland genes, the coats were thick, long, and most often soft and with a silky finish. Through Ginta, Moscow Waterdogs presented with this ample coat type that was passed to offspring. When combined with Giant Schnauzer and Airedale Terrier, a rougher/harsher texture was most often established.

With the combining of Moscow Waterdog Ledi and Hybrid Demon came an exceptional mixing of the size, power, and aggression of the Moscow Waterdog with the muscular brawn, athletic vigour, and intelligence of the Rottweiler. All this blended with the trainability and working proficiency of the Giant Schnauzer and East European Shepherd, along with the perseverance, unwavering devotion, and speed of the Airedale Terrier.

The first breeding of Hybrid Demon and Moscow Waterdog Ledi at the Moscow City Club produced a litter from which one of the pups was a new hybrid, Ashye (1961). A repeat breeding in 1963 produced a litter containing the female Dzhessi (1963) who became the property of Red Star Kennels.

These breedings of Hybrid Demon and Moscow Waterdog Hybrid Ledi were undertaken with the purpose (objective) of obtaining offspring that would have harsh, dense, long-haired coats. Dogs such as Hybrid Demon and Hybrid Arras (Rottweiler, Giant Schnauzer, Airedale Terrier) who did not have any Newfoundland genes, produced only short-haired offspring. Dogs that were primarily of Moscow Waterdog (Newfoundland) lineage almost always produced offspring with dense, long, rather soft, silky coats.

Hybrid Ayshe (1961) and **Hybrid Dzhessi (1963)** had Giant Schnauzer Roy on both sides of their linage with great grandsires Roy and Azot and great grand dam Hizha [Hinga] (Giant Schnauzer, Roy × Airedale Terrier, Sotta).

Although there are no photographs of these two females, they are reported as having common features, being of large format and representing the [appropriate/preferred] type. Their heads were of the desired type, although Ayshe had a somewhat wider skull. Both had good bone and well-developed muscular bodies with excellent hindquarters providing powerful drive and fluid movement. Both also presented with the desired harsh broken coat with more than adequate well-developed facial dressings and leg feathering. The two branches deriving from Ayshe and

Dzhessi were very different in their composition by way of the stud dogs used: (Hybrid, Dik × Hybrid, Ayshe).

Thus began a large family from Demon and Ledi, one that developed into two separate branches because of the stud dogs used for breeding to Hybrids Ayshe (1961) and Dzhessi (1963).

Family Lines

1960: Based on Giant Schnauzer Dasso f. Drahenshljuht (Giant Schnauzer, Ajax f. Kliatal × Giant Schnauzer, Azra f. Notr-Dam)

THE PEDIGREE OF MALE LITTERMATES Dasso and Ditter can be found in Appendix A, Dasso Section. The family information on Ditter is contained in the following chapter. Their sire and dam were of German ancestry but it is not clear if Dasso and Ditter were born in Germany and imported into Russia, or if they were born in Russia.

In a paper on the breed, written collectively by J.A. Lakatos, L.S. Osipova, and I.L. Owl and re-printed in the Russian Magazine *Rusdog*, they confirmed that Ditter and Dasso were in fact littermates. The paper states that Ditter was "black" coated and Dasso was "pepper and salt" coloured.

However, the only photograph available is of Dasso as recorded

Dasso f. Drahenshlyujht, 1960

in the Black Russian Terrier Database, and *he presents in a black coat*. If we accept that the photograph and record in the Database is that of Dasso, then it would have been Ditter who presented in the "pepper and salt" coloured coat. This could be assumed as correct in that there is no photograph of Ditter and no coat colour is recorded in his listing.

Other questions which one could muse about is whether one of their parents might have been "pepper and salt" coloured, and most importantly, why would Red Star cynologists use a dog at stud who was that colour? It is possible that the "pepper and salt" originated three, four or five generations back, for which there are no records available. On the other hand, Ditter may have presented sufficient positive traits that overrode his coat colour.

Apparently these two Schnauzers did not produce as successfully as anticipated by breeders, with litters being severely culled because of cryptorchidism. Nevertheless, they do show up in a number of early pedigrees, with Dasso having recorded 4 male and 5 female offspring and Ditter credited with 5 females, all of which were used in breeding programs, notwithstanding the culling processes employed.

Ditter's coat colour of "pepper and salt", by hypothesis, might have conceivably contributed to the sparse grey hairs throughout the coats of many of today's "Blackies". In addition to culling for cryptorchidism, there would have been unquestionable elimination of "coloured" puppies presenting in future litters coming through Ditter's line. Dasso might also have carried a recessive gene for that colour. However, to this date (2016) there are many dogs of coat colour other than black.

Dasso's sons and daughters, and Ditter's daughters, were successful in producing a number of exceptional offspring that were used in breeding programs at Red Star Kennel, City Clubs, and others private breeders' kennels. Some of their offspring, such as Lera, Reks, Changa, Ditta, Dzhaga, Tsezar, Alma, Terri, Meggi, Vilma, Nora, Dega, et al., played important roles in furthering Breed development.

Family Pillars of Dasso f. Drahenshljuht

In the pedigree of Lera (Appendix A, Dasso Section), note — for information purposes — that her maternal great grand dam, Chuta, was a crossbreed coming from Russian Spotted Hound Uteshay × Rottweiler, Uza. Hybrid Lera records 1 male (Darli) and 1 female (Dega) offspring in 1970 by Hybrid Nayt and 1 female offspring (Kana) in 1972 by Hybrid Atos.

The thing of interest here is that Hybrid Kana (Hybrid, Atos × Hybrid,

Lera) produced 1 recorded female offspring in Hybrid Tsuri by Hybrid Tsorn in 1979. Tsuri's paternal great grandsire(s) Hybrid Set also had Dasso f. Drahenshljuht as his paternal great grandsire. Readers will note that Hybrid Tsorn is inbred on Hybrid Set. With Dasso also a maternal great grandsire of Tsuri, we can appreciate the source of Giant Schnauzer format in the development of Hybrid breeding resources. Currently Hybrid Tsuri has no recorded offspring.

What we note in Hybrid Reks is the direct intervention of Giant Schnauzer genes on his paternal side from Dasso (1960). This, combined with his maternal great grandsire Roy on both sides, provided a very strong Giant Schnauzer base. However, when we examine his photograph we also appreciate the mass composition coming through Rottweiler Una and Moscow Waterdog Tina. Reks has only one offspring recorded in female Dezi (1971) (Reks × Lada). In 1974 Dezi produced females Ped Shanel and Ped Shelli, and male Ped Shvarc (Dan Zhan ×

Crossbreed, Cholka, 1953.

Reks, yr?

Ped Shvarc, 1974

Sherli, 1977

Dezi), and Pedi (1980), again by Dan Zhan. Ped Shvarc sired Sherli (1977) (Ped Shvarc × Daza).

Unfortunately, no photograph or expert's description of Changa was discovered. She presents an interest in her solid composition of Giant Schnauzer and Rottweiler. Of special note is that her dam, Teya, is a crossbreed of Giant Schnauzer and Rottweiler, and inbred on Roy and Rottweiler littermate sisters Una and Urma, with the added Giant Schnauzer impact coming paternally from Dasso f. Drahenshljuht.

Crossbreed Changa when bred to male Hybrid Devy (Hybrid, Demon × Crossbreed, Cholka) produced a fine "Black Terrier" specimen in Hybrid Farlaf, possibly ca. 1974. Farlaf sired Hybrid Yukon (1976) (Hybrid, Farlaf × Hybrid, Vega). From Yukon's pedigree (Appendix A, Dasso Section) readers will see some important gaps in information from his maternal side. Yukon was located in Chelyabinsk and has 3 male and 3 female recorded offspring recorded in the Database. Yukon also has Giant Schnauzer Dasso f. Drahenshljuht on his maternal side through his grandsire Al'Princ whose maternal grand dam was also Crossbreed Changa (Giant Schnauzer, Dasso f. Drahenshljuht × Crossbreed, Teya).

On the following page is a photo collage of specimens in the pedigrees of Hybrids Yukon and Al'Princ.

In examining the pedigrees of Hybrids Yukon, Farlaf, and Al'Princ (Appendix A, Dasso Section), readers can more easily see the complexities along with the wisdom in how Red Star geneticists pulled in the genes of Giant Schnauzer Dasso both paternally and maternally to arrive at Hybrid Yukon. And, of course, looking at the [big] picture we realize that the Giant Schnauzer format was based on the genes of Roy and reinforced from those of Dasso f. Drahenshljuht × Crossbreed Teya (Crossbreed, Vah (Roy × Una) × Crossbreed, Basta (Roy × Urma)). Readers will note as well that Yukon's maternal great grand dam Alba's maternal grandsire was also Dasso.

Hybrid Ditta (1964) produced some exceptional offspring including the incomparable male Hybrid Karay 1967 (Hybrid, Nayt × Hybrid, Ditta), photos of Ditta and Karay on p. 101. In that 1967 litter were also male Jar and females Dina II, Dar-Ditta, and Dzhun. Again note that Ditta's maternal grand dam Alva was a cross of Rottweiler and Airedale Terrier.

In a repeat breeding with Hybrid Nayt in 1968, Ditta produced Hybrid

Crossbreed, Cholka, 1953

Hybrid, Tom, 1964

Hybrid, Demon, 1957

Hybrid, Foka, 1960

Hybrid, Rams 1, 1966

Hybrid, Alba, 1969

Hybrid, Topaz, 1967

Farlaf, ca. 1974

males Denas, Darli, and Dinar and female Dar Ritsa. Then in 1972, she was bred to Hybrid Dzhaga (Giant Schnauzer, Dasso f. Drahenshljuht × Hybrid, Berta) and produced Hybrid Danchar making Danchar inbred on Dasso f. Drahenshljuht. Hybrid Danchar was bred to Hybrid Setti and sired Hybrid male Re-Milford and female Re-Dzhessi.

Although Dzhaga's pedigree (Appendix A, Dasso Section) is somewhat sketchy, he brings a solid gene structure of the major foundation breeds through Brayt and Chonga. Brayt contributes strengths coming

Hybrid, Ditta, 1964   *Hybrid, Karay, 1967*

from the combinations of Giant Schnauzer, Rottweiler, and Moscow Waterdog, with Changa adding Giant Schnauzer and Airedale Terrier genes. Hybrid Bars was by Hybrid, Brayt (Crossbreed, Azart × Moscow Waterdog, Hanka) out of Crossbreed, Chonga (Giant Schnauzer, Roy × Airedale Terrier, Salma).

Hybrid Dzhaga sired 7 male and 7 female recorded offspring from 1968 through 1973 out of Hybrid Yuta [Yutta], Hybrid Ata, Hybrid Karmen, Hybrid Raksha, and Hybrid Yuna.

Hybrid Danchar currently shows only 1 male (Hybrid, Re-Milord) and 1 female (Re-Dzhessi) recorded offspring with Hybrid Setti in 1976.

Although **Crossbreed Tsezar**'s breeding record is not remarkable in itself, a current limited amount of directional information does not preclude his offspring having a workable impact on the developing breed structure in the mid 1960s. Of somewhat limited interest on the maternal side of his offspring is that Hybrid Kassij shows his great grandsire as Moscow Dog Hybrid Chuk and his great grand dam as Moscow Waterdog

Hybrid Volga. The interest here is in Kassij's [bulky] appearance. His great grandsire Moscow Waterdog Hybrid Brayt was also 50% Moscow Waterdog.

Hybrid, Kassij, 1969

Bred to Hybrid Dzhek in 1970, Alma produced 1 male Karu and 3 females Karolina, Kristi and Kassi. These offspring were actively involved in the Breed development in St. Petersburg in the 1970s. Offspring of Hybrid Karu were inbred on Dasso f. Drahenshljuht. These specimens will be highlighted in Volume 6, *Leningrad Families*.

Hybrid Lira (1966) was bred to Hybrid Lord (1966) recording only 1 male (Ljuter) and 1 female (Loli) offspring in 1969. Hybrid Terri (1966) currently show no recorded offspring.

Family Lines

1960: Based on Giant Schnauzer Ditter f. Drahenshljuht (Giant Schnauzer, Ajax f. Kliatal × Giant Schnauzer, Azra f. Notr-dam)

Family Pillar of Ditter f. Drahenshljuht

Hybrid Meggi female (Ditter f. Drahenshljuht × Hybrid, Gayda)

IN 1964, MEGGI WAS BRED to Vah and produced females Velta and Darling and male Oskar. These three Hybrid Black Terriers carried the colour genes of Ditter into the late 1960s and early 1970s. By examining the pedigrees (Appendix A, Ditter Section), one can appreciate the effects of the perpetuation of a diluted "pepper and salt effect" probably coming through Ditter, given the base [male] breed being Giant Schnauzer.

A later Meggi (1985) (Hybrid, Sid × Hybrid, Rona) carried the genes from Ditter's litter brother Dasso on both sides of her lineage.

Hybrids Vilma, Veda, Nora (Giant Schnauzer, Ditter f. Drahenshljuht × Hybrid, Vanda) (Ditter's pedigree is combined with Dasso's in Appendix A, Dasso Section.)

Bred to Ditter in 1962, Vanda produced 3 female offspring, Vilma, Veda, and Nora. Vilma has one recorded female offspring with Daks; Veda records 1 male and one female with Daks; and Nora's record lists 2 females and 1 male also with Daks. Nora was also was bred to Dik, producing female Tishka in 1967.

Of note with this group is that Hybrid Nora is recorded as having a "cloudy" [grey shaded?] coat colour. Nora produced 2 male and 3 female offspring all of whose coat colour is stated as black — but?.

Hybrid Dega (Giant Schnauzer, Ditter f. Drahenshljuht × Hybrid, Mirta): In 1969 at Leningrad, Dega (1963) was described as meeting the established requirement as a large, powerful, well-muscled bitch with a good head, dark eyes, complete teeth with scissors bite, flat lying ears, and even temperament.. Her back was reported to be solid and she had a free flowing movement. She also had a rough black coat. Hybrid Dega (1963) was born at Red Star Kennel in Moscow but was sent to a private owner at Leningrad. Given the "experts' description" above, Dega (1963) was or could have been, an important brood bitch through the mid 1960s into the early 1970s, recording 5 male and 4 female offspring: Zahanna (female) (1965) (Viy × Dega); Gana (female), and Girey, Gosha, and Grayt (males) (1967) (Nayt × Dega); Beta (female) and Borey (male) (1969) (Nayt × Dega); Nur (male) (1971) (Torri × Dega). In every case, these dogs were recorded as having black coats.

It appears in records that this Dega (1963) went to St. Petersburg but curiously, not one of her offspring shows any record of producing offspring of their own. Could it possibly be that none was bred because of their coat colour? Or that none of their offspring was recorded for that reason?

An interesting point of view is that there are no available photographs of offspring sired by Ditter, or of their offspring, until we get to Hybrid Muza (Hybrid, Ajaks × Hybrid, Beta). Given the general breeding practices throughout much of the early "Black Terrier" development and Muza's dam Beta having been born in February 1969, it might safely be considered that Muza could have been born in early Spring 1971.

Hybrid Muza was an exceptionally fine looking specimen possibly being born in or close to 1971 given her dam Hybrid Beta was born in 1969. Although both Muza and her dam were born in St. Petersburg, she/they are included here as well because of their family line's connection to Muza's maternal great grandsire, Giant Schnauzer Ditter f. Drahenshljuht. This anomaly occurs occasionally because of the limited breeding base that was shared throughout much of Russia and particularly between Red Star Kennel, Moscow City Club, and Leningrad/ St. Petersburg City Club.

Hybrid Beta (1969) was also was bred to male Lord (1966) (Tom ×

Muza	Ajaks, 1967	Karat, 1964
Nayt, 1964	Nastya, 1962	Foka, 1960

Dik, 1958

Dina I) and in March 1971 produced a large litter of 4 male and 4 female offspring. It must be recognized that all of these offspring coming from Beta carried the coat-colour genes of Ditter. This litter consisted of females Masha, Malva, Malta, and Mik, and males Molloh, Misha, Mavr, and Mars.

Although the coat colour genes of Giant Schnauzer, Ditter f. Drahenshljuht are fading through the input of sires hopefully not carrying a gene for "pepper and salt" colour, the fact remains that sparse white/grey hairs were quite prevalent in the "black terriers".

Many of Masha's offspring were used within the advancing breeding programs, ergo, the possibility of a perpetuation of the sparse white/grey hairs throughout the black coats. Masha's offspring included: in 1974,

106 | Donald B. Anderson: The Creation of the Black Russian Terrier

females Molli Set, Maykl Silva Set, Mani Set, and Meri, and males Monstr-Dzhimmi Set, Mayk Set, Mozes Set, and Morris Set (Set × Masha); in 1976, female Mashka and males Michel and Mishka (Urban × Masha); and in 1979, female Moya Mariya (Oksay × Masha).

Of these offspring, Mashka went to Sweden and was used in breeding until the mid 1980s. Michel was used with females Roksa II and Doris, producing 4 male and 5 female recorded offspring.

Probably the most prolific of this group was **Monstr-Dzhimmi-Set (1974)** (Set × Masha) who sired a great looking early "black terrier" in Pluton (1976) (Monstr-Dzhimmi-Set × Ora). Other offspring sired by the "Monstr" included: in 1976, female Leda, and males Lel, Labi, and Layf (Monstr-Dzhimmi-Set × Ilona), and Prelli (Monstr-Dzhimmi-Set × Ora); females Tinga and Talya (1977) (Monstr-Dzhimmi-Set × Ustya); females Gloriya and Gayana (1978) (Montr-Dzhimmi-Set × Ilona); female Nega and male Nik (1979) (Monstr-Dzhimmi-Set × Tinga); female Dilli (1981) (Monstr-Dzhimmi-Set × Baska).

The pedigree of Hybrid Monstr-Dzhimmi-Set in Appendix A is a good example of the locations of members of his lineage showing Red Star as the primary breeding location advancing to include Leningrad/St. Petersburg, some private owners [which may well have been shared with Red Star and City Clubs] advancing to the point of Monstr being located in Tallin, Estonia, were he had considerable influence on the breed there with some of his "get" going back to St. Petersburg and some to private owners/breeders.

For example, in the mid 1980s, female Hybrid Gloriya (1978) was bred to male Hybrid Zorro (1978) and produced 5 male and 1 female recorded offspring. One of Gloriya's offspring was Hybrid Erhan (1984) male (Hybrid, Zorro × Hybrid, Gloriya). Hybrid Erhan was privately owned and sired 15 male and 28 female offspring from 1986 through 1990 with a number of females, producing some excellent specimens going into private ownership and to St. Petersburg.

Knowing **Hybrid Set**'s paternal grandsire was Giant Schnauzer Dasso and Masha's maternal great grandsire was Ditter, let's examine the pedigree of Hybrids Nega and Nik (Monstr-Dzhimmi-Set × Hybrid, Tinga) in Appendix A, Ditter Section. Readers will see the spread of private owners. Note the added influence from Hybrid Nayt, back from Hybrid Monstr-Dzhimmi-Set, in Hybrids Nik and Nega.

Hybrid, Set, 1971

Hybrid, Ustya, 1974,
Rated Breed Champion

Monstr-Dzhimmi-Set, 1974

Gayna, 1978

Layf, 1976

Pluton, 1976

Note that Hybrids Masha and Lusha (Hybrid, Skif × Hybrid, Dar Ritsa) in Nik's pedigree were not littermates. Given the geographical closeness of Tallin, Estonia, and St. Petersburg, they could have been located at either location. Hybrid Lusha was bred to Hybrid Set in 1974 to produce males Urban and Ulvik and female Ustya. Her privately owned offspring will be covered in Volume 6, *Leningrad Families*.

Female **Hybrid Talya (1977)** (littermate of Hybrid Tinga; see pedigree of Hybrid Nik (1979) in Appendix A, Family Lines of Ditter) was homed at

St. Petersburg and produced 1 recorded female offspring Hybrid Chara 1980 (Hybrid, Labi × Hybrid, Talya) located at Petrozavodsk, capital of the Republic of Karelia, Russia, on the western shore of Lake Onega [1,010 km from Moscow and 412 km from St. Petersburg]. A map of Russia will demonstrate the compactness of this area within the massive geography of Russia [Tallin, Estonia, to Petrozavodsk, Russia, 790 km].

Hybrids Set and Masha also had a profound impact on the Black Terrier/Black Russian Terrier in the advancing development stages of the 1970s and onward.

Family Lines

1961: Based on Hybrid Ayshe (Female)
(Hybrid, Demon × Hybrid, Ledi)

WE WILL FIRST EXAMINE THE "line" developed through Ayshe and follow with that of Dzhessi in the next chapter. Again, it is a great loss not to have photographs of these two important foundation females. An absolute truth from an ancient Chinese proverb is: "a picture is worth a thousand words." Or possibly more appropriate in this instance, from the Russian writer Ivan Turgenev (in *Fathers and Sons*, 1862): "A picture shows me at a glance what it takes dozens of pages of a book to expound."

Hybrid Ayshe's recorded offspring (2 male and 6 female) provide a limited picture of the initial involvement of Ledi's contribution through a single recorded litter by Hybrid Dik in 1964 that included the females, Aydina, Adzhi-Shahra, Ayda, Adi, Aida, and Dzhan, and the male Dzhin (Dik × Ayshe). The male Dzhin had no recorded offspring in the Database.

Of interest is that Hybrid Dik was a prolific breeder having been bred to Ayshe, Sarra, Nastya, Velta, Nora, and probably others, both at Red Star kennel and at the Moscow City Club of Service Dogs.

Despite the reported unsound bite formation of many dogs in the lineage of both Ayshe and Dik, apparently the male Dzhin and female Adi had "good" bite structure. There are no records of Dzhin having been used in the breeding programs at Red Star Kennel or the Moscow City Club. No photographs were located of Ayshe, Adi, or Aidi.

Adi and *Aida* had a strong Moscow Waterdog influence in their lineage on both sides coming from their paternal great grand dam Hanka (Newfoundland, Lord × Moscow Waterdog, Tiza) and from their maternal great grandsire Grum and maternal grand dam Ledi (Moscow Waterdog

Grum × Hybrid, Ginta). Hybrid Ginta was also 50% Moscow Waterdog through her dam Hanka.

Hybrid Aydina (1964) female (Hybrid, Dik × Hybrid, Ayshe) produced 3 recorded male offspring: Hybrid Atos (1969) (Hybrid, Lord × Hybrid, Aydina) Moscow, who sired 4 female offspring in the 1970s, 1 each with Hybrids Dar Karmen, Kheppi, Lera, and Raffi. All are recorded as privately owned in Russia.

Hybrid Adzhi-Shahra (1964) female (Hybrid, Dik × Hybrid, Ayshe) produced 3 male and 2 female recorded offspring with Hybrid Bechel in 1969. All were recorded as privately owned in Moscow and St. Petersburg.

Hybrid Ayda (1964) female (Hybrid, Dik × Hybrid, Ayshe) produced 1 male and 1 female recorded offspring by Hybrid Bechel in 1969. Hybrid Chari (female) was located in Novocherkassk and Hybrid Men (male) at Moscow.

Hybrid Dzhan (1964) female (Hybrid, Dik × Hybrid, Ayshe) produced 1 female (Diva) recorded offspring by Hybrid Viy (yr?) in Moscow.

Hybrid Diva produced 2 male offspring, Rams 2 and Devi , by Hybrid Vud in 1971, and male Din (1973) by Hybrid Kapitan Flint. All recorded offspring of Diva are recorded as privately owned.

Offspring of Hybrid Adi

Adi belonged to "Red Star" and was bred there to Karat, producing female Zitta (no date of birth recorded). In 1967, bred to Tom, Adi produced female Dinka; and in 1969, by Topaz, females For-Zhanna, Tana, and Tapa. In examining the pedigree of Zitta (Appendix A, Ayshe Section) it becomes visibly evident how the early Demon × Ledi line was blended with other crossbreeds and hybrids, morphing together into a more harmonious Black Terrier.

Zitta was bred twice at Moscow City Club to Dzhek, producing female Dzhe-Zitta, and to Chingiz-Rhan, producing female Tan Irza. Dates of birth of these females were not recorded. There are no recorded offspring of Dzhe-Zitta. In 1978 Tan Irza was was bred to Artosha producing one recorded male offspring, Sen Ikir, who records only 1 male offspring (Ker Rambul) 1981 out of Hybrid Ketti (Hybrid, Anchar × Hybrid, Feya).

In 1966, Hybrid Aida was was bred to Giant Schnauzer, Dasso f.

Drahenshljuht, producing Hybrids female Alma and male Terri. The interest here is in breeding Hybrid Aida back to the Giant Schnauzer. Terri and Alma were sent for breeding to Moscow City Club. (See pedigree of Aida and Adi in Appendix A, Ayshe Section.)

Hybrid Terri (1966) currently has no recorded offspring in the Database, making it impossible to know what impact, if any, he had within the breeding program at Moscow and/or at any of the City Breed Clubs or private breeders. However, Terri's litter sister, Alma, was was bred to male Dzhek in 1970, producing 3 hybrid females: Karolina, Kristi, and Kassi, and the male Karu. Dzhek traces back through Foka and Nayda to Moscow Waterdog, Hanka, and from Alma through Ayshe to Moscow Waterdog Hybrid, Ledi. Hybrids Karolina and Karu went to Leningrad/St. Petersburg. In 1973, Karolina was bred to male Chard-Han and produced the female Alkara who was bred to male Bim 1 in 1977 to produce male Sherif. Litter sisters Kristi and Kassi were privately owned and currently show no offspring recorded.

Hybrid Sherif (1977) would extend Ayshe's family line on his maternal side in 1983 in a breeding with Dolli producing females Astra, Ata, and Ayka, and males Ars and Araks.

Readers will note how Sherif, through his sire, Bim 1, goes back to stud dogs Foka and Uran, and females, Nayda and Alfa, all very important Hybrid foundation contributors. Blending together the lines of Dzhek (1966) × Alma (1966), and adding into the mix the line of Bim 1, was sheer genius. The impact on Sherif in this gene blending from Hybrid Dzhek's grandsire, Foka, and grand dam, Nayda, was substantially reinforced through Bim I and his paternal grandsire and grand dam who were also Hybrids Foka and Nayda. Although Hybrid Sherif was located in St. Petersburg, his pedigree is included in Volume 5, *Moscow Families* to again demonstrate the combinations of specimens intermixed from different locations and Clubs.

Hybrid Karu contributed a major impact on the developing breed. In 1973, bred to the female Dar Ritsa, he sired female Vaksa. In 1976, Karu was backcrossed to his daughter Vaska, and they produced females Kroshka and Krezi. This mating of father and daughter demonstrates the intensity of the Moscow breeding program. Vaksa's dam Dar Ritsa's maternal grandsire was also Giant Schnauzer Dasso. All other specimens in this line trace back to Giant Schnauzer Roy. This is a powerful family line with its Giant Schnauzer foundation base coming from Dasso f. Drahen-shljuht (1960) (Giant Schnauzer, Ajax f. Kliatal × Giant Schnauzer, Azra f. Notr-Dam).

Hybrid, Irtish, 1976

Hybrid, Karay, 1967

Hybrid, Ayna, 1967

Hybrid, Dzhek, 1966

Hybrid Bim I, yr?

Hybrid Krezi was bred to male Irtish in 1979 and produced females Hybrid Rona and Ragda and males Rey and Rayt. Hybrid Rona was to have a significant impact on the breed in the mid 1980s. Hybrid Ragda went to Krivoy, Ukraine, and records 2 female offspring by Hybrid Din-

Hybrid, Ayman, 1964

Hybrid, Nayt, 1964

Hybrid, Karat, 1964

Hybrid, Ditta, 1964

Giant Schnauzer, Dasso f. Drahenshljuht, 1960

Dzhin: Hybrid Dzhina (1984) in Nikolayev, Ukraine, and Hybrid G-Purga (1984) in Novocherkassk, Russia. Some of these specimens are covered more in Volume 6, Leningrad Families.

Hybrid Kroshka was bred to male Hybrid Irtish (1976) (Karay × Irisha) in 1978 and produced female Zolli and male Zorro. Bred to Irtish again in 1980, she produced females Cinta and Tsimmi. This repeat breeding demonstrated "the proof in the pudding" of their offspring quality. There are no available photographs of offspring from Kroshka.

Pedigrees of Irtish, Zorro, and Zolli are included (Appendix A, Ayshe Section) to demonstrate the sharing of breeding stock between Red Star/ Moscow and St. Petersburg and the export of Irtish to Estonia.

Combining the pedigrees of Hybrid Irtish (1976) and Hybrid Kroshka (1976) again demonstrates the intense breed development planning in blending together two exceptional lines in a family building process. Moving into the 1980s, Hybrid Zorro sired 7 male and 5 female recorded offspring with Hybrids Gloriya and Nora. His female littermate, Zolli, currently shows 1 male offspring in Hybrid Ramzay sired by Hybrid Nik (1979). Hybrid Nik was inbred on Hybrid Monstr-Dzhimmi-Set.

Family Lines

1963: Based on Hybrid Dzhessi (Female) (Hybrid, Demon × Hybrid, Ledi)

HYBRID DZHESSI (1963) (HYBRID, DEMON × Hybrid, Ledi) was a half-sibling of Ayshe (1961) from a second breeding of Demon × Ledi. Although there is currently limited information available on the family developed through Dzhessi, she comes from a very impressive lineage and shows up in many Hybrid pedigrees.

Hybrid Dzhessi was the property of Red Star Kennel and in 1964 was bred to Tom, producing female Arma. From a litter in 1966 with Viy, Dzhessi produced the female Hybrid Sarra and the male Robin. In 1963, bred to Giant Schnauzer Dasso f. Drahenshljuht, she produced female Hybrid Roza who in turn, bred to Hybrid Uran, produced Hybrid Nord in 1969.

Hybrid Sarra [Sara, Sarah] can present in the Database occasionally spelled differently on multiple searches. Again, this is a situation created through the computer translation system that is not always consistent. Computer translation programs are — as yet? — not capable of interpreting meaning.

There are no offspring recorded in the database for female *Hybrid Arma (1964?)* (Hybrid, Tom × Hybrid, Dzhessi). On the other hand, she presents an exceptional recorded family tree of half-siblings on her paternal side through her sire Tom.

In examining Arma's pedigree (Appendix A, Dzhessi Section), it is interesting to note that Aray (1954) and Borka (1955) are by Giant Schnauzer, Roy × Rottweiler, Urma, and Tuman's paternal grandparents were also (Roy × Urma). Arma's great grand dam, Fimka, is of unknown

115

heritage. Given her lineage, it is inconceivable that Arma would not have been used at least once with one of the many exceptional studs at Red Star or the Moscow City Club. Archival information suggests that Dzhessi's daughters Arma and Sarra were kept as brood bitches at the Moscow Club. This information in itself would indicate the strong probability that a number of litters would have been produced, with a consequent larger number of acceptable offspring for further breeding.

Hybrid Sarra (1966) is a half-sibling to Arma on their maternal side through their dam Dzhessi. Sarra has only one offspring recorded in the female Hybrid Re-Byuti (Hybrid, Dik × Hybrid, Sarra). Re-Byuti is a granddaughter of Dzhessi, and records suggest that two granddaughters of Dzhessi were used in the breeding program at Moscow City Club— but this information I could not confirm. Database records no offspring from Hybrid Re-Byuti.

Family Lines

Family Pillar of Nayt

Although it could be argued that Nayt was a Hybrid (by distant past), it could also be argued that he was basically a crossbreed of Giant Schnauzer × Rottweiler. Nayt represents one of those cases in the creation of the Black Russian Terrier where one set of great great grandparents has effectively faded from his genetic makeup, while accepting the possibility of those genes being a measurable factor in some of Nayt's offspring, dependent entirely on the specimens he was was bred to. That factor might also be considered measurable dependent on the specimens his offspring were bred to. A comparable argument could be raised regarding the fading genetic input to the [breed] coming from the early use of dogs such as the South Russian and Central Asian Ovcharka and the Moscow Dog that included the genes of the Great Dane.

This point comes to light in reference to male *Crossbreed Chubarik (1953)* who was by Giant Schnauzer, Roy × Moscow Waterdog, Ufa (Newfoundland, Negus f. Mangeym × East European Shepherd, Rina).

Female Crossbreed Chadra (1953) was also by Giant Schnauzer, Roy × Rottweiler, Una.

Hybrid Nayt (photos next page) played a major role through 11 male and 8 female offspring recorded from a number of high quality females that included Dzhina, Ditta, Dega, and Lera in the late 1960s and in 1970. Those 19 offspring by Nayt included: female Miledi (yr?); males Karay, Jar, and females Dina II, Dar-Ditta, and Dzhun (1967); males Girey, Gosha, and Grayt and female Gana (1967); males Dena, Darli, Dinar, and

Hippi and female Dar Ritsa (1968); male Borey and female Beta (1969); male Darli and female Dega (1970).

Moving forward 3 generations, readers can see the impact coming through Hybrid Nayt in the pedigree of his great grand son Hybrid, Monstr-Dzhimmi-Set (Appendix A, Nayt Section) who sired 5 male and 8 female recorded offspring in the late 1970s. Monstr-Dzhimmi-Set's offspring included Hybrid Layf (1976), male from Hybrid, Ilona; Hybrid, Pluton (1976) male from Hybrid, Ora; Hybrid, Gayna (1978) female from Hybrid, Ilona. For more detailed information on Monstr-Dzhimmi-Set [Tallin, Estonia] see his listing in Volume 6.

Readers will note that Hybrid Nayt sired Hybrid Karay and Hybrid Beta in the pedigree of Monstr-Dzhimmi-Set placing Nayt on both sides of Monstr's lineage. Also note in the pedigree of Hybrid Layf, that Hybrid Karay is his paternal *and* maternal great grandsire. Clearly, Hybrid Nayt (1964) delivered a positive genetic family impact on the developing Black Terrier Group from the mid 1960s onward, coming from his strongly constructed lineage of Giant Schnauzer × Rottweiler.

As can be seen from photographs, Nayt appears to have been a fine upstanding dog of fairly good quality. In profile, he might seem only very slightly high at the rump. However, the face-on shot portrays a nice dog indeed.

Hybrid Miledi (yr?) produced male Yarayt (Darli × Miledi) and female Kleopatra (Vud × Miledi) (1971). Yarayt was inbred on Nayt and currently shows no recorded offspring.

Hybrid Nayt, 1964

Hybrid Ditta, 1964

Crossbreed Chubarik, 1953

Hybrid Kleopatra, on the other hand, records one offspring in the male Hybrid Len Klaus (1974) (Hybrid, Artosha × Hybrid, Kleopatra) who presented as what was then considered as typical for a "Black Terrier".

It is also known that Hybrid Nayt was the sire of Hybrid Karay (1967) male (Hybrid, Nayt × Hybrid, Ditta). Both Nayt and Ditta were Red Star residents but Hybrid Karay was sent to St. Petersburg where he sired 9 male and 2 female recorded offspring. A number of his offspring were dispersed within Russia, Estonia and Finland and will be look at in more detail in Volume 6, *Leningrad Families*.

Readers may wish to be aware of the two male dogs in this family carrying the name Dik: **Hybrid Dik (1956)** (Crossbreed, Chubarik × Crossbreed, Chadra) sired male Hybrids Shaytan (sire of Nayt) and Sambo; and Hybrid, Dik (1958) (Crossbreed, Haytar × Hybrid, Vishnya) sired Hybrid Vud (1967) (sire of Kleopatra).

Crossbreed Ahta, 1954

Len Klaus sired 3 male recorded offspring by different females in 1977, 1978, and 1980, including the male Hybrid Le Kuchum (1977) (Hybrid, Len Klaus × Hybrid, Leda). Le Kuchum was inbred on Vud (1967) (Dik × Velta).

With the arrival of Hybrid Le Kuchum, we witness that Nayt, a powerful influence on this family line, has faded into the past through Miledi. Hybrid Leda is recorded as a half-sibling of Hybrid Kleopatra.

Hybrid, Vud, 1967

Hybrid, Len Klaus, 1974

Hybrid, Artosha, 1971

Hybrid, Le Kuchum, 1977

Hybrid, Alba, 1969

Hybrid, Krimson Glo, 1982

Hybrid Le Kuchum show 5 male and 5 female recorded offspring (1981–85) — all of whom appear to have been privately owned — with a number of females. One of his offspring, male Hybrid Krimson Glo (1982) is especially interesting in that he shows as having sired 35 male and 43 female offspring through the 1980s into 1992. Note Hybrid Vud on both sides of Le Kuchum, again demonstrating close line-breeding. Krimson Glo is described as being small but powerful, and sporting a big head with a large muzzle, short neck and deep chest.

Family Lines

1964: Based on Hybrid Tom (Male) (Crossbreed, Gay × Hybrid, Dina)

HYBRID TOM (1964) THROUGH HIS large family had a profound effect on the early development of the new breeding stock coming through Red Star and Moscow City Club. Tom's lineage is interesting in setting the early stage through the strengths of Giant Schnauzer and Rottweiler [Crossbreed, Aray on both sides], with Htora (Giant Schnauzer, Roy × Airedale Terrier, Sotta) bringing an early contribution of the Airedale. Tom's maternal great grandsire Araj is of unknown ancestry and his great grand dam is completely unknown, leaving readers to speculate. Although Tom was used extensively at stud, the Database currently records only 7 male and 7 female offspring: Yuta (female) (Tom × Unknown); Nora (female) (Tom × Irda); Topaz (male) (Tom × Lada); Dzhim (male) (Tom × Panta); Cherri (female) (Tom × Dzhina); Yutta (female) (Tom × Rokki); Arma (female) (Tom × Dzhessi): Lord (male) (1966) (Tom × Dina I): Dinka (female) (1967) (Tom × Adi); Dzhoya (female) (1967) (Tom × Dega); Tuman (male) (1967) (Tom × Dega). Pedigrees in Appendix A under Tom Section..

Family Pillar of Hybrid Tom (1964) × Hybrids Dega (1962) and Rokki

Tom, bred to an unknown female, sired the recorded female Hybrid Yuta (date unknown). Yuta, bred to male Tuman (1967) (Tom × Dega), produced one recorded female offspring Yuna. Of note is that both Yuta and Tuman were sired by Tom. Dega was inbred on Demon. Yuna's only recorded offspring was female Vesta (1973) (Dzhaga × Yuna). Also note Tuman (1956?) in pedigree of Topaz (1967).

Vesta has 1 male and 3 female recorded offspring: Layka [Layna] (yr?) female (Lo-Rom × Vesta); Soldi (1977) female (Charli II × Vesta); Viy, male, and Varta, female (1979) (Lo-Rom × Vesta). These offspring of Vesta were no significant producers as recorded in the Database. They also were born after 1980 which is outside the terms of reference for this study so were not investigated further.

Family Pillar of Hybrid Tom (Male) (1964) × Hybrid Lada (1964)

Records indicate that Topaz (1967) was born at Red Star in Moscow. He is recorded as having sired 4 male and 9 female offspring. Following back through Topaz's pedigree (Appendix A), one notes that he is connected to the Moscow Waterdog through Foka, Bara, and Brayt to Hanka on his paternal side, and Brayt again on his maternal side, and again from Volga, Hanka, and Tiza (Newfoundland, Negus f. Mangeym × Caucasian Ovcharka, Karabashka). We also discover a touch of Moscow Dog coming by way of Chuk (1956) (Roy × Chili) through Toddi (German Great Dane, Ralf × East European Shepherd, Pretti). Note that Gay's sire, Aray, and dam, Borka, are both from Giant Schnauzer Roy × Rottweiler Urma, born in separate litters one year apart.

The Database record shows Hybrid Topaz having sired 4 male and 9 female offspring from females Nayda, Dina II, Adi, Changa, and Sekki. Interestingly, Topaz is recorded as having been born in 1967 with most of his offspring recorded as 1969. Of these offspring, his main successor is recorded as being Hybrid Kapitan Flint.

- Hybrid Ata (yr?) female (Hybrid, Topaz × Hybrid, Nayda)
- Hybrid Ayda (yr?) female (Hybrid, Topaz × Hybrid, Nayda)
- Hybrid Tapa (yr?) female (Hybrid, Topaz × Hybrid,Nayda)
- Hybrid Tana (1969) female (Hybrid, Topaz × Hybrid, Nayda)
- Hybrid Ulma (yr?) female (Hybrid, Topaz × Hybrid, Dina II)
- Hybrid Todi (1969) male (Hybrid, Topaz × Hybrid, Dina II)
- Hybrid Agat (1969) male (Hybrid, Topaz × Hybrid, Dina II)
- Hybrid For-Zhana (1969) female (Hybrid, Topaz × Hybrid, Adi)

- Hybrid Tana (1969) female (Hybrid, Topaz × Hybrid, Adi)
- Hybrid Tapa (1969) female (Hybrid, Topaz × Hybrid, Adi)
- Hybrid Alba (1969) female (Hybrid, Topaz × Hybrid, Changa)
- Hybrid Agat (1969) male (Hybrid, Topaz × Hybrid, Changa)
- Hybrid Kapitan Flint (1969) male (Hybrid, Topaz × Hybrid, Sekki)

Historically, Hybrid Topaz is an exciting representative of the developing Black Terrier and a dog I would very much like to have seen. Check out his overall format [photo follows]: balance of head and neck to body, straight back, strong powerful stance, coarse coat and overall bulk. It is really too bad that there are no current particulars available about him. Readers can only make assumptions at this point, based on a relatively good photo collage covering his lineage. Topaz has no siblings recorded but half siblings from his sire Tom included: Nora, Cherri, Yuta, Dzhim, Lord, Dzhoya, and Tuman. Most of Topaz's offspring were used within the breeding programs at Red Star, Moscow City Club of Service Dogs, and other Clubs.

No photo of Hybrid Lada (1964) dam of Topaz, but her pedigree extends back to Moscow Dog Hybrid Chuk × Moscow Waterdog Hybrid Volga, to Moscow Dog Chili and Moscow Waterdog Hanka.

Hybrid Alba was bred to Hybrid Rams I in 1971 and produced 3 male recorded offspring in Hybrids Bush, Al' Princ, and Artosha.

Kapitan Flint (1969), son of Topaz out of female Hybrid Sekki, is of particular interest in that he was bred to females Dezi, Ulma, Dzhudi,

Hybrid, Topaz, 1967, male. Hybrid, Tom × Hybrid, Lada

Hybrid, Alba, 1969, female. Hybrid, Topaz × Crossbreed, Changa

Hybrid, Bush, male

Hybrid, Artosha

Hybrid, Rams I × Hybrid, Alba

Diva, Deya, and Chara throughout the 1970s at Moscow and Leningrad City Clubs. As can be seen, Flint's paternal grand dam Sekki also contributed the genes of Demon. See full pedigree of Hybrid Kapitan Flint in Appendix A, p. 194.

Hybrid Kapitan Flint has 5 male and 6 female offspring currently recorded in the Database. The first litter (no recorded birth date) included females Gerda and Gertruda and male Grey (Kapitan Flint × Dezi). He also sired 3 recorded litters in 1973 with females Ulma (Sunika Un, Santa Un, Sello Un); Dzhudi (Dzhina); and Diva (Din). Of these three litters, only the female Sunika Un and the male Sello Un have available photographs. Sello Un went to Latvia, however there is no current record of his offspring.

In 1975 Kapitan Flint sired female Changa (Kapitan Flint × Deya); in 1976 female Dodzh (Kapitan Flint × Unknown); and male Zhan Grey

Sunika Un, 1973

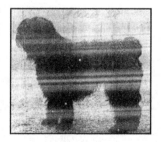

Sello Un, 1973

(Kapitan Flint × Chara).

If one studies the pedigree of Kapitan Flint and his offspring, it becomes interesting to visualize the complexities involved in breeding selection and the [growing] importance of genetic contributions that are blended together and then change position on the breeding map. Sometimes, a line presents as paternal and then re-presents in another pedigree as maternal. Occasionally, that process is reversed again, continuing to intensify genetic structure.

Readers might want to keep in mind that the BRT Virtual Database by Y. Semenov is a relatively new undertaking of gargantuan proportions, and as such new data is added on a continuing basis as discovered, from records of many sources. As time goes on the Database will grow to include pertinent historical information on many early dogs and their offspring, not yet available to the canine fancy.

Included here are photographs of three littermates of Hybrid Brayt and Moscow Waterdog Hybrid Volga (Crossbreed, Azart × Moscow Waterdog, Hanka) for the purpose of extending readers' visual appreciation of the Moscow Waterdog contribution.

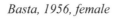

Vishnya, 1956, female   *Basta, 1956, female*   *Velta, 1956, female*

The following photo collage is of members of the lineage of Topaz (1967?). See photo of Topaz on p. 124.

Hybrid, Tom: Sire of Topaz. (Crossbreed, Gay × Hybrid, Dina).

Crossbreed, Aray, 1954: Great Grandsire of Topaz (Giant Schnauzer, Roy × Rottweiler, Urma).

Giant Schnauzer, Roy, 1947?. Greay great grandsire of Topaz.

Rottweiler Urma, 1950. Great great grand dam of Topaz.

Brayt, 1956: Great grandsire (Azart × Hanka).

Volga, 1956: Great grand dam (Azart × Hanka).

Azart, 1954: Great great grandsire (Roy × Una).

Hanka, 1952: Great great grand dam (Lord × Tiza).

Chuk, 1956: Great Grandsire (Roy × Chili).

Family Pillar of Hybrid Tom (1964) × Hybrid Dega

Hybrid Dzhoya (1967) female (Hybrid, Tom × Hybrid, Dega) was a prolific dam producing 7 male 11 female recorded offspring from different males from 1969 through 1975. The name of every one of her offspring began with the prefix Dan, regardless of the sire. For example: Dan-Darsi, Dan-Zhenni, Dan-Zhan, Dan-Zhan, Dan-Orta …

Hybrid, Dzhoya, 1967 (Hybrid, Tom × Hybrid, Dega)

Hybrid, Dan-Darsi, 1969 (Hybrid, Viy × Hybrid, Dzhoya)

Hybrid, Dan-Zhenni, 1970 (Hybrid, Dzhim × Hybrid, Dzhoya)

Dan-Zhan, 1970 (Hybrid, Dzhim × Hybrid, Dzhoya)

Dan-Orta, 1972 (Hybrid, Ajaks × Hybrid, Dzhoya)

Hybrid, Dan-Olchigem, 1972 (Hybrid, Ajaks × Hybrid, Dzhoya)

Hybrid Tuman (1967) male (Hybrid, Tom × Hybrid, Dega) was really some potent contributor to the Black Terrier group, siring 8 male and 22 female recorded offspring with females Ulma, Sekki, Panta, Meri, Yuta, Chana, Nim Eva, Chapa, Rynda, Raksha, Nayda, and Dan-Dingo. He was also a littermate of Dzhoya; half sibling on his sire's side of Topaz, Nora, Cherri, Yutta, Arma, Dzhim, Lord, and Dinka; and half sibling on his dam's side of Rams I. Purely for comparative interest see photographs of Hybrid Tuman 1967 and his paternal great grandsire Aray 1954.

It is unfortunate indeed that at this time there is somewhat limited information available on Hybrid Tuman's breeding history, particularly when we are privileged to have photographs [next page] of his offspring; female Karina-Un (Tuman × Ulma), and males Kras-Boss (Tuman × Ulma) and Zhuk (1970) (Tuman × Raksha).

One of Hybrid Tuman's female offspring, Kora

Hybrid, Tuman, 1967 (1972) ((Tuman × Hybrid, Nayda), whose maternal grandsire was Karat)), was bred to Dzhek (1966) (Karat × Ata), producing female Radin (1976). Unfortunately, no photograph of Hybrid Kora (1972) was located in available archive files.

Another of Tuman's daughters, Chara (1972) (Tuman × Hybrid, Nayda) was bred to Kapitan Flint, producing male Hybrid Zhan Grey (1976), an interesting combination indeed. A close examination of Zhan Grey's pedigree shows his paternal great grand sires

Crossbreed, Aray, 1954

were Hybrid Tom and Hybrid Demon. His maternal grandsire was Tuman and Tuman's sire was Hybrid Tom and Tuman's dam Hybrid Dega was sired by Hybrid Demon. Dega's dam Galka's paternal and maternal grandsire on both side was Hybrid, Demon. That is some tightly knit pedigree requiring concentration to follow. Zhan Grey's pedigree goes a long way to explaining the "why" of the same dogs repeated numerous times. Thus was the [families] pathway of the creation of the Black Russian Terrier. Hybrid Tuman (1967) is not to be confused with Hybrid Tuman (1956) sire of Hybrid Dina (1956?).

Karina-Un   *Krass-Boss*   *Zhuk, 1970*

Radin, 1976?   *Dzhek, 1966*   *Karat, 1964*

Other offspring from Hybrid Tuman (1967) × Hybrid, Nayda (1966) also included:

- Kora (female) (1972) (Tuman × Nayda) 2 recorded female offspring
- Dzhulja (female) (1972) (Tuman × Nayda) 1 recorded female offspring
- Dor-Ditta (female) (1973) (Tuman × Dan-Dingo) inbred on Tom × Dega; 2 male, 1 female recorded offspring
- Dor-Deri (female) (1973) (Tuman × Dan-Dingo) as Dor-Ditta above; no recorded offspring
- Dor-Dintay (male) (1973) (Tuman × Dan-Dingo) as Dor-Ditta above; 1 male and 1 female recorded offspring

Hybrid Zhan Grey proved a good sire with a number of females in the late 1970s and early 1980s. Among his offspring was the male Kim Boy (1979) (Zhan Grey × Tim Ilza) who became a sire of note in Germany. Currently, Kim Boy has 8 male and 8 female recorded offspring during the 1980s, mostly with female Gipsy (Grand × Aza-1). Gipsy's grandsires being Bars (1970) (Agat × Chara) and Atos (year?) (Tishka × Chara). The dam of both Bars and Atos was Chara (Karat × Irda).

Through his great grand dam Adzhi-Shahra, *Kim Boy* has the genes of Moscow Waterdogs Hanka and Grum. Additionally, Adzhi-Shahra, through her maternal great grand dam Ginta, intensifies the Moscow Waterdog genes again from Hanka and by extension Hanka's dam Tiza (1949) (Newfoundland, Negus f. Mangeym × Caucasian Ovcharka, Karabashka).

Hybrid Kim Boy's pedigree (Appendix A, Tom`s section) demonstrates an interesting disbursement perspective of the developing breed from Russia to Lithuania to Germany. Members of Kim Boy's lineage were prolific breeders not only for numbers [because we only have those that were recorded] but for quality. Many of Kim Boy's offspring names contain the German prefix "*von der*" or "*von den*".

Another daughter of Tuman was [another] *Hybrid Lada (1970)* (Hybrid, Tuman × Crossbreed, Panta). The interest here comes from Lada's maternal lineage and both of her great grand dam(s), the

Hybrid, Kim Boy, 1979

Hybrid, Radzh-Mira, 1971

Hybrid, Barhan-Zhan, 1969

Hybrid, Dzhaga, 1965

crossbreed Dila (Rottweiler, Farno × Crossbreed, Chuta). Readers will note the [genetic power] coming together with the blending of these Lines into a solid family structure.

Crossbreeds Dila and Ila are a definite study in genetic dominance. It is extremely unfortunate that to date there are no photographs available of crossbreed Chuta or Russian Spotted Hound, Uteshay. The photographs clearly show the result of crossing Rottweiler Farno with crossbreed Chuta (Russian Spotted Hound, Uteshay × Rottweiler, Una) creating crossbreed Dila.

Crossbreed Dila was then was bred to Rottweiler, Geyni, creating crossbreed Ila who was 75% Rottweiler and 25% Russian Spotted Hound. Dila presents as a tight-knit, athletic, streamlined, easily recognized Rottweiler type. By crossing Dila with Rottweiler, Geyni, their offspring, as presented in Ila, have reverted back to present as a fabulous Rottweiler. Geyni and Dila also produced Ila's female littermate Ilma, shown in Lada's (1970) pedigree.

For further interest, Dila was bred to Hybrid Karat (Foka × Nayda) to produce female Hybrid Rokki who bred with Tom, to produce female Yutta. Dila was also the dam of male Karen 1 (1963) (Rottweiler, Linch × Dila). Again, it is unfortunate that birth dates are not available. Also of

Crossbreed, Dila, 1958   *Rottweiler Geyni, 1955*   *Crossbreed, Ila, 1960*

Rottweiler Farno, 1951   *Rottweiler Birma, yr?*

interest is that Ilma was bred to Karen 1 and produced Crossbreed Panta (1965) female (Crossbreed, Karen 1 × Crossbreed, Ilma).

Hybrid, Dzhim, male

Crossbreed Panta produced male Dzhim with Tom; females Dina and Lada, and male Timur, with Tuman, possibly in 1970. Note that Panta is inbred on Dila. Malva is also by Rottweiler Farno × Crossbreed Chuta (Russian Spotted Hound, Uteshay × Rottweiler, Uza), *but is also recorded in the Database as being a Rottweiler.*

Crossbreed Karen 1 with Ila also produced male Bezeviht in 1967 [see Adolf following]. This story becomes a little bit strange in that a male offspring Adolf (Crossbreed, Bezeviht × Rottweiler, Lasta) *is recorded as a Rottweiler.* This is all presented for its research value and understanding of possible challenges with language interpretations and computer translations. Nevertheless, the study is fascinating to engage in. Note that Malva (above) dam of Linch, *is recorded as being a Rottweiler* when in fact she is a crossbreed. The same designation applies to Linch with Malva coming from Rottweiler, Farno × Crossbreed Chuta (Russian Spotted Hound, Uteshay × Rottweiler, Uza).

Because of the intricacies of such a subject as this book, it is easy for me as the author/compiler of information to get just a wee bit off track from time to time. However, one must admit that this road travelled is both exciting and mind challenging, for which I apologize not.

Take a good look at the pedigree of Adolf (Appendix A, Tom section). Readers have already made note that the dam of Dila is Chuta (above) and that Bezeviht is inbred on Dila. Moving to Adolf's dam Lasta, we see that her dam was also Chuta. And of course Farno and Chuta also produced Dila. Now back up and take another look at the photographs of Dila, Geyni, Ila, Farno, and Birma. What a mind-exercising genetics history lesson. Note in Adolf's pedigree that his dam, Lasta, is recorded as a Rottweiler. She is of course a crossbreed of 75% Rottweiler and 25% Russian Spotted Hound. Adolf may be more Rottweiler than Russian Spotted Hound, but in taking a close look at his pedigree, he is not a "purebred" Rottweiler.

Crossbreed Adolf was bred to Hybrid Aza to produce female Hybrids

Lir Lita and Rada in 1976 adding a more dominantly forceful contribution of Rottweiler genes from Aza through her paternal grandsire Karat and both maternal grand dams, Irda and Teya, with the addition of Giant Schnauzer Dasso f. Drahenshljuht. Again it is unfortunate that no photographs could be discovered of Adolf, Aza, or Lir Lita.

Lir Lita was was bred to Hybrid Zhan Grey bringing forward an additional powerful genetic contribution from Kapitan Flint and Hybrid Topaz. Hybrid Log-Magri's pedigree presents a power [line] in its own right.

Hybrid Log-Magri brought her incredible lineage into the 1980s to be matched in a farsighted selection with the incredible *Hybrid Bim II*. These two exceptional "Black Terriers" produced offspring with superb qualities in Black Russian Terrier males Vanish and Vir and female Vesta, whelped at Red Star Kennel in December 1987. Vanish was privately owned at Moscow and sired 5 male and 11 female recorded offspring with a number of well-bred females. From this point forward, almost all the early Hybrids have disappeared from [short] pedigrees with the official recognition of the Black Russian Terrier by the Fédération Cynologique Internationale (FCI).

Pedigree of *Black Russian Terrier Vanish* who straddles the [line] separating the Black Terrier development and the official Black Russian Terrier may better be placed at the end of this treatise but is here to demonstrate his lineage (Appendix A, Tom section) with both the complexity and ease of following it back to its early conception. History appears to us when tracing members of this line through Log-Magri/Lir Lita/Adolf/ Bezeviht/Zhan Grey/Kapitan Flint/Topaz, Sekki, *et al.* to the beginning.

Vanish sired 5 male and 11 female recorded offspring of superior quality into the 1990s with the greatest impact coming through his female offspring who were housed as adults throughout Russia, Lithuania, Ukraine and other locations. *Alea iacta est* ("the die is cast"). BRT Vanish was bred at Red Star and is reported to have been owned by V. Spiridonov and Margarita Begal and homed at Moscow.

The selection of Rams II by Red Star to pair with Log-Magri was another of those strokes of genius in moving the breed closer to the goal of determined perfection. Bim II's lineage went back to include the early "greats"" Foka, Dega, Karat, Sekki, Bechel, Adzhi-Shahra, Tuman, and Rynda. The earlier multiple inbreeding combinations on Demon, Foka,

Brayt, Aray, Beniamino, and Roy set a powerful foundation for future combinations — witness BRT Vanish.

Family Pillar of Hybrid Tom (1964) × Hybrid Dina I

Dina I, through her sire Foka, grandsire and great grandsire Brayt, plus her great grand dam Gayda, brings a multiplicity of Moscow Waterdog genes originating from Hanka and Tiza (Newfoundland, Negus f. Mangeym × Caucasian Ovcharka, Karabaska).

Dina I had only one recorded offspring from Tom, that being the male Lord, born in 1966. She did, however, produce other recorded offspring in breedings with Crossbreed Gay and Hybrid Tsezar.

Another interesting [relevant] side-bar is in the pedigree of **Hybrid Lord 1966** (Hybrid, Tom × Hybrid, Dina I), who shows up in a number of pedigrees, being credited with 10 male and 11 female recorded offspring, including: Atos (male) (1969) (Lord × Aydina); Vays and Viking (males) (1969) (Lord × Roksa); Tseron (male) (1972) (Lord × Roksa).

Dina I, 1964

Other equally important offspring from Lord were: Venta and Varya (females) and Yard (male) (1969) (Lord × Roksa); Loli (female) and Ljuter (male) (1969) (Lord × Lira); Dar-Ena and Dar-Elsa (females) (1969) (Lord × Darling); Masha, Malva, Malta, and Mika (females) and Molloh, Misha, Mavr, and Mars (males) (1971) (Lord × Beta); Tsatsa and Tseyla (females) (1972) (Lord × Roksa).

Foka, 1960

In more closely analyzing Lord's pedigree, an extended examination of the great grandsire and great grand dam column reveals:

●Aray and Borka were siblings from different litters (Giant Schnauzer, Roy × Rottweiler, Urma).

●Tuman was by Aray (Giant Schnauzer, Roy × Rottweiler, Urma) × Htora (Giant Schnauzer,

Brayt, 1956

Atos, 1969

Vays, 1969

Viking, 1969

Roy × Airedale Terrier, Sotta).

- Fimka's lineage was recorded as unknown.
- Vah was a crossbreed of Giant Schnauzer, Roy × Rottweiler, Una.
- Bara was a hybrid coming from Brayt × Hybrid, Appa (Rottweiler, Beniamino × Hizha [Hinga] (Giant Schnauzer, Roy × Airedale Terrier, Sotta)).
- Brayt was by Crossbreed, Azart (Giant Schnauzer, Roy × Rottweiler, Una) × Moscow Waterdog, Hanka (Newfoundland, Lord × Moscow Waterdog, Tiza).

Tseron 1972

- Nelma was by Crossbreed, Haytar (Giant Schnauzer, Roy × Airedale Terrier, Sotta) × Hybrid Gayda (Crossbreed, Azot × Moscow Waterdog, Hanka).

Family Pillar of Hybrid Tom (1964) × Hybrids Dega

Hybrid Yuna (yr?) female (Hybrid, Tuman × Hybrid, Yuta) presents an interesting pedigree in that her maternal great grand dam, Dila, traces back to Russian Spotted Hound Uteshay. Readers will also note that Yuna is inbred on Tom. Her daughter Vesta reintegrates the Giant Schnauzer through Dasso f. Drahenshljuht from her paternal side. Also note that Yuna's sire Hybrid Tuman (1967) (Tom × Dega) is not the same Hybrid Tuman (1956?) (Aray × Htora) who was the maternal grandsire of of Hybrid Tom (1964). Hybrid Dega's sire was Hybrid, Demon, and her dam Galka was inbred on Demon.

Hybrid Tom (1964) was a powerful contributor, producing offspring of outstanding value, in building on his family line, with the females described in his family structure (Hybrids Panta Dzhina, Dzhessi, Irda, Dina I, Adi, Lada, Dega, Rokki.)

Hybrid Vesta (1973) is recorded as having produced 3 female and 1 male offspring: Layka [Layna] (female) (Lo-Rom × Vesta); Soldi (female) (1977) (Charli II × Vesta); female Varta and male Viy (1979) (Lo-Rom × Vesta). Vesta's offspring by Lo-Rom may have been born in the same litter, but are recorded as two separate litters, with no date of birth recorded for Layka [Layna].

The pedigree of Varta and Viy is included for its blending interest

Tom, 1964

Dan Zhan, 1970

Hybrid, Dzhoya, 1967

Hybrid, Dzhim, 1966

Hybrid, Dzhaga, 1965

Hybrid, Atos, 1980

Hybrid, Demon, 1957

Hybrid, Lo-Rom, 1973

which is easily followed through the pedigrees in this section. An interesting discovery showed Hybrid Lo-Rom, owned by Red Star, to have been selected for military service in the Moscow District of Dmitriyevsky. Lo-Rom is currently credited as having sired 5 male and 5 female offspring from 1975 through 1981 including Hybrids male Volf-Gross and female Vaska (1978) (Lo-Rom × Hybrid, Chezetta). Hybrid Atos (1980) male (Hybrid, Lo-Rom × Hybrid Sabina-Diana) is credited with siring 11 male and 13 female offspring in the 1980s.

Family Pillar of Hybrid Tom (1964) × Hybrid Irda (1962)

Hybrid Irda produced female Nora coming from Tom. Given the date of Irda's grand dam Charva, her dam, Binta, might have been born in 1955 or 1956. Note the intensity of Giant Schnauzer genes coming through Roy.

Hybrid Nora carried the family genes of Tom forward through her breeding with Karat, producing the male Hybrid Dzhim in 1968. Nora's dam, Hybrid Irda, was triple inbred on Giant Schnauzer Roy and through her maternal great grand dam, Aza, contributed the genes from the Moscow Waterdog, Fomka.

Although *Hybrid Dzhim (1968)* currently records only 1 female offspring, Poldi Char (1972) (Hybrid, Dizhim × Hybrid, Chari), in the Database, his pedigree makes it inconceivable that he would not have contributed significantly within the Group breeding program. His photograph offers a fabulous presentation of a Black Terrier from 1968. Every

Dzhim, 1968 (Hybrid, Karat × Hybrid, Nora)

Dzhim, 1966 (Hybrid, Karat × Crossbreed, Teya)

Dzhim (yr? (Hybrid, Tom × Crossbreed, Panta)

member of Dzhim's lineage was an exceptional winner in their individual and collective contributions to the breed.

Hybrid Dzhim (male) (1968) (Karat × Nora) with 1 recorded female offspring in Poldi Char (1972) (Dzhim × Chari) brings into the mix a large measure of Moscow Waterdog through his great grandsires and great grand dams: Bara, Brayt, Nelma, and Bul. Other great grandparents Vah, Gay, and Binta, were crossbred Giant Schnauzer and Rottweiler, while Dina contributed a blending of Giant Schnauzer, Rottweiler, and Airedale Terrier, plus whatever came through Fimka and her sire, Araj, of unknown lineage.

In studying the pedigrees, readers can appreciate how Lines morphed and grew with each succeeding blending within the limited but increasing gene pool. Although some lines died out, they nevertheless contributed to the evolution of the Black Terrier Group.

Note that Dzhim was a popular male name. Others had added prefix and/or suffix; e.g., Oldzhim Lot, Nboy-Dzhim, M-Dzhim, et al.

- Hybrid Dzhim (yr?) male (Hybrid Tom × Crossbreed, Panta)
- Hybrid Dzhim (1966) male (Hybrid, Karat × Crossbreed, Teya)
- Dzhim (1967) male (Hybrid, Tom × Hybrid, Dzhina)
- Hybrid Dzhim (1968) male (Hybrid, Karat × Hybrid, Nora)
- BRT Dzhim (1989) male (Hybrid, Araks (1983) × BRT Arna (1986))

Family Pillar of Hybrid Tom (1964) × Hybrid Panta (1965)

Note that Panta is a crossbreed of Rottweiler and Russian Spotted Hound on both sides coming through Chuta (Russian Spotted Hound, Uteshay × Rottweiler, Uza). Panta has 2 male and 3 female offspring recorded and only one male in Dzhim from Tom. The others, male Timur and females Dina and Lada, were by Tuman. Tuman was by Hybrid, Tom × Hybrid, Dega. See Panta's partial pedigree in the Appendix, Tom's section.

Once again, we run into the conundrum of same-name usage, this time with a second Hybrid Dzhim embedded within the Tom Family (Hybrid, Tom × Hybrid, Panta). This Dzhim (yr?) sports a much different pedigree but with ancestors of equal value and importance.

Hybrid Dzhim (yr?) had no recorded offspring, but from his pedigree and photograph (opposite), it seems unlikely that he was not used as a sire, at least for the speculation of determining what he might produce. This Dzhim's half siblings from Tom included Topaz, Nora, Cherri, Yutta, Arma, Lord, Dinka, Dzhoya, and Tuman, and Dina, Timur and Lada from Tuman.

As another sidebar, a third male Hybrid Dzhim (1966) (Hybrid, Karat × Crossbreed, Teya) adds another exciting dimension to the genius of Red Star and Moscow Club breeding programs (sired 8 male and 3 female recorded offspring).

Family Pillar of Hybrid Tom (1964) × Hybrid Dzhina (1965)

Following Hybrid Dzhina's (1965) pedigree (see Cherri's as well) we note that her maternal grandsire was Ditter f. Drahenshljuht who was a littermate of Dasso, with their sire and dam coming from Germany. Hybrid Dzhina (1965) is credited with producing 2 male and 5 female offspring with Hybrids Nayt and Tom in 1967–68.

Both Dasso and Ditter (despite their litters being severely culled because of cryptorchidism), nevertheless, do show up in a number of early pedigrees, with Dasso having recorded 4 male and 5 female offspring and Ditter credited with 5 females, all of which were used in breeding programs, notwithstanding the culling processes employed. Dasso's sons and daughters, and Ditter's daughters, were successful in producing a number of exceptional offspring.

Somewhat perplexing is the breeding of Hybrid, Daks × Hybrid, Nora (Giant Schnauzer, Ditter × Hybrid, Vanda) given that Hybrid Nora is recorded as having had a cloudy coloured coat, which could have ranged from a shade of grey to a dirty white. Hybrid Dzhina is recorded as black coated as are her offspring.

Hybrid Dzhina (1965) was bred to Hybrid Tom and produced hybrid females Cherri and Nensi, and male Dzhim possibly around 1967. The adverse effects of Ditter's shortcomings may have been somewhat diluted through the gene input from Daks's breeding to Nora to produce Dzhina. Additionally, the strong input from Tom bred to Dzhina (Daks × Nora) should have further improved the genetic structure in their offspring.

Dan Zhan, 1970

Dzhim, 1966

Dzhoya, 1967

Chanita, 1966

Tom, 1967

However, Dzhina's offspring would have carried forward to some degree the off-colour coat gene coming through Ditter and Nora. Hybrid Dzhina's breeding to Hybrid Tom produced 3 recorded offspring who would have been carriers of the non-black gene. It would have been helpful to have had access to a photograph of Hybrid Nora to visualize her physical attributes.

Hybrid Cherri was bred to the exceptional male Shaytan (Hybrid, Dayv × Hybrid, Kara) who was inbred on Demon. However, one might wonder about litter culling related to both Nora and Dzhina. Hybrids Cherri and Shaytan produced the female Rika in 1973, and Rika was bred to Char-Tuman producing the female Dzherri in 1979. Dzherri was a prolific producer and was bred to male Atos in 1983, 1984, and 1985, and to Lin Sharman in 1987.

A curiosity in Hybrid Dzherri lies in her maternal side with her grand dam, Cherri, and great grand dam, Dzhina, carrying forward the cloudy/ pepper and salt colour genes from Giant Schnauzer Ditter and Hybrid Nora.

A major interest arises in examining available photographs of Dzherri's lineage. Readers get an appreciation of the quality of some of her ancestors. Although **Hybrid Chanita** is not directly connected to Tom, it is interesting to observe the quality she contributed through Char-Tuman to Dzherri. Chanita presents in a gorgeous format for a dog born in 1966. Hybrid Chanita (Hybrid, Karat × Crossbreed, Teya), was a littermate of Hybrid Dzhim. Ergo, the strong genetic base in Hybrid Dzherri plus an interesting contemplation with regard to the question of [lineage] coat colour.

Family Pillar of Hybrid Tom (1964) × Hybrid Rokki

Hybrid Yuta (1968) (Tom × Rokki), was bred to male Hybrid Dzhaga (1965) [pedigree in Appendix A, Tom section] in 1970 produced male Urchan, who was bred to female Kora, to produce the male Nemfred and female Unga in 1976.

Hybrid Nemfred was the sire of the excellent producer Hybrid Sid who was used extensively, siring among others, Santa, Stella, Bora,

Meggi, Marta, and Mer. As a reminder to readers, I would like to repeat that Hybrid Karat, sire of Hybrid Rokki, has 8 male and 22 female recorded offspring. Only Rokki is recorded as coming from Crossbreed Dila. For detailed information on Hybrid, Sid (1979) refer to Vol. 6, *Leningrad Families*.

Dzhaga, 1965

The female *Hybrid Unga* was bred to Irbis in 1973 and produced a litter of 12 offspring: females, Yanka, Yarta, Yatanka, Yarika, Yasi, and Yanika, and males Yarrey, Jazur [possibly Yazur], Yanbek, Yago, Yargus, and Yarvik. With the exception of male Hybrid Yarrey, this entire litter currently has no recorded offspring in the Database. In 1976, Hybrid Yarrey was bred to privately owned Hybrid Aza and sired 1 male recorded offspring in Hybrid Abrek, also privately owned and with no individual data recorded. Abrek was bred in 1979 to females in the area of Chelyabinsk and the town of Chebarkul, approximately 1,500 km from Moscow and 2,426 km from Leningrad/St. Petersburg.

As noted above, male *Hybrid Dzhaga (1965),* bred to female Hybrid, Yuta, combined some exceptional qualities that contributed

Dasso, 1960

substantially to the male line creating Hybrid, Sid. Dzhaga was also a prolific sire with a number of different females from 1969 through 1973 and whose offspring played major roles in the 1970s: Dzhin (1969?) (Dzhaga × Unknown) male; Kora (1969?) (Dzhaga × Nayda) female; Demon (1969?) (Dzhaga × Alfa) male [not Demon (1957) (Arras × Chomga) that we started with]; Unga (1970) female and Urchan, male (Dzhaga × Yutta); Zhela (1971) (Dzhaga × Ata) female; Urs (1971) (Dzhaga × Karmen) male; Radzh-Mira, Radzh-Mymra, Radzh-Mayra, females and Radzh-Muk, male (1971); Danchar (1972) (Dzhaga × Ditta) male; Vesta (1973) (Dzhaga × Yuna) female.

*Hybrid, Darti, 1970?
(Hybrid, Dzhaga ×
Hybrid, Yutta)*

Hybrid Dzhaga's pedigree is included to demonstrate his lineage in comparison with Yutta's. Hybrid Brayt, as we know, traces back to the original Giant Schnauzers, Rottweilers, and Karabashka. Crossbreed Chonga contributes Giant Schnauzer and Airedale Terrier while the lineage of Fimka and Araj is unknown. Readers will recall the statement made regarding Dasso and his littermate Ditter (re coat colour and cryptorchidism) in the section regarding the family of Tom and Dzhina.

Hybrid Dzhaga, bred to Hybrid Yuta, sired Hybrid Darti (yr?) male (Hybrid, Dzhaga × Hybrid, Yuta). Darti's photograph, although not very clear, does present an upstanding large male of quality construction.

Unfortunately, there are currently no recorded offspring of Hybrid Darti.

Family Pillar of Hybrid Tom (1964) × Hybrid Dzhessi (1963)

Hybrid Dzhessi (1963) was a sibling of Hybrid Ayshe (1961) (Hybrid, Demon × Moscow Waterdog, Grum). Her pedigree adds the fourth generation dimension when compared with the pedigree of her sibling Ayshe. Ayshe was the dam of Hybrid Adi of the family of Tom and Adi.

The family lineage of Hybrid Dzhessi (1963) presents a strong interest in its strength in genes emanating from the Moscow Waterdog through her dam, Ledi. One has to wonder about the physical structure and presentation format of Ledi given her preponderance of Moscow Waterdog, and asking what influence Azot contributed given he was a cross of Giant Schnauzer Roy and Rottweiler Firma. We currently have only photographs of Ledi's sire, Moscow Waterdog, Grum, and her dam Ginta. Ledi was a combination of 75% Moscow Waterdog with 12.5% each of Giant Schnauzer and Rottweiler. Adding Demon to the mix in creating Dzhessi would definitely dilute the physical format coming through Moscow Waterdog Grum.

Hybrid Dzhessi has 3 female offspring recorded in the Database only one of which is by Tom: Hybrid Arma (female) (Tom × Dzhessi). Arma has no currently recorded offspring and no photograph could be located.

For reader information, Dzhessi's other 2 recorded offspring were: **Hybrid Roza** (female) (1963) (Giant Schnauzer, Dasso f. Drahenshljuht × Dzhessi) and **Hybrid Sarra** (female) (1966) (Hybrid, Viy × Dzhessi).

For the available photographs of the Tom and Dzhessi family refer to those of Family Tom and Adi with reference to the corresponding pedigrees.

Family Pillar of Hybrid Tom (1967) × Hybrid Adi

Hybrid Adi (1964) has 5 female and 1 male offspring recorded but only female Dinka and male Osman (1967) were with Tom. Although Dinka and Osman currently have no offspring recorded in the Database, they do present an impressive lineage. Again, readers should keep in mind that although there is no current recorded information on these Hybrids and many others that does not confirm that they were not used within the massive breeding program(s) in the early years of the creation of the Black Russian Terrier.

Family Lines

1964: Based on Hybrid Karat (Male)
(Hybrid, Foka × Hybrid, Nayda)

HYBRID, KARAT WAS THE PICK of the litter. He was one of the exceptional stud representatives of the developing "Black Terrier" and a prolific
breeder with 8 male and 19 female recorded offspring. Karat had all the
right lines, a beautiful large head, and good movement. Two of Karat's
daughters from different dams are shown below with him for comparison
of format. It should be noted that Hybrid Karat was used extensively at
Leningrad. See pedigree of Hybrid Stesha and littermates in Appendix A,
Karat section.

Karat, 1964   *Chanita, 1966*   *Chada, 1968*

His littermates from that extraordinary 1964 litter included males
Ayman and Fang. Ayman was a very large and powerful dog with a strong
coarse constitution and who sired another strong stud dog in male Bim I
(Ayman × Alfa). Fang was also an exceptional stud dog, siring the female
Jolka (1969) (Fang × Ruza). Jolka was a bitch of very high quality, going
to Finland were she established the Jolkas family line.

Family Pillars of Karat

Karat produced a large family line of many excellent offspring that would carry forward his solid, upstanding format, with 8 male and 19 female recorded offspring. Karat was matched with a number of exceptional females, producing many offspring of extraordinary acceptable type and format, well represented in the limited number of available photographs.

Raksha (female) (Karat × Irda) 3 male and 5 female recorded offspring: females Zhaklin and Zhulya and males Zhurd, Zhuk (1970) (Tuman × Raksha) and females Radzh-Mira, Radzh-Mymra, Radzh-Mayra and male Radzh-Muk (1971) (Dzhaga × Raksha).

Chara (female) (Karat × Irda) 2 male and 4 female recorded offspring: male Atos (Tishka × Chara); females Kerri, Dzhilda, Leda (Vud × Chara); female Charda (Roy × Chara) [Note that this Roy is not the original Roy of 1947?); male Bars (1970) (Agat × Chara).

Zhuk, 1970

Chuta (female) (Karat × Irda) 3 female recorded offspring: Eva and Charodeyka (Rams 2 × Chuta).

Lada (female) (Karat × Irda) no recorded offspring.

Chuk (male) (Karat × Irda) 2 female recorded offspring: Aza and Algreda (1973) (Chuk × Changa).

Radzh-Mira

Hybrid Blek-Veda (female) (Karat × Sekki) 1 male recorded offspring: Hybrid Argo (1971) (Alf × Blek-Veda). Argo presents an inquiring interest in that, bred to Silva-Bagira, he sired male Grey f. Raakzeje [Raakze] and female Gabi. Silva-Bagira not only adds a direct influence of Giant Schnauzer through Akbar f. Raakzeje [Raakze] but also carries the genes of Hybrid Karat. Again showing the spread of breeding stock from Red Star into the public domain, it is noted that Hybrid Blek-Veda was homed at Sarov, a town approximately 400 km (250 mi) east of Moscow in the region of Nizhny Novogard (Gorky).

Readers will have recognized the Giant Schnauzer kennel name of "f. Raakzeje [Raakze]" and that it had taken on the developing Black

Hybrid, Alf, 1966, male (Hybrid, Daks × Hybrid, Veda)

Hybrid, Veda, 1962, female
(Giant Schnauzer, Ditter ×
Hybrid, Vanda)

Hybrid, Sekki, 1962, female
(Hybrid, Demon × Hybrid,
Arsa)

Hybrid, Bleck-Veda, 1968, female (Hybrid, Karat × Hybrid, Sekki)

Terrier in 1977 with the naming of Grey f. Raakzeje [Raakze]. One might also wonder why Grey f. Raakzeje [Raakze] currently shows no recorded offspring. Grey's female sibling Gabi records 2 female offspring with Hybrid Filipp (I) in Glora-Fil Ganna-Fil (1980). Hybrid Glora-Fil records 7 male and 4 female offspring with a number of males in 1982–89. Glor-Fil was privately owned at Moscow. Hybrid Ganna-Fil records 3 male and 8

Hybrid, Ayaks [Ajaks], 1967, male (Hybrid, Karat × Hybrid, Stesha)

female offspring in 1984–89 also with a selection of males. Ganna-Fil's home location is not currently recorded.

Bechel

Hybrid Bechel (male) (Hybrid, Karat × Hybrid, IIa) sired 4 male and 4 female recorded offspring: female Chari (1969) and male Men (Bechel × Ayda); females Bella and Basma and males Barhan-Zhan, Bahor Boss, and Burkhan (1969) (Bechel × Adzhi-Shahra); female Basya (1970) (Bechel × Dinga).

Hybrid Chari (1969) privately owned at Novocherkassk produced Hybrid Poldi Char (1972) female (Hybrid, Dzhim × Chari). Hybrid Men (1969) shows no recorded offspring. Hybrid Bella (1969) female (Hybrid, Bechel ×

Hybrid, Adzhi-Shahra) records 1 offspring in Hybrid Nerhan (1973) male (Hybrid, Nord × Hybrid, Bella). Hybrid Nerhan sired female Gamma with Hybrid Tim Ilza and male Blord with Hybrid Re-Dzhessi both in 1979, and Hybrid Dani-Nandi (1981) female (Hybrid, Nerhan × Hybrid, Le Dani Mir).

Bechel

Hybrid Blod is of interest in that he sired 7 male and 15 female offspring with a selection of females from 1982 through 1987.

Readers will note the different Rottweilers coming into the blend through Bechel's dam, IIa. The parentage of Bechel's maternal great grandparents, Armin and Kora are unknown. Through Dila and Chuta came the blending of Russian Spotted Hound Uteshay × Rottweiler Uza. An added touch of interest is the reminder that Chuta also produced

Females Lasta and Malva with Rottweiler, Farno, and females Ohta and Zubra with Rottweiler Sultan-2.

Zitta (female) (Karat × Adi) 2 recorded female offspring: female Dzhe-Zitta (Dzhek × Zitta); and female Tan Irza (Chingiz Rhan × Zitta) — no recorded dates of birth. Note that Airedale Terrier genes are present in the mix through Haytar (1952) (Giant Schnauzer, Roy × Airedale Terrier, Sotta). Vishnya (1956) is a hybrid combination of Giant Schnauzer, Rottweiler, and Moscow Waterdog.

Also of interest in Zitta's lineage is the early concentration of Moscow Waterdog from Bray and Vishnya but more so coming from Ledi who, but for a touch of Giant Schnauzer Roy × Rottweiler Firma, is a Moscow Waterdog. Ledi's sire, Grum, also provided the genes of East European Shepherd (Rina). Zitta presents quite an interesting genetic combination, the story of which could have been greatly enhanced by a photograph of her. Hybrid Ledi was the dam of Hybrid females Ayshe and Dzhessi by Hybrid Demon.

Hybrid Dzhek (1966) male (Hybrid, Karat × Hybrid, Ata) 5 male and 10 female recorded offspring. As seen above and throughout this study, Hybrid Karat has been a major contributor to the development of the Black Terrier Group. Unfortunately, there is no photograph of Hybrid Ata and she records only 1 offspring in male Dzhek (1966) although she comes with a powerful background of exceptional lineage. As seen in his photograph, Hybrid Dzhek not only presents as a solid upstanding male, but we again witness a large number of recorded female offspring.

As is known, Karat was a serious sire in the development process but Dzhek's dam Hybrid Ata records only 1 offspring in Hybrid Dzhek (1966). Together Dzhek and Karat currently record a total of 13 male and 32 female offspring which was exceptional for record-keeping in the mid-1960s timeframe.

Hybrid Dzhek 1966 *Hybrid Radin (yr?)* *Hybrid Anchar (1971)*

In taking a close look at Dzhek's great grandsires and great grand dams we discover the extended lineage and recorded offspring of each.

- Vah Crossbreed (Giant Schnauzer, Roy × Rottweiler, Una) 3 male and 3 female offspring
- Bara Hybrid (Moscow Waterdog Hybrid, Brayt × Crossbreed, Appa) 2 male offspring
- Brayt Moscow Waterdog Hybrid (Crossbreed, Azart × Moscow Waterdog, Hanka) 10 male and 7 female offspring
- Nelma Hybrid (Crossbreed, Haytar × Hybrid, Gayda) 1 female offspring
- Aray Crossbreed (Giant Schnauzer, Roy × Rottweiler, Urma) 2 male offspring
- Borka Crossbreed (Crossbreed, Aray × Rottweiler, Urma) 2 male offspring
- Tuman Crossbreed (Crossbreed, Aray × Airedale Terrier, Htora) 1 female offspring
- Fimka unknown ancestry 3 female offspring
- Crossbreeds Aray and Azart were half siblings sired by Giant Schnauzer Roy and dams Rottweiler littermates Una and Urma.

Hybrid Anchar sired 5 hybrid female offspring in Ketti (1973) (Anchar × Hybrid, Feya); Dan-Yaza, Dan-Yamika, and Dan-Jana (1974) (Anchar × Hybrid, Dzhoya); Ulma (1977) (Anchar × Hybrid, Purga).

Hybrid Ulma (1977) produced 3 female offspring in 1981 (Hybrid, Ted Tulat × Hybrid, Ulma).

Hybrid Karu (1970) male (Hybrid, Dzhek × Hybrid, Alma) sired 3 female offspring:

- Hybrid Vaksa (1973) female (Karu × Hybrid, Dar Ritsa) 2 females
- Hybrid Kroshka (1976) female (Karu × Hybrid, Vaksa) Hybrids male Zorro, female Zolli (1978) (Irtish × Kroshka) and females Cinta and Tsimmi (1980) (Hybrid, Irtish × Hybrid, Kroshka)
- Hybrid Krezi (1976) female (Karu × Hybrid, Vaksa) 2 male and 3 female offspring

Note that female littermates Kroshka and Krezi were inbred on their sire Hybrid Karu.

Hybrid Nayda (1966) female (Hybrid, Karat × Crossbreed, Teya) 3 male and 8 female recorded offspring. In Nayda we again witness a strong

*Hybrid Nayda
(female), 1966
(Hybrid, Karat ×
Crossbreed, Teya) 3
male and 8 female
recorded offspring*

*Chanita (female),
1966 (Karat × Teya)
3 male and 4, female
recorded offspring.*

*Hybrid Dzhim (male),
1966 (Hybrid, Karat
× Crossbreed, Teya) 8
male and 3 female
recorded offspring*

*Hybrid Chingiz (male),
1969 (Hybrid, Rom ×
Hybrid, Chanita) 3 male
and 5 female recorded
offspring*

*Hybrid Tap Arto (male),
1975 (Hybrid, Chingiz
Rhan × Hybrid, Tapa) 1
male and 7 female recorded
offspring*

lineage primarily structured on Giant Schnauzer and Rottweiler genes with the somewhat durable effect of Moscow Waterdog coming through Bara, Brayt, and Nelma who also contributed a touch of Airedale Terrier from her sire, Crossbreed Haytar, and grand dam Airedale Terrier Sotta.

Hybrid Nayda, bred and homed at Red Star, did not appear to have the bulk of her female littermate Hybrid Chanita. However, she did carry the "big dog" genes passed on through her offspring sired by Dzhaga, Topaz, Nord, and Tuman. [Some confusing dates are recorded in the Database.]

Hybrid Chanita is referred to throughout this Volume by way of her contributions as a premium producer with Hybrid Rom siring 3 male and 5 female offspring in 1969.

There is no available photograph of Hybrid Vita who records 1 female offspring Hybrid Zitta (yr?) (Hybrid, Chingiz Rhan × Hybrid, Vita). Hybrid Zitta records 1 female offspring in Hybrid Dzherri (1974) (Hybrid, Vays × Hybrid, Zitta). Dizherri produced 3 recorded female offspring in 1978 in Hybrids Dalila, Dali, Dinara (Hybrid, Artosha × Hybrid, Dzherri).

Hybrid Chanita (1966) was paternal grand dam of Hybrid Tap Arto (1975) and also his maternal great grand dam who along with Hybrid Rom brought forward a powerful genetic package in creating this line moving into the 1980s. Note that Hybrids Chingiz Rhan and Charmi were littermates.

It is easy to appreciate the genetic power and involvement of private breeders/owners coming into the development of the Breed in the late 1960s and forward through this line containing 27 female and 18 male recorded offspring from just these five "Black Terriers". The effect is magnified by a large factor, not only by these specimens, but by many others given the geographic spread of individual "dogs" and the inter-breeding processes across Russia (and USSR) and other European nations.

Hybrid Vita (1966) female (Karat × Teya) shows 1 female recorded offspring in female Zitta (Hybrid, Chingiz Rhan × Vita). Hybrid Zitta was inbred on Karat and Teya, but has only 1 recorded offspring female Dzherri (1974) (Hybrid, Vays × Zitta). Hybrid Dzherri was bred to Hybrid Artosha and produced 3 (privately owned) female offspring in Dalila, Dali, and Dinara (1978).

Hybrid Dzhim (1966) male (Karat × Teya) shows 8 male and 3 female recorded offspring: female Delsi and male Dzherri (1969) (Dzhim × Nensi); males Damir and Dan (1970) (Dzhim × Aydina); males Max and Nim-Mir (1970) (Dzhim × Inga); females Dan-Zhenni, Dan-Zhaklin, and males Dan-Zhan, Dan-Zhuan, and Dan-Zhak (1970) (Dzhim × Dzhoya). Dzhoya was also a productive female in the 1970s with 7 male and 11 female recorded offspring with different males. Of these offspring, Dan-Zhan is of particular interest in that he sired 11 male and 14 female recorded offspring.

Dan-Zhan (male) (1970 (Dzhim × Dzhoya) 11 male and 14 female recorded offspring:

It is of note that Galka, maternal great grand dam of Dan-Zhan and dam of Dega, is inbred on Demon, and through her dam, Yaga, and grand

Dan Zhan, 1970

dam, Mirta, contributes the genes of Moscow Dog Hybrid Chuk and Moscow Waterdog Hybrid Volga.

Hybrid Dan Zhan (1970) sired some exceptional offspring with a considerable number of quality females:

- Irma (yr?) (female) Dan Zhan × Unknown): 1 male, 1 female offspring
- Purga (yr?) (female) (Dan Zhan × Lera): 1 female offspring
- Roy (yr?) (male) (Dan Zhan × Alfa): 3 male, 1 female offspring
- Filipp (yr?) (male) (Dan Zhan × Zlyuka Yuk): 1 female offspring
- Char-Tuman (1973) (male) (Dan Zhan × Chara): 1 male, 2 female offspring
- Char Tedzheri (1973) (female) (Dan Zhan × Chara): 2 male offspring
- Lo-Rom (1973) (male) (Dan Zhan × Rayma): 5 male, 5 female offspring
- Gil-Assol (1974) (female) (Dan zhan × Dan-Dasi): 2 male, 3 female offspring
- Ped Shvarc (1974) (male) (Dan Zhan × Dezi): 2 female offspring
- Ped Shanel (1974) (female) (Dan Zhan × Dezi): 2 male, 5 female offspring
- Ped Shelli (1974) (female) (Dan Zhan × Dezi): 1 female offspring
  Elza (1974) (female) (Dan Zhan × Eva): no recorded offspring
- Ned Nays (1975) (male) (Dan Zhan × Neda): 5 female offspring
- Duglas (1976) (male) (Dan Zhan × Rin-Deza): 3 male offspring
- Derda (1976) (female) (Dan Zhan) × Rin-Deza): 1 male, 1 female offspring).

- Dali (1976) (female) (Dan Zhan × Rin-Deza): 1 male offspring
- Din-Dzhin (1976) (male) (Dan Zhan × Daza): 2 male, 11 female offspring).
- Gil-Raut (1976) (male) (Dan Zhan × Dan-Darsi): no recorded offspring
- Gil-Reda (1976) (female) (Dan Zhan × Dan-Darsi): 2 female offspring
- Gil-Relli (1976) (female) (Dan Zhan × Dan-Darsi): 1 male, 1 female offspring

Pet Shvarc 1974

Reks

Dzhim, 1966

- Gerta (1977) (female) (Dan Zhan × Lera): 1 male, 1 female offspring
- Chada (1977) (female) (Dan Zhan × Seggi): 1 male, 1 female offspring
- Atos (1978) (male) (Dan Zhan × Lera): 5 female offspring
- Filipp 2 (1978) (male) (Dan Zhan × Feya): 5 male, 9 female offspring
- Pedi (1980) (female) (Dan Zhan × Dezi): 1 female offspring

Examining the incredible lineage structure of Hybrid Atos, one can only imagine how complete this portrait could have been with a photographic collage of every member of his lineage back to the original breeds. Hybrid Atos is credited with siring 5 female offspring in the 1980s and 1990.

Let us take a quick look at the great grandsires and great grand dams of Atos (1978). All four were exceptional specimens and producers of the early 1960s. With the exception of Crossbreed Teya, all were excellent hybrid representatives of the evolving "Black Terrier Group". Teya was a

Tuman, 1967

Nayda, 1966

[double] cross of Giant Schnauzer and Rottweiler (paternally Vah (Roy × Una) and maternally (Roy × Urman)).

Hybrid Karat (Foka × Nayda) was an impressive large dog of fine quality in all respects. His sire, Foka, was a large, strongly developed dog, heavy in Giant Schnauzer and Rottweiler with the added advantages of Moscow Waterdog and Airedale coming from his maternal side. The maternal great grandsires of Karat were Azart (1954) and Haytar (1952). Azart was a crossbreed of Giant Schnauzer Roy × Rottweiler Una, presenting in the format of the Giant Schnauzer but heavier and stronger. Haytar on the other hand was a crossbreed of Giant Schnauzer Roy and Airedale Terrier Sotta, presenting as a large, dry-type dog of good substance, with a Giant-Schnauzer-type head with substantial furnishings. These early dogs were quite on the mark in exhibiting the style(s) envisioned by Red Star breeders.

Hybrid Tom (1964) (Gay × Dina) was a large upstanding dog of excellent proportions. He was a powerful mixture of Giant Schnauzer Roy and Rottweiler Urma, coming through his sire Gay (Aray × Borka). From his dam, Dina, through Tuman, came the genes of Aray (Giant Schnauzer, Roy × Rottweiler, Urma), with Tuman also contributing the genes of Airedale Terrier through Htora (Giant Schnauzer, Roy × Airedale Terrier, Sotta). Also through Dina (Tuman × Fimka) was the unknown parentage of Fimka.

Crossbreed Teya (Vah × Basta) was a (pure) crossbreed from Vah (Giant Schnauzer, Roy × Rottweiler, Una) × Basta (Giant Schnauzer, Roy × Rottweiler, Urma). There are no available photographs of Teya or Basta. Based on his genetic composition, Vah was an exceptional representation of what a Giant Schnauzer × Rottweiler crossbreed should be. One could safely make the presumption that Basta was [likely] to be the same.

Hybrid Dega (Demon × Galka) would have presented a very different format in coat style and texture. She was of a more complex composition, combining genes from all of the major breeds. First, Dega is inbred on Demon (Arras × Chomga), a powerful combination of Giant Schnauzer, Rottweiler, and Airedale Terrier. Dega's dam Galka's parents, Negus × Yaga, were sired by Demon, and Yaga's dam Mirta (Moscow Dog Hybrid, Chuk × Moscow Waterdog Hybrid, Volga) completed the picture. Unfortunately, there are no photographs of Atos or his female siblings Purga and Gerta. There are also no photographs of his offspring from the early 1980s.

Photographic collage of Hybrid Atos (1978) male (Hybrid, Dan Zhan (1970) × Hybrid, Lera (1972)). No photograph of Atos or his dam, Lera, was discovered.

Dan-Zhan, 1970   Dzhim, 1966   Dzhoya, 1967

Karat, 1964   Tom, 1964   Foka, 1960

Vah, 1956   Brayt, 1956   Chuk, 1956

Volga, 1956   Azart, 1954   Haytar, 1952

Hybrid, Ayna, 1967,   *Ayaks [Ajaks], 1967, male*
female (Hybrid, Karat ×   *(Hybrid, Karat × Hybrid,*
Hybrid, Stesha)   *Stesha)*

Ayna (female) (1967) (Karat × Stesha) shows 2 male and 2 female recorded offspring: females Irisha and Inza, and males Irbis and Ildar (1970) (Karay × Ayna): Irisha produced some significantly important offspring in the 1970s. Locations for Arni, Arisha, Ada, Atika, and Arta are not currently recorded. Offspring in this litter were privately owned.

Ada, Atika, *and* **Arta** (females) (1967) (Karat × Stesha) show no recorded offspring.

Ayaks [Ajaks] (male) (1967) (Karat × Stesha). Ayaks [Ajaks] was also an exceptional producer, sire of 6 male and 6 female recorded offspring, and probably many others both in Moscow and possibly Leningrad.

Antey (male) (1967) (Karat × Stesha) no recorded offspring. In examining the photograph and "experts descriptions" of Antey, it is inconceivable that he would not have been used at stud with the abundant exceptional females that were available at Red Star Kennel and both Moscow and Leningrad City Clubs. It is highly likely that breeding records of this fine specimen will eventually surface from the myriad of records that exist in Russia and with Russian breeders who have immigrated throughout Europe and North America. It also seems reasonable that offspring of the fine specimens that were both Ajaks [Ajaks] and Antey would have been line bred/inbred with each other.

Antey 1957

Pedigree of **Hybrid Charli 1** is included here to display his extensive inbred lineage on Demon. In following his lineage readers will note that

Charli 1's maternal great grand dam, Galka, is also inbred on Demon, which exponentially increases the genetic input of Demon through Dega. Foka also played a significant role in both sides of his pedigree. Charli 1's pedigree is indeed an interesting study. Charli 1 sired 2 male and 2 female recorded offspring: female Peppi (1977) (Charli 1 × Ped Shanel); male Shvarts 2 (1977) (Charli 1 × Kerri); female Birza and male Bim II (1979) (Charli 1 × Sabina-Diana).

Hybrid Peppi produced 2 male and 8 female recorded offspring from 1980 through 1983. Bred to Hybrid Chester in 1983, she produced female Hybrid Onika who in turn produced 3 male and 9 female recorded offspring from 1985 through 1990.

Hybrid, Peppi, 1977

Hybrid Birza produced 2 male and 7 recorded female offspring from 1981 through 1986 including female Ayna (1986) (Hybrid, Lafler × Hybrid, Birza) who in turn records 2 male and 7 female offspring 1988–89.

Hybrid Bim II sired 3 male and 7 female offspring from 1981 through 1987 including female Hybrid Vesta (1987) (Hybrid, Bim II × Hybrid, Log-Magri).

Hybrid, Onika, 1983

Hybrid, Ayna, 1986

Hybrid, Vesta, 1987

Hybrid, Sekki, 1962

It is important to include the pedigree of *Hybrid Galka* (Appendix A, Karat section) in reference to the pedigree of Charli 1 to show the additional influence coming through Hybrid Demon (1957). Readers will note that Hybrid Galka is a paternal great grand dam of Charli 1 and was inbred on Hybrid Demon. Through Galka comes a powerful genetic boost to Hybrid Dega who was sired by Hybrid Demon.

It is important to show the pedigree of Hybrid Dega (1962) to demonstrate her importance on the trailway to Charli 1 with the genetic input coming to him from both Hybrid Foka and Hybrid Demon. Readers will also recall that Hybrid Dega (1962) was the dam of male Hybrids Rams I (1966), Tuman, and Jermak, and female Dzhoya (1967).

Family Lines

VUD WAS A PRODUCER IN the late 1960s and in his photograph, he presents as a rather heavily built, solid animal with a thick black coat and considerable facial furnishing. Little information is available on this stud dog other than his impressive lineage and few recorded offspring.

Family Pillars of Vud

Hybrid Rams 2 (Vud × Diva), no date of birth, is the only male offspring recorded from Vud, coming from a third litter sired by him. Hybrid Vud was the sire of six recorded female offspring: Kerri, Dzhilda, and Leda (Vud × Chara) (yr?); Dinga (Vud × Dzhulja) (yr?); Kleopatra (1971) (Vud × Miledi); and Dzhudi 1971) (Vud × Diva).

Rams 2 is particularly interesting with Dik appearing in his paternal third and maternal fourth generation, and with the extended family of crossbreed Vah, also on both sides in his fourth generation. Through his fourth generation maternal great grand dam, Meggi, comes Giant Schnauzer Ditter f. Drahenshljuht, who readers will recall is reported as being pepper and salt coloured. See pedigree of Vud in Appendix A, Vud section.

Rams 2 sired 2 recorded females in Eva and Charodeyka (Rams 2 × Chuta), no recorded date of birth.

Of Vud's female offspring, Kerri produced male Shvarts 2 (1977) (Charli 1 × Kerri); Leda produced male Le Kuchum (1977) (Len Klaus × Leda); Kleopatra produced male Len Klaus (1974) (Artosha × Kleopatra); and Dzhudi produced female Dzhina (1973) (Kapitan Flint × Dzhudi).

161

In Shvarts 2's pedigree, Foka presented as a fine hybrid "Black Terrier" specimen who produced some fine breed representatives including Nastya, Dina I, Karat, Ayman, and Rams I; Dega is triple inbred on Hybrid Demon (Arras × Chomga); superdog Karat, with 8 male and 19 female recorded offspring, is inbred on Brayt; Sekki's sire was Demon; Dik was also a super producer with 10 male and 15 female recorded offspring; Velta was strongly composed of Giant Schnauzer and Rottweiler, with a touch of Moscow Waterdog through Hanka. Velta's maternal grandsire, through her dam, Meggi, was Giant Schnauzer Ditter f. Drahenshljuht, of pepper and salt colour; Irda was triple inbred on Giant Schnauzer Roy with a balance of Rottweiler and Moscow Waterdog. Unfortunately, Shvarts 2 did not present with heavy facial furnishings. Note that Hybrid Foka was the sire of Hybrid Karat.

Rams 2

Vud, 1967

Dik, 1958

Viy, 1960

Haytar, 1952   *Vishnya, 1956*   *Vah, 1956*

There are many "Black Terriers" carrying the name Shaytan. For interest there is one by Shvarts 2 × Arna, photo below with no date of birth. Note that Arna's dam, Dzhilda, is also by Vud × Chara, as with Kerri, dam of Shvarts 2.

Le Kuchum, 1977

Len Klaus, 1974

Hybrid, Karat, 1964,

Hybrid, Shvarts 2, 1977, male

Hybrid, Foka, 1960, male

Hybrid, Shaytan (male)
(Hybrid, Shvarts 2 ×

Arna, 1979, female (Hybrid, Ned-Nays ×
Hybrid, Dzhilda)

Ned-Nays, 1975, male
(Hybrid, Dan Zhan ×
Hybrid, Neda)

Dan Zhan, 1970, male
(Hybrid, Dzhim ×
Hybrid, Dzhoya)

Dzhim, 1966, male
(Hybrid, Karat ×
Crossbreed, Teya)

Dzhoya, 1967, female
(Hybrid, Tom × Hybrid,
Dega)

Vud, 1967, male
(Hybrid, Dik × Hybrid,
Velta)

Tishka, 1967, male
(Hybrid, Dik × Hybrid,
Nora)

Family Lines

1967: Based on Hybrid Tuman (Male) (Hybrid, Tom × Hybrid, Dega)

HYBRID TUMAN (1967) SIRED 8 male 22 female recorded offspring, with a number of excellent representative females in the time-frame of 1969 through 1973. Note that Aray (1954) was a paternal great grandsire of Tuman (1967). Crossbreed Aray was also the sire of Tuman (1956?).

Once again, we have two important stud dogs with the same name in the evolution of the Black Terrier, in the same family line. Tuman (1967) sports an impressive lineage that is extended here to include the line of the two Tumans, tracing Tuman (1967) (Tom × Dega) backward through Tom and Dina to Tuman (1956?), to Aray (1954) (Roy × Urma), and Htora (1952) (Giant Schnauzer, Roy × Airedale Terrier, Sotta).

Hybrid Tuman (1967)'s dam, Hybrid Dega (Hybrid, Demon × Hybrid, Galka), is triple inbred on Demon, with both Galka's grandsires being Demon. Also note that Hybrid Dega's paternal great grand dam was Rottweiler Femka (1951). Similar name confusion with Unknown, Fimka (1951) and Rottweiler, Femka (1951). Crossbreed Femka (1951) female (Rottweiler, Kastor × Rottweiler, Tina) was a paternal great grand dam of Hybrid Dega. So Tuman (1967), from his sire, Hybrid Tom, has Unknown Fimka on his paternal side and Rottweiler Femka maternally through his dam Hybrid Dega. See pedigree of Dega (1962) in Appendix A, Tuman (1967) section.

Note that *Fimka (1951)*, a paternal great grand dam of Tuman (1967), is of unknown parentage. Her dam was unknown and her sire, Araj, has no recorded parentage. Unfortunately, there is no photograph of Fimka's only recorded daughter, Dina, which might have allowed liberty for some speculation. The interest in Dina's lineage comes from the fact that her

sire, Tuman (1956?), paternally came from Crossbreed Aray (Roy ×
Rottweiler, Urma) and maternally from (Roy × Airedale Terrier, Sotta),
and that she was was bred to Gay who was by Crossbreed, Aray × Crossbreed, Borka who were both from Giant Schnauzer Roy × Rottweiler
Urma, born one year apart. More of the stuff of fascination.

Looking back from the pedigree of Hybrid Tuman (1967) we see that
his paternal great grandsire was the earlier Hybrid Tuman (1956?) who
was a combination of Giant Schnauzer, Rottweiler, and Airedale Terrier.

Family Pillars of Tuman (1967)

A problem with many of Tuman's recorded offspring is that there are no
dates of birth. Hybrid Chagi (Tuman × Unknown) produced one recorded
male offspring Ralf Chang (Bim 1 × Chagi) 1975.

Kras-Boss (1971?) male (Hybrid, Tuman × Hybrid, Ulma) is truly an
interesting specimen by his photograph. His parentage is excellent and
he is most probably a dog I would like to have known. He looks to me like
a dog that was upstanding, self-assured, and at the same time ready for a
good go at anything. He was a big lad, with good bone, large format, and
an acceptable coat for the time. I would love to have seen his eyes. He
was definitely an exciting evolution of his lineage that included Tuman,
Tom, Topaz, Demon, and Nayt. His sire Tuman (1967) produced 9 male
and 23 female offspring from a number of females from 1969 into 1973.
Given that Tuman was born in 1967 and that there is recorded no date of
birth for Ulma, dam of Kras-Boss, one might reasonably assume that
Kras-Boss could have been born around 1971. Unfortunately, Kras-Boss
currently has no recorded offspring nor does his littermate female, Karina-
Un. Tuman's litter sister, Dzhoya, has currently recorded 7 male and 12
female offspring with a number of exceptional males including Viy, Dzhim,
and Ajaks [Ayaks], from 1969 through 1975.

Dega, paternal grand dam of Kras-Boss, was triple inbred on Demon
(1957). Gay was inbred on Giant Schnauzer Roy and Rottweiler Urma.
Galka was inbred on Demon. Lada was a hybrid of Giant Schnauzer,
Rottweiler, Moscow Waterdog, and Moscow Dog.

Nayt (1964) was composed of 90 percent Giant Schnauzer ×
Rottweiler plus 10 percent Giant Schnauzer × East European Shepherd
through Chubarik (1953).

Hybrid Maur (yr?) male (Hybrid, Tuman × Hybrid, Sekki) recorded 2 female offspring (yr?) (Maur × Vlasta) and Hybrid, Vega (1974) (Magnitogorsk) (Maur × Vil'da). Sekki (photo next page) was sired by Demon. Dega was sired by and triple inbred on Demon. Galka was also inbred on Demon.

As well, *Sekki* was a good producer producing offspring that included Hybrids Maur, Kitri, Chada, Blek-Veda, and Kapitan Flint.

Hybrid Dina female (Hybrid, Tuman × Hybrid, Panta) 1 recorded female offspring in Le Dani Mir (Dzhin × Dina). Note that Panta was inbred on Dila (Russian Spotted Hound, Uteshay × Rottweiler, Uza). Karen 1 and Ilma are crossbreeds of Rottweiler and Russian Spotted Hound.

Hybrid Timur male (Tuman × Panta) recorded male Vajs and female offspring Virta, Verda, and Vietta (yr?) (Hybrid, Timur × Hybrid, Vayda).

Kras-Boss *Tuman*

Tom, 1964 *Demon, 1957* *Topaz*

Topaz *Karina-Un* *Chubarik*

Hybrid, Sekki, female, 1962
(Hybrid, Demon ×
Hybrid, Arsa)

Other offspring recorded from Hybrid Tuman include: Hybrid Yuna (female) (Tuman × Yuta) (1 recorded female offspring, Vesta (1973) (Dzhaga × Yuna)); Hybrid Gayda female (Tuman × Chana) (1 recorded male offspring, Ertzog (King × Gayda)); Hybrid Karem male (Tuman × Nim Eva) (1 male Dallar and 2 female recorded offspring Darvi (1974) (Karem × Gerda), and Dezi (1976) (Karem × Gerda)); Hybrid Yarcha female (1970) (Tuman × Chapa) no recorded offspring; Hybrid Lada female (1970) (Tuman × Panta) no recorded offspring; Hybrid Feya female (Tuman × Meri) (1 recorded female offspring, Ketti (1973) (Anchar × Feya)).

Hybrid Rema Greza (1970) female (Tuman × Rynda) 3 recorded female offspring: Sabina-Diana, Setti, and Seggi (1973) (Barhan-Zhan × Rema Greza). One interesting aspect of Rema Greza is that one of her maternal great grandsires was Giant Schnauzer Ditter f. Drahenshljuht (pepper and salt coat colour). Another interest is in her 3 daughters who were sired by Barhan-Zhan who, in turn, was sired by Bechel, bringing Karat back into the mix.

Zhulya (1970) female (Tuman × Raksha) 2 male and 3 female recorded offspring: females Ora, Oyta, and Olesya and males Oksay and Om (Set × Zhulya) (1973). Oksay was a sire of some exceptional off-spring.

Hybrid Tuman × Hybrid Raksha also produced females Zhaklin and Zherika and males Zhurd and Zhuk (1970). Following photographs of Hybrids Zhul and Zhaklin show two littermates with considerable differences in physical format.

Hybrid, Vajs, yr?, male

(Hybrid, Timur × Hybrid, Vayda)

Hybrid, Virta, yr?,

Hybrid, Vays, 1969, male (Hybrid, Lord × Hybrid, Roksa)

The following photographic collage (next page) presents a relatively good speculative picture of Zhulya through her offspring and lineage. She was sired by Tuman (1967) and her dam, Raksha, was sired by Karat. This again expresses very close breeding practices within a limited genetic base. The photos begin with Olesya, Oksay, and Om. Note also that Arni, dam of Set was also sired by Karat.

Other offspring by Tuman (1967) covered elsewhere included:

- Yanga (female) (1970) (Tuman × Unknown) no recorded offspring
- Yard (male) (1970) (Tuman × Unknown) no recorded offspring
- Lera (female) (1972) (Tuman × Nayda) 1 male and 3 female offspring
- Chara (female) (1972) Tuman × Nayda) 1 male offspring Zhan Grey (1976) (Kapitan Flint × Chara)

Hybrids Set and Zhulya present another marvel in inbreeding in the production of hybrid offspring Oksay, Om, Ora, Oyta, and Olesya in one litter in 1973. Littermates Oksay and Oyta were bred together in 1977 to produce one recorded offspring in male Hybrid Tsorn. Tsorn was bred to Hybrid Kana in 1979 to sire female offspring Hybrid Tsuri who currently shows no recorded offspring. In 1980, Tsorn was bred to Hybrid Charda and sired female offspring, Panta who, in her own right, produced 1 male and 5 female recorded offspring with Hybrid Atos. No littermates of Hybrid Tsorn nor other offspring are currently recorded from littermate Hybrids Oksay × Hybrid, Oyta.

Hybrid Tsuri is recorded as having been housed at Red Star and Hybrid Panta was located in Magnitogorsk, Russia. Hybrid Panta bred to Hybrid Atos produced 1 female Hybrid Danka Pabo (yr?) who is listed as being in Hungary. Again, with Hybrid Atos, she produced 1 male Hybrid O Bim and 5 female offspring (Orli, Osta, Olga, and Olda) in 1982 at Magnitogorsk, Russia. It appears that this group produced a solid base of female offspring for future breeding stock. Hybrid O Bim sired 12 male and 21 female offspring, with his female littermates contributing another 17 female offspring. One of Orli's male offspring, Hybrid Zhakila Charli (1986), produced 8 male and 10 female offspring in Magnitogorsk and Chelyabinsk from 1989 through 1995.Hybrid Oksay sired 3 male and 5 female recorded offspring.

- Oksay was bred to Hybrid Hilda and sired male Oks Hort Hilda, and females Oks Hristina Hilda and Oks Hanta Hilda (1976)
- Oksay was bred to Hybrid Molli Set and sired male Hybrid Yard (1977)
- Oksay was bred to Hybrid Gera and sired female Hybrid Baska (1977)
- Oksay was bred to Chelza and sired female Hybrid Linda (1979)
- Oksay was bred to Hybrid Masha and sired female Hybrid Moya Mariya (1979)
- Hybrid Oyta currently shows 1 male recorded offspring
- Oyta was was bred to her sibling, Oksay, producing male Tsorn (1977)
- Hybrid Ora currently shows 1 male and 1 female recorded offspring
- Ora was was bred to Monstr-Dzhimmi-Set producing male Pluton and female Prelli (1976)
- Hybrid Om currently shows no recorded offspring
- Hybrid Olesay currently shows no recorded offspring

Olesya, 1973   *Oksay, 1973*   *Om, 1973*

Set, 1971   *Karay, 1967*   *Tom, 1964*

Two things need to be kept in mind here. First, the quality appearing in the photographs of these 3 littermates, and secondly, that the BRT Database is still in its infancy so records will continue to be added with time and the supreme efforts of the Russian fanciers who manage the Database.

Hybrid Baska (1981) is here to represent the line coming from Tuman moving into the 1980s and approaching the official recognition of the Black Russian Terrier by FCI. Hybrid Baska also demonstrates that Russian breeders in 1981 were still employing breeding stock of unknown lineage; to wit, Baska's dam, Dzhenni, grandsire Chernish and grand dam Alpha-Malyshka. Hybrid Baska produced 3 currently recorded offspring in Hybrid Bari (1985) male (Hybrid, Bonni-Dinar × Baska); Hybrid Vanda (1986) female (Hybrid, Das-Gaston × Baska); and Hybrid Gella-Linda (1988) female (Hybrid, Laf Dzherom × Baska).

The interesting pedigree of Hybrid Zhan Grey (1976), who is currently the only recorded offspring of Hybrid Kapitan Flint (1969) × Hybrid Chara (1972), can be viewed in Appendix A, Tuman (1967) section.

Karat, 1964

Nayt, 1964

Foka, 1960

Demon, 1957

Brayt, 1956

Arras, 1954

Hybrid, Zhuk, male,
1970

Hybrid, Zhaklin, female,
1970

Hybrid, Tuman,
1967

Family Lines

1975: Based on Hybrid Tap Arto (Male) (Hybrid, Chyingiz Rhan × Hybrid, Tapa)

THE PHOTOGRAPHS AVAILABLE OF FAMILY members of Tap Arto show an incredible, well-developed standardized format. Readers would be more appreciative of the physical similarities presented in this line had the available photographs been more clear. See next page. However, no imagination is required to visualize the genetic structure passed on from the early generations and particularly those coming through Hybrid Chanita. A large number of female offspring were produced by this line of Black Terriers.

Hybrid Tap Arto is recorded as having sired 1 male and 7 female currently recorded offspring from 1978 through 1981, including Hybrid Tarzan (1981) male (Hybrid, Tap Arto × Hybrid, Kara).

173

*Hybrid, Tap Arto, 1975,
male*

*Hybrid, Chingiz Rhan,
Sire of Hybrid, Tap Arto
1969*

*Hybrid, Chanita,
(Paternal Grand Dam
and Maternal Great
Grand Dam of
Hybrid, Tap Arto)*

*Hybrid, Karat, 1964,
male*

*Hybrid, Tyapa, 1959,
male*

*Hybrid, Tarzan, 1981,
male. Privately owned at
Armavir*

Family Lines

1976: Based on Hybrid Mashka (Female) (Hybrid, Urban × Hybrid, Masha)

A LINE BUILT DIRECTLY ON Hybrid Mashka from 1979 through 1983 established a migration of high-quality breeding stock into private ownership throughout Sweden, The Netherlands, and Finland. Hybrid Mashka's pedigree is in Appendix A, p. 175.

- Hybrid Calov (1979) male (Hybrid, Jolkas Genij × Hybrid, Mashka) 9 male/5 female offspring
- Hybrid Cacsha (1979) female (Hybrid, Jolkas Genij × Hybrid, Mashka) 4 male/4 female offspring
- Hybrid Gritt (1982) male (Hybrid, Hrabrij Foka × Hybrid, Mashka) 2 male/3 female offspring
- Hybrid Grisja (1982) female (Hybrid, Hrabrij Foka × Hybrid, Mashka) 1 male offspring
- Hybrid Harpo (1983) male (Hybrid, Deiko × Hybrid, Mashka) 6 male/9 female offspring

Although offspring coming from the above specimens are recorded in the BRT Virtual Database, offspring coming from them are not as yet recorded.

Family Lines

1977: Based on Hybrid Lord (Male)
(Hybrid, Atos × Hybrid, Virta)

IT IS OF INTEREST TO note that Red Star Kennel was continuing to be active within the breeding program it created [as it continues to be in 2016]. This fact presents a good reason for examining a breeding utilizing another of the male hybrid specimens named Atos. This dog also does not record a date of birth but his male offspring Hybrid Lord was born at Red Star in 1977 (Hybrid, Atos × Hybrid, Virta). Hybrid Lord is credited with siring 3 male and 10 female recorded offspring from 1981 through 1985. His offspring provided a power source for breed advancement moving into the 1980s. Lord was privately owned at Moscow and his sire, Atos, and dam, Virta, were owned by, and resident at, Red Star. Continuing interest witnesses that again the breeding stock was a combination of well-recognized proven specimens.

Hybrid, Vays, 1969, male

As in many other cases, it is unfortunate that no photograph of Hybrid Lord (1977) could be located. Although there are photographs elsewhere of many members of Lord's lineage, it is appropriate to include here photos of his maternal great grandsire Vays and great grand dam Chada to demonstrate the quality from which he came. All of his great grandsires and great grand dams were of exceptional quality.

Hybrid, Chada, 1968, female

176

Family Lines

1979, 1982, 1983: Based on Offspring of Hybrid Mashka (Female) (Hybrid, Urban × Hybrid, Masha)

HYBRID MASHKA, HOMED IN SWEDEN, was bred to Hybrid Jolkas Genij in 1979, Hybrid Hrabrij Foka in 1982, and to Hybrid Deiko in 1983. Pedigrees of her recorded offspring are in Appendix A, 1979, 1982, 1983 Mashka section. Hybrid Mashka (1976) produced some exceptional offspring who themselves produced more exceptional offspring, advancing the Black Russian Terrier into its future.

Family Lines

1980: Based on Hybrid Panta (Female) (Hybrid, Tsorn × Hybrid, Charda)

MOVING INTO 1980, FEMALE HYBRID Panta (1980) was born at Red Star Kennel and, bred to Hybrid Atos, produced 1 male and 5 female recorded offspring in 1982. [Don't confuse this Panta with Hybrid Panta (1965) (Crossbreed, Karen 1 × Crossbreed, Ilma).] One female offspring, Danka Pabo, does not record a birth date so it is possible she was the only recorded offspring from an earlier litter. This female is recorded as having gone to Timber Wolf Kennel in Hungary. It is important to note that Hybrids Oksay and Oyta were littermates. Of the other 5 offspring, the 1 male, O Bim, is the only one presenting with a photograph in the Database. It is presented in a collage of members of his lineage, which notably are only male specimens on his maternal side.

- Hybrid O Bim sired 12 male and 21 female recorded offspring
- Hybrid Atos sired 11 male and 13 female recorded offspring
- Hybrid Panta produced 1 male and 5 female recorded offspring
- Hybrid Lo-Rom sired 5 male and 5 female recorded offspring
- Hybrid Sabina-Dianna produced 3 male and 2 female recorded offspring
- Hybrid Tsorn sired 2 female recorded offspring
- Hybrid Charda produced 2 female recorded offspring

Hybrid Atos (1980) was privately owned and homed at Magnito-gorsk, Chelyabinsk region, 1,400 air km and 1,680 road km southeast of Moscow.

The male name Atos was extensively used which can create some

178

degree of consternation when searching through considerable records. The BRT Virtual Database lists fifteen individuals named Atos and another twenty-two using Atos as the prefix.

On **O Bim**'s extended paternal side [sire Atos], the luck is only somewhat better with pictures of female Hybrids Dzhoya and Adzhi-Shahra.

Hybrid, O Bim, male, 1982   *Hybrid, Atos, male, 1980*   *Hybrid, Oksay, male, 1973*   *Hybrid, Set, male, 1971*

Hybrid, Dan Zhan, male, 1970   *Hybrid, Karat, male, 1964*

Hybrid Dzhim, male, 1966   *Hybrid, Dzhoya, female, 1967*

Hybrid, Tuman, male, 1967   *Hybrid, Bechel, male, 1966*

Hybrid, Adzhi-Shahra, female, 1964

Addendum

1978: Family Lines Based on Giant Schnauzer Females Ledi 1945 and Anni f. Raakzeje [Raakze]

Anni f. Raakzeje [Raakze]

INFORMATION EXAMINED DURING THIS RESEARCH project [suggested/stated] that no Giant Schnauzer females had been successfully used in developing a line(s) employing females of that breed. And to some extent that could be assumed to be true given that no female Giant Schnauzers are discovered in available pedigrees. However, that is not quite the case at all. Our famous Giant Schnauzer, Roy, considered the father of the Black Terrier breeding Group, ergo the Black Russian Terrier, was, of course, the product of/from a pair of Giant Schnauzers (Zorab × Ledi). From these two pre-origin-BRT Giant Schnauzers came both Roy and his male littermate Boj. Early on I had thought that Roy and Boj were one and the same with different spelling. That has proven to not be the case. Also interesting is the discovery of Ledi's pedigree no. D018K. Without knowing Red Star's registration process, it is exciting to think of Ledi as being the

Anni f. Raakzeje [Raakze]

eighteenth specimen of the original selection of breeding participants. She would have been born in or before 1945 given Roy and Boj's birth date as 1947. Adding to the challenge is Zorab's pedigree no. 741GD.

BRT breed father Roy has recorded currently (2016) in the BRT

Virtual Breed Database 36 male and 45 female offspring. His male litter-mate Boj, as of 2012, has only male Kalyan and female Kal'ma recorded as offspring from one litter in 1949 (Giant Schnauzer, Boj × Giant Schnauzer, Mira). Mira's ancestry is currently listed as Unknown. Also no photographs have been discovered of Giant Schnauzers Zorab, Ledi, Mira, Kalyan, or Kal'ma.

Here follows what appears to have happened: female Kal'ma was bred to Crossbreed Chudniy (Giant Schnauzer, Roy × Rottweiler, Uda) producing female Crossbreed Kemi in 1955. Kemi was was bred to Crossbreed Azart producing Crossbreed Kerri in 1958. Here, that line ends with Kerri showing no recorded offspring. This is very interesting with a huge question mark — why? Crossbreed Kerri's pedigree in Appendix A, Addendum shows powerful first crosses of Giant Schnauzer and Rottweiler.

The [available] story of male *Giant Schnauzer Kalyan* is somewhat the same but definitely different. Kalyan is credited with 6 male and 6 female recorded offspring. Kalyan sired males Bagor and Bazar and 3 females Balka, Barka, and Banda in 1955 with Crossbreed Chadra (Giant Schnauzer, Roy × Rottweiler, Una). Only the male Bagor shows a re-corded offspring in female Tjapa (1956) (Crossbreed, Bagor × Cross-breed, Mukha). Hybrid Tjapa records no offspring. Crossbreed Mukha was sired by Giant Schnauzer, Roy × Moscow Waterdog Tiza).

A second litter sired by Kalyan was with Crossbreed Hroma (Giant Schnauzer, Roy × Airedale Terrier, Sotta) also in 1955, and producing males Bay, Bak, Bor, and Bas and females Bega, Bita, and Brada. None of these early specimens currently shows any recorded offspring. Again comes the question — why?

Just as with Giant Schnauzer Roy, his littermate Boj may well have sired one or more female lines coming from (their) dam Giant Schnauzer Ledi [with help from Giant Schnauzer Zorab].

Quite possibly, references to no successful lines developed from female Giant Schnauzers may have come from the non-performance of a line developing from Boj. [There were plenty coming from Roy.] Also, no female Giant Schnauzers could be discovered other than Anni f. Raakzeje [Raakze]. At this point, one can only wonder what might have happened.

The other female Giant Schnauzer story is that of *Anni f. Raakzeje* [*Raakze*] (yr?) (Ekso f. Rozeggers-Haus [Exo v. Roseggerhaus] × Brotta f. Haus Brekker [Bitta v. Haus Brekker]).

Anni was located at Red Star and is currently credited with producing 2 female Hybrid offspring in Gayde and Tishka (1975) with Hybrid Kuchum. Hybrid Gayde currently shows 1 male recorded offspring in Hybrid Bes (1979) (Hybrid, Bars × Hybrid, Gayde). Hybrid Bes is credited with siring males Sherri Bek and Sholom, and female Shella (1982) (Hybrid, Bes × Hybrid, Ped Shanel); female Hybrids Naira and Nika and male Nord (1985) (Hybrid, Bes × Hybrid, Dolli Bek); Hybrid Tom-Tifrina (1987) female (Hybrid, Bes × Hybrid, Sherri-Torri).

• Hybrid Sherri Beck sired 1 male and 1 female offspring in 1985 and 1987
• Hybrid females Sholom and Shella show no recorded offspring
• Hybrid female Naira records 3 female offspring in 1989 and 1990
• Hybrid female Nika records 2 female offspring in 1988
• Hybrid male Nord records 13 male and 18 female offspring in 1988, 1989 and 1990
• Hybrid female Tom-Tifrina records 2 female offspring in 1990

Suffice it to say that a strong argument could be offered in support of a BRT line created through female Giant Schnauzer Anni f. Raakzeje [Raakze] whose genes were carried into the developing Black Russia Terrier into the 1990s.

The pedigree of Hybrid Nord (1985) male (Hybrid, Bes × Hybrid, Dolli Bek) (Appendix A, Addendum) demonstrates the influence coming from female Giant Schnauzer Anni f. Raakzeje [Raakze] whose contribution of new Giant Schnauzer genes moved forward into the 1980s and 1990s. The main purpose is to query the contention that no female Giant Schnauzer was successfully bred from, and thereby to confirm that a female Giant Schnauzer *did* play an integral part in the creation of the Black Russian Terrier. Readers cannot help but notice that Anni's lineage is of pure German Giant Schnauzer genes.

Another conundrum arises in the discovery in the BRT Virtual Database of a lesser recorded Giant Schnauzer line originating with a half sibling of Giant Schnauzers (male) Akbar and (female) Anni f. Raakzeje

[Raakze], by the name of Artus v. Sachsenring (Giant Schnauzer, Ekso f. Rozeggers-Haus [Exo v. Roseggerhaus] × Giant Schnauzer, Burga v.d. Stefanidrunnen) and Giant Schnauzer Hella v.d. Wallwitzburg (Unknown Parentage).

This presents a number of Giant Schnauzers that, according to available records, do not seem to have come into the BRT until the birth of Hybrid Laf-Vayda (1985) female (Hybrid, Lafler × Hybrid, Reda) and Hybrid Fal Dezi (1986) female (Hybrid, Lafler × Hybrid, Rena). Although information on this breeding group/line is currently sketchy at best, one cannot but wonder about the effect of [new] Giant Schnauzers being introduced in the 1980s into an already-established Breed and what would have been the reasoning? Apparently these two females were bred by a Maria Yakunchikova and owned by one Efimov with no recorded home location. Records show these Giant Schnauzers to have been of imported German origin. See pedigree of Gainar v. Virker Park in Appendix A, Addendum.

Although the "terms of reference" of this study was to not delve into the Breed beyond 1980, I feel it is important to point out that there may have been an important impact on the Black Russian Terrier structure with the addition of purebred Giant Schnauzers into the breed in 1988–89 moving into the 1990s. Hybrid Wojtek Dzsek (born in Moscow and resident in Hungary) has 6 male and 13 female offspring recorded in the BRT Virtual Database. One of Wojtek Dzsek's male offspring, Hybrid Amur Z Ro-Da-Gu (born in Moscow and resident in Czech Republic), also shows 6 male and 13 female recorded offspring. Many of the offspring of these two males remained in Hungary or went to the Czech Republic, Poland, Germany, Italy, Slovakia, Denmark, et al. Amurka Z Ro Da Gu, female littermate of Amur, currently records 1 male and 2 female offspring in the Database.

Considering the number of currently recorded offspring coming through Hybrids Grey and Wojtek, et al., one appreciates the influence that might possibly have come about through the reintroduction of the Giant Schnauzer as late as 1979 from Hybrid Grey through Wojtek Dzsek to his offspring and forward.

What impact this might have had, I do not have sufficient background data to comment on. Therefore, this limited [but intriguing] observation is provided for information purposes only.

The pedigree of Giant Schnauzer Gainar v. Virker Park is presented (Appendix A, Addendum section) to demonstrate the additional Giant Schnauzer input into the Black Russian Terrier development process approaching, and into, the 1990s. Gainar currently shows no recorded siblings in the Database. Note that Anni f. Raakzeje [Raakze]'s paternal lineage is the same as that of Gainar. Also note the designation call letters DDR (*Deutsche Demokratische Republik*) and GDR (German Democratic Republic); both refer to East Germany during post WWII and "Cold War" period of 1949 to 1990. Both designations appear in pedigrees of Giant Schnauzers.

As one last step in this study of Moscow Families the pedigree of Hybrid Zeman is presented in Appendix A to show the addition to the breeding process of Giant Schnauzer Jaguar in 1982 and his lineage.

These "late" appearing Giant Schnauzers present interesting questions for future study.

Giant Schnauzer, Kris f. Rortrayh, 1980

Only a Small Part

The foregoing is only a small part of the story of the undertakings of Red Star Kennel and the Moscow City Club of Service Dogs. The full account would comprise volumes and require access to the official military records and the discovery of masses of unavailable and missing records. It would also require the personal memories of the specialists who were the early breeders experimenting with mixing and matching the best of those "Black Terriers" that were available in the 1950s, 1960s, and 1970s. And that would be only the beginning — that first thirty years from 1950 to 1980 which was the difficult part, a time of breed selections and pairing, a time of vision, a time of format and temperament establishment and development — a time of evolution.

The universal Breed acceptance part began with the 1980s. This second thirty years — 1980 to 2010 — was the period of refinement and polishing. It was also the time for discovering the modern period fraught with debilitating ailments and genetic problems that needed to be recognized, accepted as reality, and dealt with, to save the Black Russian

Terrier breed from traveling that road to destruction suffered by many other Breeds abused by the canine fancies of the modern world.

The third thirty-year period of 2010 to 2040 will require a "master plan" to analyze and address the future challenges of health and structure stability.

Moscow, Russia, was the birth-cradle of the Black Russian Terrier. It was the starting place from which this new breed would evolve, branching out first to Leningrad (now St. Petersburg) then across the USSR member states, populating the great hinterland of modern Russia, spreading throughout all of Europe, the United Kingdom, the Americas, and around the world, in the timeframe of six decades.

The world has become the home of this marvellous canine breed and the place in which it will be perfected.

From the accounts and information contained in this undertaking it is hoped that readers will appreciate the constitution that is the Black Russian Terrier Family, from its beginning, through the developmental period, to the dog of today: a family member and a working dog that requires interesting and challenging activities.

Volume 6: *Leningrad Families* will explore the continued advancement of Breed development emanating from Leningrad City Kennel (St. Petersburg) and into private hands, spreading into the Baltic States and Scandinavian countries.

Appendix A

1954: Family Lines Based on Crossbreed Aray (Male) (Giant Schnauzer, Roy × Rottweiler, Urma)

		Roy (Schn.) 1947?, Red Star
	Aray (Cx.) 1954, Red Star	
		Urma (Rtw.) 1950, Red Star
Gay (Cx.), Red Star		
		Roy (Schn.) 1947?, Red Star
	Borka (Cx.) 1955, Red Star	
		Urma (Rtw.) 1950, Red Star

Dega (♀) Aktaj [Aktay] (♂) (Hyb.), Red Star

		Vah (Cx.) 1956, Red Star
	Foka (Hyb.) 1960, Red Star	
		Bara (Hyb.) 1957, Red Star
Dina I (Hyb.) 1964, Red Star		
		Brayt (M.Wdg.Hyb.) 1956, Red Star
	Nayda (Hyb.) 1961, Red Star	
		Nelma (Hyb.), Red Star

Tuman (Hyb.),
1956?, Red Star

Aray (Cx.) 1954,
Red Star

Roy (Schn.) 1947?, Red Star

Urma (Rtw.) 1950, Red Star

Htora (Cx.) 1952,
Red Star

Roy (Schn.) 1947?, Red Star

Sotta (Aired.) 1948, Red Star

Dina (♀) (Hyb.), Moscow

Fimka (Unkn.)

Araj (Unkn.)

Unknown

Unknown

Unknown

Unknown

Unknown

Unknown

Gay (Cx.) ,
Red Star

Aray (Cx.) 1954,
Red Star

Roy (Schn.) 1947?, Red Star

Urma (Rtw.) 1950, Red Star

Borka (Cx.) 1955,
Red Star

Roy (Schn.) 1947?, Red Star

Urma (Rtw.) 1950, Red Star

Tom (♂), Ata (♀) (Hyb.) 1964, Red Star

Dina (Hyb.),
Moscow

Tuman (Hyb.) 1956?,
Red Star

Aray (Cx.) 1954, Red Star

Htora (Cx.) 1952, Red Star

Fimka (Unkn.)

Araj (Unkn.)

Unknown

1954: Family Lines Based on Crossbreed Azart (Male) (Giant Schnauzer, Roy × Rottweiler, Una)

Azart (Cx.) 1954, Red Star	Roy (Schn.) 1947?, Red Star	Zorab (Schn.)
		Ledi (Schn.)
	Una (Rtw.) 1950, Red Star	Kastor (Rtw.) 1947, Moscow
		Birma (Rtw.), Moscow

Azor (♂) (Hyb.) 1961, Red Star/St. Petersburg (Privately Owned)

Bayta (Hyb.) 1955, Red Star	Chudniy (Cx.) 1953, Red Star	Roy (Schn.) 1947?, Red Star
		Uda (Rtw.) 1950, Red Star
	Cheka (Cx.), Red Star	Roy (Schn.) 1947?, Red Star
		Finta (S.R.Ovch.) 1951, Red Star

Abbreviations: ♀, bitch; ♂, dog; Aired., Airedale; C.Ovch., Caucasian Ovcharka; C.A.Ovch., Central Asian Ovcharka; Cx., Crossbreed; E.E.Shep., East European Shepherd; G.G.Dane, German Great Dane; Hyb., Hybrid; M.Dvr, Moscow Diver; M.Dog, Moscow Dog; M.Wdg., Moscow Waterdog; Newf., Newfoundland; R.S.Hnd., Russian Spotted Hound; Rtw., Rottweiler; Schn., Schnauzer; S.R.Ovch., South Russian Ovcharka.

		Roy (Schn.) 1947?, Red Star
	Azart (Cx.) 1954, Red Star	
		Una (Rtw.) 1950, Red Star
Brayt (M.Wdg.Hyb.) 1956, Red Star		
		Lord (Newf.) 1948-50?, Moscow
	Hanka (M.Wdg.) 1952, Red Star	
		Tiza (M.Wdg.) 1949, Red Star

Bars [Baron] (Hyb.) 1958 (♂), Red Star

		Zorab (Schn.)
	Roy (Schn.) 1947?, Red Star	
		Ledi (Schn.)
Chonga (Cx.) 1953, Red Star		
		Bil f. Askania (Aired.) 1944, Moscow
	Salma (Aired.) 1949, Red Star	
		Teffi (Aired.), Moscow

		Vah (Cx.) 1956
	Foka (Hyb.) 1960, Red Star	
		Bara (Hyb.) 1957
Ayman (Hyb.) 1964, Red Star		
		Brayt (M.Wtg.Hyb.) 1956, Red Star
	Nayda (Hyb.) 1961, Red Star (Privately Owned)	
		Nelma (Hyb.), Red Star

Bim I (♂) (Hyb.) 1969–70?, Red Star

		Chani (Hyb.) 1962, Red Star
	Uran (Hyb.) 1966, Red Star	
		Ohta (Cx.), Red Star
Alfa (Hyb.) 1968?, Red Star		
		Chuk (M.Dog Hyb.) 1956, Red Star
	Alfa (Hyb.) 1961, Red Star	
		Volga (M.Wdg.Hyb.) 1956, Red Star

		Roy (Schn.) 1947?, Red Star
	Azart (Cx.) 1954, Red Star	Una (Rtw.) 1950, Red Star
Brayt (M.Wdg.Hyb.) 1956, Red Star		Lord [Newf.] 1948-50?
	Hanka (M.Wdg.) 1952, Red Star	Tiza (M.Wdg.) 1949, Red Star

Chani (Hyb.) Nord 1962?, ♂, Red Star

		Armin f. Tize Turm (Rtw.)
	Geyni (Rtw.) Moscow	Kora f. Schneidenplatz (Rtw.)
Ira (Cx.), Red Star		Unknown
	Meri (Aired.), Moscow	Unknown

		Vah (Cx.) 1956, Red Star
	Foka (Hyb.) 1960, Red Star	Bara (Hyb.) 1957, Red Star
Rams I (Hyb.) 1966, Red Star		Demon (Hyb.) 1957, Red Star/Saratov (Privately Owned)
	Dega (Hyb.) 1962, Red Star	Galka (Hyb.) (Privately Owned)

Charli 1 (Hyb.) 1979?, ♂, Red Star

		Foka (Hyb.) 1960, Red Star
	Karat (Hyb.) 1964, Red Star	Nayda (Hyb.) 1961, Red Star
Chada (Hyb.) 1968, Red Star		Demon (Hyb.) 1957, Red Star/Saratov (Privately Owned)
	Sekki (Hyb.) 1962, Red Star	Arsa (Hyb.) Red Star

```
                                             | Unknown
                        | Ajax f. Kliatal (Schn.)
                        |                    | Unknown
        Ditter f.
        Drahenshljuht                        | Unknown
        (Schn.) 1960,   | Azra f. Notr-Dam
        Moscow          | (Schn.)             | Unknown
```

Dega (♀) (Hyb.) 1963, St. Petersburg (Privately Owned)

```
                                             | Roy (Schn.) 1947?, Red Star
                        | Chuk (M.Dog Hyb.)
                        | 1956, Red Star      | Chili (M.Dog), Red Star
        Mirta (Hyb.) 1960,
        Red Star                             | Azart (Cx.) 1954, Red Star
                        | Volga (M.Wdg.Hyb.)
                        | 1956, Red Star      | Hanka (M.Wdg.) 1952, Red Star
```

```
                                             | Ajax f. Kliatal (Schn.) 1954, Germany
                        | Dasso f. Drahenshljuht
                        | (Schn.) 1960, Moscow | Azra f. Notr-Dam (Schn.) Germany
        Reks (Hyb.) (yr?),
        Red Star                             | Azart (Cx.) 1954, Red Star
                        | Gloriya (Hyb.) 1959,
                        | Red Star            | Cholka (M.Wdg.Hyb.) 1953, Red Star
```

Dezi (Hyb.) 1971, ♀, Red Star

```
                                             | Brayt (M.Wdg.Hyb.) 1956, Red Star
                        | Nord (Hyb.) 1962,
                        | Red Star            | Ira (Cx.), Red Star
        Lada (Hyb.) 1968,
        Red Star                             | Chani (Hyb.) 1962, Red Star
                        | Nelli (Hyb.) 1966,
                        | Red Star            | Ohta (Cx.), Red Star
```

Haytar (Cx.) 1952,
Red Star

Roy (Schn.) 1947?,
Red Star

Zorab (Schn.)

Ledi (Schn.) Moscow

Sotta (Aired.) 1949,
Red Star

Bil (fon) Askania (Aired.) Moscow

Teffi (Aired.) Moscow

Dik (Hyb.) 1958, ♂, Red Star

Vishnya
(M.Wdg.Hyb.) 1956,
Red Star

Azart (Cx.) 1954,
Red Star

Roy (Schn.) 1947?, Red Star

Una (Rtw.) 1950, Red Star

Hanka (M.Wdg.) 1952,
Red Star

Lord [Newf.] 1948–50?, Moscow

Tiza [M.Wdg.] 1949, Red Star

Bul (Cx.) 1956,
Red Star

Roy (Schn.) 1947?,
Red Star

Zorab (Schn.)

Ledi (Schn.) 1953, Moscow

Aza (M.Wdg.Hyb.) 1954,
Red Star

Roy (Schn.) 1947?, Red Star

Fomka (M.Wdg.), Moscow

Irda (♀) (Hyb.) 1962, Red Star

Binta (Cx.) 1955,
Red Star

Farno (Rtw.) 1951,
Red Star

Kastor (Rtw.) 1947, Moscow

Birma (Rtw.), Moscow

Charva (Cx.) 1953,
Red Star

Roy (Schn.) 1947?, Red Star

Una (Rtw.) 1950, Red Star

		Gay (Cx.) Red Star
	Tom (Hyb.) 1964, Red Star	
		Dina (Hyb.), Moscow
Topaz (Hyb.) 1967, Red Star		
		Nord (Hyb.) 1962, Red Star
	Lada (Hyb.) 1964, Red Star	
		Alfa (Hyb.) 1961, Red Star

Kapitan Flint (♂) (Hyb.) 1969, Red Star

		Arras (Hyb.) 1954, Red Star
	Demon (Hyb.) 1957, Red Star/Saratov	
		Chomga (Cx.) 1953, Red Star
Sekki (Hyb.) 1962, Red Star	(Privately Owned)	
		Azart (Cx.) 1954, Red Star
	Arsa (Hyb.), Red Star	
		Arsa (Hyb.) 1954, Red Star

		Vah (Cx.) 1956, Red Star
	Foka (Hyb.) 1960, Red Star	
		Bara (Hyb.) 1957, Red Star
Karat (Hyb.) 1964, Red Star		
		Brayt (M.Wdg.Hyb.) 1956, Red Star
	Nayda (Hyb.) 1961, Red Star	
		Nelma (Hyb.) Red Star

Kitri (♀) (Hyb.) 1957, Red Star

		Arras (Hyb.) 1954, Red Star
	Demon (Hyb.) 1957, Red Star/Saratov	
		Chomga (Cx.) 1953, Red Star
Sekki (Hyb.) 1962, Red Star	(Privately Owned)	
		Azart (Cx.) 1954, Red Star
	Arsa (Hyb.), Red Star	
		Arsa (Hyb.) 1954, Red Star

		Azart (Cx.) 1954, Red Star
	Brayt (M.Wdg.Hyb.) 1956, Red Star	
Nord (Hyb.) 1962, Red Star		Hanka (M.Wdg.) 1952, Red Star
		Geyni (Rtw.), Red Star
	Ira (Cx.), Red Star	
		Meri (Aired.), Red Star

Lada, Alfa (♀), Agat (♂) (Hyb.) 1964

		Roy (Schn.) 1947?, Red Star
	Chuk (M.Dog Hyb.) 1956, Red Star	
Alfa (Hyb.) 1962, Red Star		Chili (M.Dog), Red Star
		Azart (Cx.) 1954, Red Star
	Volga (M.Wdg.Hyb.) 1956, Red Star	
		Hanka (M.Wdg.) 1952, Red Star

		Roy (Schn.) 1947?, Red Star
	Azart (Cx.) 1954, Red Star	
Dzhoy (Hyb.) 1957, Red Star		Una (Rtw.) 1950, Red Star
		Beniamino (Rtw.) 1949, Red Star
	Arsa (Hyb.) 1954, Red Star	
		Hadzhi [Hodzha] (Cx.) 1952, Red Star

Lada Tag (♀) (Hyb.) 1959, Moscow

		Zorab (Schn.)
	Roy (Schn.) 1947?, Red Star	
Dzhena (Cx.) 1956, Red Star		Ledi (Schn.), Moscow
		Kastor (Rtw.) 1947, Moscow
	Una (Rtw.) 1950, Red Star	
		Birma (Rtw.), Moscow

Shvarts 2 (Hyb.)
1977, Red Star

Charli 1 (Hyb.),
Red Star

Rams I (Hyb.) 1966, Red Star

Chada (Hyb.) Red Star

Kerri (Hyb.),
Red Star

Vud (Hyb.) 1967

Chara (Hyb.) 1968, Red Star

Lin Sharman (Hyb.) 1984, ♂, Moscow

Linda Bek (Hyb.)
1980, Moscow

Bill (Hyb.) 1977,
Moscow

Ort-Zaur (Hyb.) 1974

Layna (Hyb.) 1973, Moscow

Dalila (Hyb.) 1978,
Moscow

Artosha (Hyb.) 1971

Dzherri (Hyb.) 1974

Tuman (Hyb.) 1967,
Red Star

Tom (Hyb.) 1964,
Red Star

Gay (Cx.) Red Star

Dina (Hyb.) Moscow

Dega (Hyb.) 1962,
Red Star

Demon (Hyb.) 1957, Red Star/Saratov
(Privately Owned)

Galka (Hyb.) (Privately Owned)

Maur (♂) (Hyb.) 1969?, Red Star/Ekaterinburg* (Privately Owned)

Sekki (Hyb.) 1962,
Red Star

Demon (Hyb.) 1957,
Red Star/Saratov
(Privately Owned)

Arras (Hyb.) 1954, Red Star

Chomga (Cx.) 1953, Red Star

Arsa (Hyb.),
Red Star

Azart (Cx.) 1954, Red Star

Arsa (Hyb.) 1954, Red Star

*Note: Ekaterinburg, Russia also known as Yekaterinburg and Sverdlovsk.

```
                                                    | Zorab (Schn.)
                            Roy (Schn.) 1947?,
                            Red Star                | Ledi (Schn.), Moscow
            Azart (Cx.) 1954,
            Red Star                                | Kastor (Rtw.) 1947, Moscow
                            Una (Rtw.) 1950,
                            Red Star                | Birma (Rtw.), Moscow
```

Mirta (♀) (Cx.) 1958?, Red Star/Ivanovo (Privately Owned)

```
                                                    | Kastor (Rtw.) 1947, Moscow
                            Farno (Rtw.) 1954,
                            Red Star                | Birma (Rtw.), Moscow
            Binta (Cx.) 1955,
            Red Star                                | Roy (Schn.) 1947?, Red Star
                            Charva (Cx.) 1953,
                            Red Star                | Una (Rtw.) 1950, Red Star
```

```
                                                    | Zorab (Schn.)
                            Roy (Schn.) 1947?,
                            Red Star                | Ledi (Schn.), Red Star
            Chuk (M.Dog Hyb.)
            1956, Red Star                          | Beniamino I (Rtw.) 1949, Red Star
                            Chili (M.Dog),
                            Red Star                | Toddi (M.Dog), Red Star
```

Mirta 1960, Alfa 1961 (♀) (Hyb.), Red Star

```
                                                    | Roy (Schn.) 1947?, Red Star
                            Azart (Cx.) 1954,
                            Red Star                | Una (Rtw.) 1950, Red Star
            Volga (M.Wdg.Hyb.)
            1956, Red Star                          | Lord (Newf.) 1948–50?, Moscow
                            Hanka (M.Wdg.) 1952,
                            Red Star                | Tiza (M.Wdg.) 1949, Red Star
```

		Haytar (Cx.) 1952, Red Star
	Dik (Hyb.) 1958, Red Star	
		Vishnya (M.Wdg.Hyb.) 1956, Red Star
Vud (Hyb.) 1967, Red Star		
		Vah (Cx.) 1956, Red Star
	Velta (Hyb.) 1964, Red Star	
		Meggi (Hyb.) 1961, Red Star

Rams 2 (Hyb.) 1969?, ♂, Moscow

		Vah (Cx.) 1956, Red Star
	Viy (Hyb.) 1960, Red Star	
		Bara (Hyb.) 1957, Red Star
Diva (Hyb.), Moscow		
		Dik (Hyb.) 1958, Red Star
	Dzhan (Hyb.) 1964, Moscow	
		Ayshe (Hyb.) 1961, Red Star

		Beniamino I (Rtw.) 1949, Red Star
	Arras (Hyb.) 1954, Red Star	
		Hizha [Hinga] (Cx.) 1952, Red Star
Demon (Hyb.) 1957 Red Star/Saratov (Privately Owned)		
		Roy (Schn.) 1947?, Red Star
	Chomga (Cx.) 1953	
		Femka (Rtw.) 1951, Red Star

Sekki (♀) (Hyb.) 1962, Red Star

		Roy (Schn.) 1947?, Red Star
	Azart (Cx.) 1954	
		Una (Rtw.) 1950, Red Star
Arsa (Hyb.), Red Star		
		Beniamino I (Rtw.) 1949, Red Star
	Arsa (Hyb.) 1954	
		Hadzhi [Hodzha] (Cx.) 1952, Red Star

		Roy (Schn.) 1947?, Red Star
Azart (Cx.) 1954, Red Star	
		Una (Rtw.) 1950, Red Star
Brayt (M.Wdg.Hyb.) 1956, Red Star		
		Lord (Newf.) 1949–50?, Moscow
Hanka (M.Wdg.) 1952, Red Star	
		Tiza (M.Wdg.) 1949, Red Star

Shrek (♂) (Hyb.) 1958, Red Star

		Kastor (Rtw.) 1947, Moscow
Farno (Rtw.) 1951, Red Star	
		Birma (Rtw.), Moscow
Binta (Cx.) 1955, Red Star		
		Roy (Schn.) 1947?, Red Star
Charva (Cx.) 1953, Red Star	
		Una (Rtw.) 1950, Red Star

		Azart (Cx.) 1954, Red Star
Brayt (M.Wdg.Hyb.) 1956, Red Star	
		Hanka (M.Wdg.) 1952, Red Star
Chani (Hyb.) 1962, Red Star		
		Geyni (Rtw.) 1955, Moscow
Ira (Cx.), Red Star	
		Meri (Aired.) Unknown, Moscow

Shrek (Hyb.) 1966, ♂, Red Star

		Roy (Schn.) 1947?, Red Star
Chuk (M.Dog Hyb.) 1956, Red Star	
		Chili (M.Dog), Red Star
Alfa (Hyb.) 1961, Red Star		
		Azart (Cx.) 1954, Red Star
Volga (M.Wdg.Hyb.) 1956, Red Star	
		Hanka (M.Wdg.) 1952, Red Star

Azart (Cx.) 1954,
Red Star

Roy (Schn.) 1947?,
Red Star

Zorab (Schn.)

Ledi (Schn.), Moscow

Una (Rtw.) 1950, Red Star

Kastor (Rtw.), 1947, Moscow

Birma (Rtw.), Moscow

Vishnya, Volga, Vesna, Basta, Velga (♀), Vityaz, Brayt (♂) (M.Wdg.Hyb.) 1956, Red Star

Hanka (M.Wdg.)
1952, Red Star

Lord (Newf.) 1948–50?,
Moscow

Halori Astor (Newf.)

Cuna f. Gayberg (Newf.)

Tiza (M.Wdg.) 1949,
Red Star

Negus f. Mangeym (Newf.),
1943, Moscow

Karabashka (C.Ovch.),
Red Star

Demon (Hyb.)
1957,
Red Star/Saratov
(Privately Owned)

Arras (Hyb.) 1954,
Red Star

Beniamino I (Rtw.) 1949, Red Star

Hizha [Hinga] (Cx.) 1952, Red Star

Chomga (Cx.) 1953,
Red Star

Roy (Schn.) 1947?, Red Star

Femka (Rtw.) 1951, Red Star

Yaga (♀) (Hyb.) (1962?), Red Star

Mirta (Hyb.) 1960,
Red Star

Chuk (M.Dog Hyb.)
1956, Red Star

Roy (Schn.) 1947?, Red Star

Chili (M.Dog), Red Star

Volga (M.Wdg.Hyb.)
1956, Red Star

Azart (Cx.) 1954, Red Star

Hanka (M.Wdg.) 1952, Red Star

1955: Family Lines Based on Rottweiler Geyni (Male) (Rottweiler, Armin f. Tize × Rottweiler, Kora f. Schneidenplatz)

```
                                            | Vah (Cx.) 1956
                        | Foka (Hyb.) 1960,
                        | Red Star          | Bara (Hyb.) 1957
      Karat (Hyb.) 1964,
      Red Star                              | Brayt (M.Wdg.Hyb.) 1956, Red Star
                        | Nayda (Hyb.) 1961,
                        | Red Star          | Nelma (Hyb.), Red Star
```

Bechel (♂) (Hyb.) 1966, Red Star (Privately Owned)

```
                                            | Armin f. Tize Turn (Rtw.)
                        | Geyni (Rtw.) 1955,
                        | Moscow            | Kora f. Schneidenplatz (Rtw.)
      Ila (Cx.) 1960,
      Red Star                              | Farno (Rtw.) 1951, Red Star
                        | Dila (Cx.) 1958,  | (Privately Owned)
                        | Red Star          | Chuta (Cx.), Red Star
```

Abbreviations: ♀, bitch; ♂, dog; Aired., Airedale; C.Ovch., Caucasian Ovcharka; C.A.Ovch., Central Asian Ovcharka; Cx., Crossbreed; E.E.Shep., East European Shepherd; G.G.Dane, German Great Dane; Hyb., Hybrid; M.Dvr, Moscow Diver; M.Dog, Moscow Dog; M.Wdg., Moscow Waterdog; Newf., Newfoundland; R.S.Hnd., Russian Spotted Hound; Rtw., Rottweiler; Schn., Schnauzer; S.R.Ovch., South Russian Ovcharka.

Tuman (Hyb.) 1967,
Red Star

Tom (Hyb.) 1964,
Red Star

Gay (Cx.) Red Star

Dina (Hyb.) Moscow

Dega (Hyb.) 1962,
Red Star

Demon (Hyb.) 1957, Red Star/Saratov
(Privately Owned)

Galka (Hyb.) (Privately Owned)

Dina, Lada (♀), Timur (♂) (Hyb.) (1967?), Red Star (Privately Owned)

Panta (Cx.) 1965,
Red Star

Karen 1 (Cx.) 1963,
Red Star

Linch (Rtw.) 1960, Red Star

Dila (Cx.) 1958, Red Star

Ilma (Cx.) 1960,
Red Star

Geyni (Rtw.) 1955, Moscow

Dila (Cx.) 1958, Red Star

Tom (Hyb.) 1964,
Red Star

Gay (Cx.), Red Star

Aray (Cx.) 1954, Red Star

Borka (Cx.) 1955, Red Star

Dina (Hyb.), Moscow

Tuman (Hyb.) 1956?, Red Star

Fimka (Unkn.)

Dzhim (♂) (Hyb.), Red Star

Panta (Cx.) 1965,
Red Star

Karen 1 (Cx.) 1963,
Red Star

Linch (Rtw.) 1960, Red Star

Dila (Cx.) 1958, Red Star

Ilma (Cx.) 1960,
Red Star

Geyni (Rtw.) 1955, Moscow

Dila (Cx.) 1958, Red Star

```
                                      | Unknown
                    | Linch (Rtw.) 1960,
                    | Red Star         | Unknown
   Karen 1 (Cx.) 1963,
   Red Star                            | Farno (Rtw.) 1951, Red Star
                    | Dila (Cx.) 1958,
                    | Red Star         | Chuta (Cx.) Red Star
```

Panta (Cx.) 1965, ♀, Red Star

```
                                      | Armin f. Tize Turm (Rtw.)
                    | Geyni (Rtw.) 1955,
                    | Moscow           | Kora f. Schneidenplatz (Rtw.)
   Ilma (Cx.) 1960,
   Red Star                            | Farno (Rtw.) 1951, Red Star
                    | Dila (Cx.) 1958, | (Privately Owned)
                    | Red Star         | Chuta (Cx.) Red Star
```

1956: Family Lines Based on Moscow Dog Hybrid Chuk (Male) (Giant Schnauzer, Roy × Moscow Dog, Chili)

Alfa (♀) (Hyb.) 1961, Red Star

Chuk (M.Dog Hyb.) 1956, Red Star	Roy (Schn.) 1947?, Red Star	Zorab (Schn.)
		Ledi (Schn.)
	Chili (M.Dog), Red Star	Beniamino (Rtw.) 1949, Red Star
		Toddi (M.Dog), Red Star
Volga (M.Wdg.Hyb.) 1956, Red Star	Azart (Cx.) 1954, Red Star	Roy (Schn.) 1947?, Red Star
		Una (Rtw.) 1950, Red Star
	Hanka (M.Wdg.) 1952, Red Star	Lord (Newf.) 1948–50?, Red Star
		Tiza (M.Wdg.) 1949, Red Star

Abbreviations: ♀, bitch; ♂, dog; Aired., Airedale; C.Ovch., Caucasian Ovcharka; C.A.Ovch., Central Asian Ovcharka; Cx., Crossbreed; E.E.Shep., East European Shepherd; G.G.Dane, German Great Dane; Hyb., Hybrid; M.Dvr, Moscow Diver; M.Dog, Moscow Dog; M.Wdg., Moscow Waterdog; Newf., Newfoundland; R.S.Hnd., Russian Spotted Hound; Rtw., Rottweiler; Schn., Schnauzer; S.R.Ovch., South Russian Ovcharka.

		Azart (Cx.) 1954, Red Star
	Brayt (M.Wdg.Hyb.) 1956, Red Star	Hanka (M.Wdg.) 1952, Red Star
Chani (Hyb.) 1962, Red Star (Privately Owned)	(Privately Owned)	Geyni (Rtw.) 1955, Moscow
	Ira (Cx.), Red Star	Meri (Aired.), Moscow

Chap (♂) (Hyb.) 1967, Red Star (Privately Owned)

		Roy (Schn.) 1947?, Red Star
	Chuk (M.Dog Hyb.) 1956, Red Star	Chili [M.Dog], Red Star
Alfa (Hyb.) 1961, Red Star		Azart (Cx.) 1954, Red Star
	Volga (M.Wdg.Hyb.) 1956, Red Star	Hanka (M.Wdg.) 1952, Red Star

---

		Unknown
	Zorab (Schn.)	Unknown
Roy (Schn.) 1947?, Red Star		Unknown
	Ledi (Schn.), Moscow	Unknown

Chuk (♂) (M.Dog Hyb.) 1956, Red Star

		Sarro (Rtw.), Moscow
	Beniamino (Rtw.) 1949, Red Star	Birma (Rtw.), Moscow
Chili (M.Dog), Red Star		Ralf (G.G.Dane), Moscow
	Toddi (M.Dog), Red Star	Pretti (E.E.Shep.), Red Star

		Beniamino (Rtw.) 1949, Red Star
	Arras (Hyb.) 1954, Red Star	
		Hizha [Hinga] (Cx.) 1952, Red Star
Demon (Hyb.) 1957, Red Star/Saratov (Privately Owned)		Roy (Schn.) 1947?, Red Star
	Chomga (Cx.) 1953, Red Star	
		Femka (Rtw.) 1951, Red Star

Dega (♀) (Hyb.) 1962, Red Star

		Demon (Hyb.) 1957, Red Star/Saratov (Privately Owned)
	Negus (Hyb.) (Privately Owned)	
		Unknown
Galka (Hyb.) (Privately Owned)		Demon (Hyb.) 1957, Red Star/Saratov (Privately Owned)
	Yaga (Hyb.), Red Star	
		Mirta (Hyb.) 1960, Red Star

		Brayt (M.Wdg.Hyb.) 1956, Red Star
	Chani (Hyb.) 1962 (Privately Owned)	
		Ira (Cx.), Red Star
Chap (Hyb.) 1967, Moscow (Privately Owned)		Chuk (M.Dog Hyb.) 1956, Red Star
	Alfat (Hyb.), Red Star	
		Volga (M.Wdg.Hyb.) 1956, Red Star

Kora (♀) (Hyb.) 1973, Leningrad (St. Petersburg) (Privately Owned)

		Dik (Hyb.) 1958, Red Star (Privately Owned)
	Skif (Hyb.) 1965 (Privately Owned)	
		Nastya (Hyb.) 1962, St. Petersburg
Oksa (Hyb.) 1971 (Privately Owned)		Deyv (Hyb.) Red Star/Chelyabinsk
	Changa (Hyb.) 1969 (Privately Owned)	
		Vesta (Unkn.) (Privately Owned)

Chuk (M.Dog Hyb.)
1956, Red Star

Roy (Schn.) 1947?,
Red Star

Zorab (Schn.)

Ledi (Schn.)

Chili (M.Dog),
Red Star

Beniamino (Rtw.) 1949, Red Star

Toddi (M.Dog), Red Star

Mirta (♀) (Hyb.) 1960, Alfa (♀) (Hyb.) 1961, Red Star

Volga (M.Wdg.Hyb.)
1956, Red Star

Azart (Cx.) 1954,
Red Star

Roy (Schn.) 1947?, Red Star

Una (Rtw.) 1950, Red Star

Hanka (M.Wdg.) 1952,
Red Star

Lord (Newf.) 1948–50?

Tiza (M.Wdg.) 1949, Red Star

Urchan (Hyb.) 1970,
Red Star

Dzhaga (Hyb.) 1965,
Red Star

Dasso f. Drahenshljuht (Schn.) 1960,
Moscow

Berta (Hyb.) 1961, Red Star

Yutta (Hyb.) 1968,
Red Star

Tom (Hyb.) 1964, Red Star

Rokki (Hyb.) Red Star

Nemfred (♂) (Hyb.) 1976, St. Petersburg (Privately Owned)

Kora (Hyb.) 1973,
St. Petersburg
(Privately Owned)

Chap (Hyb.) 1967,
Red Star /Moscow
(Privately Owned)

Chani (Hyb.) 1962, Red Star

Alfa (Hyb.) 1961, Red Star

Oksa (Hyb.) 1971
(Privately Owned)

Skif (Hyb.) 1965 (Privately Owned)

Changa (Hyb.) 1969 (Privately Owned)

Yaga (♀) (Hyb.) (yr?), Red Star

Demon (Hyb.) 1957, Red Star (Privately Owned)	Arras (Hyb.) 1954, Red Star	Beniamino (Rtw.) 1949, Red Star
		Hizha [Hinga] (Cx.) 1952, Red Star
	Chomga (Cx.) 1953, Red Star	Roy (Schn.) 1947?, Red Star
		Femka (Rtw.) 1951
Mirta (Hyb.) 1960, Red Star	Chuk (M.Dog Hyb.) 1956, Red Star	Roy (Schn.) 1947?, Red Star
		Chili (M.Dog), Red Star
	Volga (M.Wdg.Hyb.) 1956, Red Star	Azart (Cx.) 1954, Red Star
		Hanka (M.Wdg.) 1952, Red Star

1956: Family Lines Based on Moscow Waterdog Hybrid Brayt (Male) (Crossbreed, Azart × Moscow Waterdog, Hanka)

		Roy (Schn.) 1947?, Red Star
	Azart (Cx.) 1954, Red Star	
Brayt (M.Wdg.Hyb.) 1956, Red Star		Una (Rtw.) 1950, Red Star
		Lord [Newf.] 1948–50
	Hanka (M.Wdg.) 1952, Red Star	
		Tiza (M.Wdg.) 1949

Ara (♀), Dzherri, Azart II (♂) (Hyb.) 1957, Red Star (Privately Owned)

		Zorab (Schn.)
	Roy (Schn.) 1947?, Red Star	
Charva (Cx.) 1953, Red Star		Ledi (Schn.) Moscow
		Kastor (Rtw.) 1947, Moscow
	Una (Rtw.) 1950, Red Star	
		Birma (Rtw.) Moscow

```
                                                        | Roy (Schn.) 1947?, Red Star
                                    | Azart (Cx.) 1954,
                                    | Red Star
                                                        | Una (Rtw.) 1950, Red Star
          Brayt (M.Wdg.Hyb.)
          1956, Red Star
                                                        | Lord (Newf.) 1948–50?, Moscow
                                    | Hanka (M.Wdg.) 1952,
                                    | Red Star
                                                        | Tiza (M.Wdg.) 1949, Red Star
```

Bara (♀) (Hyb.) 1957, Red Star

```
                                                        | Sarro (Rtw.), Moscow
                                    | Beniamino (Rtw.) 1949,
                                    | Red Star
                                                        | Birma (Rtw.), Moscow
          Appa (Hyb.) 1954,
          Red Star
                                                        | Roy (Schn.) 1947?, Red Star
                                    | Hizha [Hinga] (Cx.)
                                    | 1952, Red Star
                                                        | Sotta (Aired.) 1949, Red Star
```

```
                                                        | Zorab (Schn.)
                                    | Roy (Schn.) 1947?,
                                    | Red Star
                                                        | Ledi (Schn.), Moscow
          Azart (Cx.) 1954.
          Red Star
                                                        | Kastor (Rtw.), 1947, Moscow
                                    | Una (Rtw.) 1950,
                                    | Red Star
                                                        | Birma (Rtw.), Moscow
```

Brayt (♂) (M.Wdg.Hyb.) 1956, Red Star

```
                                                        | Halori Astor (Newf.), Unkn.
                                    | Lord (Newf.)
                                    | 1948–50?
                                                        | Cuna f.Gayberg (Newf.), Unkn.
          Hanka (M.Wdg.)
          1952, Red Star
                                                        | Negus f. Mangeym
                                    | Tiza (M.Wdg.) 1949,   (Newf.) 1943, Moscow
                                    | Red Star              Karabashka (C.Ovch.), Red Star
```

		Roy (Schn.) 1947?, Red Star
Vah (Cx.) 1956,		
Red Star		Una (Rtw.) 1950, Red Star
Viy (Hyb.) 1960,		
(Privately Owned)		Brayt (M.Wdg.Hyb.) 1956, Red Star
Bara (Hyb.) 1957,		
Red Star		Appa (Hyb.) 1954, Red Star

Dan-Darsi (♀) (Hyb.) 1969, Red Star (Privately Owned)

		Gay (Cx.), Red Star
Tom (Hyb.) 1964,		
Red Star		Dina (Hyb.), Moscow (Privately Owned)
Dzhoya (Hyb.) 1967,		
(Privately Owned)		Demon (Hyb.) 1957, Red Star/Saratov
Dega (Hyb.) 1962,		(Privately Owned)
Red Star		Galka (Hyb.) (Privately Owned)

		Vah (Cx.) 1956, Red Star
Foka (Hyb.) 1960,		
Red Star		Bara (Hyb.) 1957, Red Star
Fang (Hyb.) 1964,		
Red Star		Brayt (M.Wdg.Hyb.) 1956, Red Star
(Privately Owned)	Nayda 1961, Moscow	
	(Privately Owned)	Nelma (Hyb.) Red Star

Jolka (♀) (Hyb.) 1969, Finland (Privately Owned)

		Haytar (Cx.) 1952, Red Star
Dik (Hyb.) 1958,		
Red Star		Vishnya (M.Wdg.Hyb.) 1956, Red Star
Ruza (Hyb.) 1966	(Privately Owned)	
(Privately Owned)		Foka (Hyb.) 1960, Red Star
Nastya (Hyb.)		
St. Petersburg		Lada Tag (Hyb.) 1959, Moscow
(Privately Owned)		(Privately Owned)

```
                                                         | Roy (Schn.) 1947?, Red Star
                                 | Azart (Cx.) 1954,
                                 | Red Star              | Una (Rtw.) 1950, Red Star
          Brayt (M.Wdg.Hyb.)
          1956, Red Star                                 | Lord (Newf.) 1948–50?, Red Star
                                 | Hanka (M.Wdg.) 1952,
                                 | Red Star              | Tiza (M.Wdg.) 1949, Red Star
```

Nayda (♀) (Hyb.) 1961, Moscow (Privately Owned)

```
                                                         | Roy (Schn.) 1947?, Red Star
                                 | Haytar (Cx.) 1952,
                                 | Red Star              | Sotta (Aired.) 1949, Red Star
          Nelma (Hyb.),
          Red Star                                       | Azot (Cx.) 1954, Red Star
                                 | Gayda (M.Wdg.Hyb.)
                                 | 1956, Red Star        | Hanka (M.Wdg.) 1952, Red Star
```

1957: Family Lines Based on Hybrid Demon (Male) (Hybrid, Arras × Crossbreed, Chomga)

		Roy (Schn.) 1947?, Red Star
	Haytar (Cx.) 1952, Red Star	
		Sotta (Aired.) 1949, Red Star
Dik (Hyb.) 1958, Red Star		Azart (Cx.) 1954, Red Star
	Vishnya (M.Wdg.Hyb.) 1956, Red Star	
		Hanka (M.Wdg.) 1952, Red Star

Aydina (♀) (Hyb.) 1964, Moscow

		Arras (Hyb.) 1954, Red Star
	Demon (Hyb.) 1957, Red Star/Saratov	
		Chomga (Cx.) 1953, Red Star
Ayshe (Hyb.) 1961, Red Star	(Privately Owned)	Grum (M.Wdg.) 1954, Red Star
	Ledi (M.Wdg.Hyb.) 1959, Red Star	
		Ginta (M.Wdg.Hyb.) 1956, Red Star

Abbreviations: ♀, bitch; ♂, dog; Aired., Airedale; C.Ovch., Caucasian Ovcharka; C.A.Ovch., Central Asian Ovcharka; Cx., Crossbreed; E.E.Shep., East European Shepherd; G.G.Dane, German Great Dane; Hyb., Hybrid; M.Dvr, Moscow Diver; M.Dog, Moscow Dog; M.Wdg., Moscow Waterdog; Newf., Newfoundland; R.S.Hnd., Russian Spotted Hound; Rtw., Rottweiler; Schn., Schnauzer; S.R.Ovch., South Russian Ovcharka.

214 | Donald B. Anderson: The Creation of the Black Russian Terrier

		Beniamino (Rtw.) 1949, Red Star
	Arras (Hyb.) 1954, Red Star	
Demon (Hyb.) 1957,		Hizha [Hinga] (Cx.) 1952, Red Star
Red Star/Saratov		Roy (Schn.) 1947?, Red Star
(Privately Owned)	Chomga (Cx.) 1953, Red Star	
		Femka (Rtw.) 1951, Red Star

Ayshe (♀) (Hyb.) 1961, Dzhessi (♀) (Hyb.) 1963, Red Star

		Fakt (M.Wdg.) 1951, Red Star
	Grum (M.Wdg.) 1954, Red Star	
Ledi (M.Wdg.Hyb.)		Ufa (M.Wdg.) 1950, Red Star
1959, Red Star		Azot (Cx.) 1954, Red Star
	Ginta (M.Wdg.Hyb.) 1956, Red Star	
		Hanka (M.Wdg.) 1952, Red Star

		Sarro (Rtw.), Moscow
	Beniamino (Rtw.) 1949, Red Star	
Arras (Hyb.) 1954,		Birma (Rtw.), Moscow
Red Star		Roy (Schn.) 1947?, Red Star
	Hizha [Hinga] (Cx.) 1952, Red Star	
		Sotta (Aired.) 1949

Demon (♂) (Hyb.) 1957, Red Star/Saratov (Privately Owned)

		Zorab (Schn.)
	Roy (Schn.) 1947?, Red Star	
Chomga (Cx.) 1953,		Ledi (Schn.), Moscow
Red Star		Kastor (Rtw.) 1947, Moscow
	Femka (Rtw.) 1951, Red Star	
		Tina (Rtw.) Red Star

```
                                                    | Roy (Schn.) 1947, Red Star
                              | Vah (Cx.) 1956,
                              | Red Star            | Una (Rtw.) 1950, Red Star
        Viy (Hyb.) 1960,
        Red Star                                    | Brayt (M.Wdg.Hyb.) 1956, Red Star
                              | Bara (Hyb.) 1957,
                              | Red Star            | Appa (Hyb.) 1954, Red Star
```

Sarra [Sara] (♀) Robin (♂) (Hyb.) 1966, Red Star

```
                                                    | Arras (Hyb.) 1954, Red Star
                              | Demon (Hyb.) 1957,
                              | Red Star/Saratov    | Chomga (Cx.) 1953, Red Star
        Dzhessi (Hyb.)        | (Privately Owned)
        1953, Red Star                              | Grum (M.Wdg.) 1954, Red Star
                              | Ledi (M.Wdg.Hyb.)
                              | 1959, Red Star       | Ginta (M.Wdg.Hyb.) 1956, Red Star
```

1958: Family Lines Based on Hybrid Dik (Male) (Crossbreed, Haytar × Hybrid, Vishnya)

		Zorab (Schn.)
	Roy (Schn.) 1947?,	
	Red Star	Ledi (Schn.) Moscow
Haytar (Cx.) 1952,		
Red Star		Bil (fon) Askania (Aired.) 1944, Moscow
	Sotta (Aired.) 1949,	
	Red Star	Teffi (Aired.) Moscow

Dik (♂) (Hyb.) 1958, Red Star

		Roy (Schn.) 1947?, Red Star
	Azart (Cx.) 1954,	
	Red Star	Una (Rtw.) 1950, Red Star
Vishnya		
(M.Wdg.Hyb.) 1956,		Lord [Newf.] 1948–50?, Red Star
Red Star	Hanka (M.Wdg.) 1952,	
	Red Star	Tiza (M.Wdg.) 1949, Red Star

Abbreviations: ♀, bitch; ♂, dog; Aired., Airedale; C.Ovch., Caucasian Ovcharka; C.A.Ovch., Central Asian Ovcharka; Cx., Crossbreed; E.E.Shep., East European Shepherd; G.G.Dane, German Great Dane; Hyb., Hybrid; M.Dvr, Moscow Diver; M.Dog, Moscow Dog; M.Wdg., Moscow Waterdog; Newf., Newfoundland; R.S.Hnd., Russian Spotted Hound; Rtw., Rottweiler; Schn., Schnauzer; S.R.Ovch., South Russian Ovcharka.

1958: Family Lines Based on Hybrid Shaytan (Male) (Hybrid, Dik × Crossbred, Ahta)

		Roy (Schn.) 1947?, Red Star
	Chubarik (Cx.) 1953, Red Star	Ufa (M.Wdg.)1950, Red Star
Dik (Hyb.) 1956, Red Star		Roy (Schn.) 1947?, Red Star
	Chadra (Cx.) 1953, Red Star	Una (Rtw.) 1950, Red Star

Shaytan (♂) (Hyb.) 1958, Red Star

		Zorab (Schn.)
	Roy (Schn.) 1948?, Red Star	Ledi (Schn.) Red Star
Ahta (Cx.) 1954, Red Star		Kastor (Rtw.) 1947, Moscow
	Una (Rtw.) 1950, Red Star	Birma (Rtw.) Moscow

217

1959: Family Lines Based on Hybrid Ledi (Female) (Moscow Waterdog, Grum × Moscow Waterdog Hybrid, Ginta)

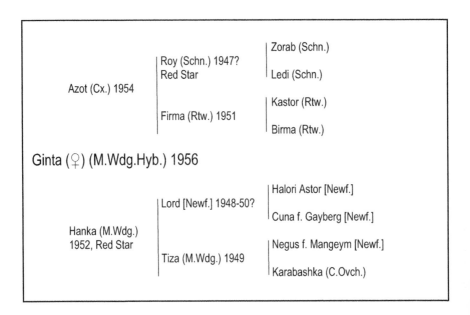

Abbreviations: ♀, bitch; ♂, dog; Aired., Airedale; C.Ovch., Caucasian Ovcharka; C.A.Ovch., Central Asian Ovcharka; Cx., Crossbreed; E.E.Shep., East European Shepherd; G.G.Dane, German Great Dane; Hyb., Hybrid; M.Dvr, Moscow Diver; M.Dog, Moscow Dog; M.Wdg., Moscow Waterdog; Newf., Newfoundland; R.S.Hnd., Russian Spotted Hound; Rtw., Rottweiler; Schn., Schnauzer; S.R.Ovch., South Russian Ovcharka.

Fakt (M.Wdg.)
1951, Red Star

   Lord (Newf.)
   1948–50?, Moscow

   Tiza (M.Wdg.) 1949,
   Red Star

      Halori Astor (Newf.)

      Cuna f. Gayberg (Newf.)

      Negus f. Mangeym (Newf.)
      1943, Moscow
      Karabashka (C.Ovch.), Moscow

Grum (♂) (M.Wdg.) 1954, Red Star

Ufa (M.Wdg.)
1950, Red Star

   Negus f. Mangeym
   (Newf.) 1943,
   Moscow

   Rina (E.E.Shep.),
   Moscow

      Unknown

      Unknown

      Unknown

      Unknown

Grum (M.Wdg.)
1954, Red Star

   Fakt (M.Wdg.) 1951

   Ufa (M.Wdg.) 1950

      Lord (Newf.) 1948–50?

      Tiza (M.Wdg.) 1949

      Negus f. Mangeym (Newf.)

      Rina (E.E.Shep.)

Ledi (♀) (M.Wdg.Hyb.) 1959, Red Star

Ginta (M.Wdg.Hyb.)
1956

   Azot (Cx.) 1954

   Hanka (M.Wdg.)
   1952, Red Star

      Roy (Schn.) 1948?, Red Star

      Firma (Rtw.) 1951

      Lord (Newf.) 1948–50?

      Tiza (M.Wdg.) 1949

1960: Family Lines Based on Giant Schnauzer Dasso f. Drahenshljuht (Male) (Giant Schnauzer, Ajax f. Kliatal × Giant Schnauzer, Azra f. Notr-Dam)

Rams I (Hyb.) 1966, Red Star
- Foka (Hyb.) 1960, Red Star
  - Vah (Hyb.) 1956, Red Star
  - Bara (Hyb.) 1957, Red Star
- Bara (Hyb.) 1957, Red Star
  - Demon (Hyb.) 1957, Red Star/Saratov (Privately Owned)
  - Galka (Hyb.)

Al` Princ (♂) (Hyb.) 1971

Alba (Hyb.) 1969, Moscow
- Topaz (Hyb.) 1967, Red Star
  - Tom (Hyb.) 1964, Red Star
  - Lada (Hyb.) 1964, Red Star
- Changa (Cx.) 1962, Red Star
  - Dasso f. Drahenshljuht (Schn.) 1960, Red Star
  - Teya (Cx.) 1961, Red Star

Abbreviations: ♀, bitch; ♂, dog; Aired., Airedale; C.Ovch., Caucasian Ovcharka; C.A.Ovch., Central Asian Ovcharka; Cx., Crossbreed; E.E.Shep., East European Shepherd; G.G.Dane, German Great Dane; Hyb., Hybrid; M.Dvr, Moscow Diver; M.Dog, Moscow Dog; M.Wdg., Moscow Waterdog; Newf., Newfoundland; R.S.Hnd., Russian Spotted Hound; Rtw., Rottweiler; Schn., Schnauzer; S.R.Ovch., South Russian Ovcharka.

```
                                                   Unknown
                            Ajax f. Kliatal SchH III
                            (Schn.) 1954, Germany   Unknown
         Dasso f.
         Drahenshljuht                              Unknown
         (Schn.) 1960,      Azra f. Notr-Dam
         Red Star           (Schn.) Germany         Unknown
```

Alma, Red Star/St. Petersburg, Lira (♀), Terri (♂) (Hyb.) 1966, Red Star

```
                                                   Haytar (Cx.) 1952, Red Star
                            Dik (Hyb.) 1958,
                            Red Star               Vishnya (M.Wdg.Hyb.) 1956, Red Star
         Aida (Hyb.) 1964,  (Privately Owned)
         Red Star/Moscow
                                                   Demon (Hyb.) 1957, Red Star/Saratov
                            Ayshe (Hyb.) 1961, Red  (Privately Owned)
                            Star (Privately Owned)  Ledi (M.Wdg.Hyb.) 1959, Red Star
                                                   (Privately Owned)
```

```
                                                   Unknown
                            Ajax f. Kliatal (Schn.)
                                                   Unknown
         Dasso f.
         Drahenshljuht                              Unknown
         (Schn.) 1960,      Azra f. Notr-Dam
         Red Star           (Schn.)                 Unknown
```

Changa (♀) (Cx.) 1962, Red Star

```
                                                   Roy (Schn.) 1947?, Red Star
                            Vah (Cx.) 1956,
                            Red Star               Una (Rtw.) 1950
         Teya (Cx.) 1961,
         Red Star
                                                   Roy (Schn.) 1947?, Red Star
                            Basta (Cx.) 1955,
                            Red Star               Urma (Rtw.) 1950, Red Star
```

		Ajax v. Kliatal SchH III (Schn.) 1954, Germany
	Dasso f. Drahenshljuht (Schn.) 1960, Red Star	
		Azra f. Notr-Dam (Schn.), Germany
Dzhaga (Hyb.) 1965, Red Star		
		Bars [Baron] (Hyb.), Red Star
	Berta (Hyb.) 1961, Red Star	
		Fimka (Unkn.) (Privately Owned)

Danchar (♂) (Hyb.) 1972, Moscow

		Ajax v. Kliatal SchH III (Schn.) 1954, Germany
	Dasso f. Drahenshljuht (Schn.) 1960, Red Star	
		Azra f. Notr-Dam (Schn.), Germany
Ditta (Hyb.) 1964, Moscow (Privately Owned)		
		Haytar (Cx.) 1952, Red Star
	Vanda (Hyb.) 1957, Red Star	
		Alva (Hyb.) 1954, Red Star

		Unknown
	Unknown	
		Unknown
Ajax f. Kliatal (Schn.)		
		Unknown
	Unknown	
		Unknown

Dasso* & Ditter† f. Drahenshljuht (♂) (Schn.) 1960, Red Star

		Unknown
	Unknown	
		Unknown
Azra f. Notr-Dam (Schn.)		
		Unknown
	Unknown	
		Unknown

*Black coat; †Pepper and salt coat.

Dasso f. Drahenshljuht (Schn.) 1960, Red Star

Ajax v. Kliatal (Schn.) SchH III 1954, Germany

Unknown

Unknown

Azra f. Notr-Dam (Schn.) Germany

Unknown

Unknown

Ditta (♀) (Hyb.) 1964, Red Star

Vanda (Hyb.) 1957, Red Star

Haytar (Cx.) 1952

Roy (Schn.) 1947?, Red Star

Sotta (Aired.) 1949, Red Star

Alva (Hyb.) 1954, Red Star

Beniamino (Rtw.) 1949, Red Star

Hizha [Hinga] (Cx.) 1952, Red Star

Dasso f. Drahenshljuht (Schn.) 1960, Red Star

Ajax f. Kliatal (Schn.)

Unknown

Unknown

Azra f. Notr-Dam (Schn.)

Unknown

Unknown

Lera (♀) (Hyb.) Red Star

Ila (Cx.) 1960, Red Star

Geyni (Rtw.) 1955, Moscow

Armin f. Tize Turm (Rtw.)

Kora f. Schneidenplatz (Rtw.)

Dila (Cx.) 1958, Red Star

Farno (Rtw.) 1951, Red Star

Chuta (Cx.) Red Star

		Unknown
	Ajax Vom Kliatal	
	SchH III (Schn.)	Unknown
Dasso f.		
Drahenshljuht		Unknown
(Schn.) 1960,	Azra f. Notr-Dam	
Red Star	(Schn.) 01208	Unknown

Reks (♂) (Hyb.), Red Star

		Roy (Schn.) 1947?, Red Star
	Azart (Cx.)] 1954,	
	Red Star	Una (Rtw.) 1950, Red Star
Gloriya (Hyb.) 1959,		
Red Star		Roy (Schn.) 1947?, Red Star
	Cholka (Cx.) 1953,	
	Red Star	Tina (M.Wdg.) 1949, Red Star

		Unknown
	Ajax f. Kliatal SchH III	
	(Schn.) 1954, Germany	Unknown
Dasso f.		
Drahenshljuht		Unknown
(Schn.) 1960,	Azra f. Notr-Dam	
Red Star	(Schn.) Germany	Unknown

Tsezar (♂) (Cx.) 1966, Red Star

		Roy (Schn.) 1947?, Red Star
	Vah (Cx.) 1956,	
	Red Star	Una (Rtw.) 1950, Red Star
Teya (Cx.) 1961,		
Red Star		Roy (Schn.) 1947?, Red Star
	Basta (Cx.) 1955,	
	Red Star	Urma (Rtw.) 1950, Red Star

		Set (Hyb.) 1971 (Privately Owned?)
	Oksay (Hyb.) 1973, St. Petersburg	
		Zhulya (Hyb.) 1970, St. Petersburg
Tsorn (Hyb.) 1977, Moscow		
		Set (Hyb.) 1971 (Privately Owned?)
	Oyta (Hyb.) 1973 (Privately Owned?)	
		Zhulya (Hyb.) 1970, St. Petersburg

Tsuri (♀) (Hyb.) 1979, Red Star

		Lord (Hyb.) 1966, Red Star
	Atos (Hyb.) 1969, Moscow	
		Elite C-10, Aydina (Hyb.) 1964, Moscow
Kana (Hyb.) 1972, Podolsk/Moscow		
		Dasso f. Drahenshljuht (Schn.) 1960, Red Star
	Lera (Hyb.) Red Star	
		Ila (Cx.) 1960, Red Star

		Demon (Hyb.) 1957, Red Star/Saratov (Privately Owned)
	Deyv (Hyb.) (yr?), Red Star/Chelyabinsk (Privately Owned)	
		Cholka (Cx.) 1953, Red Star
Farlaf (Hyb.) 1974? (Privately Owned)		
		Dasso f. Drahenshljuht (Schn.) 1960, Red Star
	Changa (Cx.) 1962, Red Star (Privately Owned)	
		Teya (Cx.) 1961, Red Star

Yukon (♂) (Hyb.) 1976, Chelyabinsk (Privately Owned)

		Rams I (Hyb.) 1966, Red Star
	Al' Princ (Hyb.) 1971 (Privately Owned)	
		Alba (Hyb.) 1969, Moscow (Privately Owned)
Vega (Hyb.) (Privately Owned)		
		Dym Varyag (Hyb.) 1969 (Privately Owned)
	Rada (Privately Owned)	
		Chayga, (Chata, Changa) Unknown (Privately Owned)

1960: Family Lines Based on Giant Schnauzer Ditter f. Drahenshljuht (Male) (Giant Schnauzer, Ajax f. Kliatal × Giant Schnauzer, Azra f. Notr-dam)

		Unknown
	Ajax f. Kliatal SchH III	
	(Schn.) 1954, Germany	Unknown
Ditter f.		
Drahenshljuht†		Unknown
(Schn.) 1960,	Azra f. Notr-dam	
Red Star	(Schn.), Germany	Unknown

Dega (♀) (Hyb.) 1963, St. Petersburg (Privately Owned)

		Roy (Schn.) 1947?, Red Star
	Chuk (M.Dog Hyb.)	
	1956, Red Star	Chili (M.Dog), Red Star
Mirta (Hyb.) 1960,		
Red Star		Azart (Cx.) 1954, Red Star
	Volga (M.Wdg.Hyb.)	
	1956, Red Star	Hanka (M.Wdg.) 1952, Red Star

†Pepper & salt coat

Abbreviations: ♀, bitch; ♂, dog; Aired., Airedale; C.Ovch., Caucasian Ovcharka; C.A.Ovch., Central Asian Ovcharka; Cx., Crossbreed; E.E.Shep., East European Shepherd; G.G.Dane, German Great Dane; Hyb., Hybrid; M.Dvr, Moscow Diver; M.Dog, Moscow Dog; M.Wdg., Moscow Waterdog; Newf., Newfoundland; R.S.Hnd., Russian Spotted Hound; Rtw., Rottweiler; Schn., Schnauzer; S.R.Ovch., South Russian Ovcharka.

		Gay (Cx.) Red Star
	Tom (Hyb.) 1964, Red Star	Dina (Hyb.) Moscow
Lord (Hyb.) 1966, Red Star		Foka (Hyb.) 1960, Red Star
	Dina I (Hyb.) 1964, Red Star	Nayda (Hyb.) 1961, Red Star

Masha (♀) (Hyb.) 1971, (Privately Owned)

		Shaytan (Hyb.) 1958, Red Star
	Nayt (Hyb.) 1964, Red Star/Moscow (Privately Owned)	Teya (Cx.) 1961, Red Star
Beta (Hyb.) 1969, St. Petersburg (Privately Owned)		Ditter f. Drahenshljuht† (Schn.) 1960, Red Star
	Dega (Hyb.) 1963, St. Petersburg (Privately Owned)	Mirta (Hyb.) 1960, Red Star

†Pepper and salt coat

		Unknown
	Ajax f. Kliatal SchH III (Schn.) 1954, Germany	Unknown
Ditter f. Drahenshljuht† (Schn.) 1960, Red Star		Unknown
	Azra f. Notr-Dam (Schn.) Germany	Unknown

Meggi (♀) (Hyb.) 1961, Red Star

		Roy (Schn.) 1947?, Red Star
	Azot (Cx.) 1954, Red Star	Firma (Rtw.) 1951
Gayda (M.Wdg.Hyb.) 1956, Red Star		Lord (Newf.) 1948–50?, Moscow
	Hanka (M.Wdg.) 1952, Red Star	Tiza (M.Wdg.) 1949, Red Star

†Pepper and salt coat

		Nayt (Hyb.) 1964, Red Star
	Karay (Hyb.) 1967,	
	St. Petersburg	Ditta (Hyb.) 1964, Red Star
Set (Hyb.) 1971		
(Privately Owned)		Karat (Hyb.) 1964, Red Star
	Arni (Hyb.) 1967	
	(Privately Owned)	Stesha (Hyb.) 1965, St. Petersburg

Monstr-Dzhimmi-Set (♂) (Hyb.) 1974, Tallin, Estonia (Privately Owned)

		Tom (Hyb.) 1964, Red Star
	Lord (Hyb.) 1966,	
	Red Star	Dina I (Hyb.) 1964, Red Star
Masha (Hyb.) 1971		
(Privately Owned)		Nayt (Hyb.) 1964, Red Star
	Beta (Hyb.) 1969,	
	St. Petersburg	Dega (Hyb.) 1963, Red Star

		Foka (Hyb.) 1960, Red Star
	Karat (Hyb.) 1964,	
	Red Star	Nayda (Hyb.) 1961, Red Star
Ayaks [Ajaks] (Hyb.)		(Privately Owned)
1967		Dik (Hyb.) 1958, Red Star
(Privately Owned)	Stesha (Hyb.) 1965,	(Privately Owned)
	St. Petersburg	Nastya (Hyb.) 1962, St. Petersburg
	(Privately Owned)	(Privately Owned)

Muza (♀) (Hyb.), St. Petersburg

		Shaytan (Hyb.) 1958, Red Star
	Nayt (Hyb.) 1964,	
	Red Star/Moscow	Teya (Cx.) 1961, Red Star
Beta (Hyb.) 1969,	(Privately Owned)	
St. Petersburg		Ditter f. Drahenshljuht† (Schn.) 1960,
(Privately Owned)	Dega (Hyb.) 1963,	Red Star
	Red Star/St. Petersburg	Mirta (Hyb.) 1960, Red Star
	(Privately Owned)	

†Pepper and salt coat

		Karay (Hyb.) 1967, St. Petersburg
	Set (Hyb.) 1971	
	(Privately Owned)	Arni 1967 (Privately Owned)
Monstr-Dzhimmi-Set		
(Hyb.) 1974,		Lord (Hyb.) 1966, Red Star
Tallin, Estonia	Masha (Hyb.) 1971	
(Privately Owned)	(Privately Owned)	Beta (Hyb.) 1969, St. Petersburg
		(Privately Owned)

Nik (♂), Nega (♀) (Hyb.) 1979, (Location?)

		Set (Hyb.) 1971 (Privately Owned)
	Monstr-Dzhimmi-Set	
	(Hyb.) 1974,	Masha 1971 (Privately Owned)
Tinga (Hyb.) 1977	Tallin, Estonia	
(Privately Owned)	(Privately Owned)	Set (Hyb.) 1971 (Privately Owned)
	Ustya (Hyb.) 1974,	
	St. Petersburg	Lusha (Hyb.) 1971 (Privately Owned)

		Unknown
	Ajax v. Kliatal (Schn.)	
	SchH III 1954, Germany	Unknown
Ditter f.		
Drahenshljuht†		Unknown
(Schn.) 1960.	Azra f. Notr-Dam	
Moscow	(Schn.), Germany	Unknown

Vilma, Veda, Nora (♀) (Hyb.) 1962, Red Star/Moscow

		Roy (Schn.) 1947?, Red Star
	Haytar (Cx.) 1952,	
	Red Star	Sotta (Aired.) 1949, Red Star
Vanda [Wanda]		
(Hyb.) 1957,		Beniamino (Rtw.) 1949, Red Star
Red Star	Alva (Hyb.) 1954,	
	Red Star	Hizha [Hinga] (Cx.) 1952, Red Star

†Pepper and salt coat

1961: Family Lines Based on Hybrid Ayshe (Female) (Hybrid, Demon × Hybrid, Ledi)

		Roy (Schn.) 1947?, Red Star
	Haytar (Cx.) 1952, Red Star	
		Sotta (Aired.) 1949, Red Star
Dik (Hyb.) 1958, Red Star (Privately Owned)		Azart (Cx.) 1954, Red Star
	Vishnya (M.Wdg.Hyb.) 1956, Red Star	
		Hanka (M.Wdg.) 1952, Red Star

Adi, Aida (♀) (Hyb.) 1964, Moscow (Privately Owned)

		Arras (Hyb.) 1954, Red Star
	Demon (Hyb.) 1957, Red Star/Saratov (Privately Owned)	
		Chomga (Cx.) 1953, Red Star
Ayshe (Hyb.) 1961, Red Star/Moscow (Privately Owned)		Grum (M.Wdg.) 1954, Red Star
	Ledi (M.Wdg.Hyb.) 1959, Red Star (Privately Owned)	
		Ginta (M.Wdg.Hyb.) 1956, Red Star (Privately Owned)

Abbreviations: ♀, bitch; ♂, dog; Aired., Airedale; C.Ovch., Caucasian Ovcharka; C.A.Ovch., Central Asian Ovcharka; Cx., Crossbreed; E.E.Shep., East European Shepherd; G.G.Dane, German Great Dane; Hyb., Hybrid; M.Dvr, Moscow Diver; M.Dog, Moscow Dog; M.Wdg., Moscow Waterdog; Newf., Newfoundland; R.S.Hnd., Russian Spotted Hound; Rtw., Rottweiler; Schn., Schnauzer; S.R.Ovch., South Russian Ovcharka.

		Beniamino I (Rtw.) 1949, Red Star
	Arras (Hyb.) 1954, Red Star	
Demon (Hyb.) 1957,		Hizha [Hinga] (Cx.) 1952, Red Star
Red Star/Saratov		Roy (Schn.) 1947?, Red Star
(Privately Owned)	Chomga (Cx.) 1953, Red Star	
		Femka (Rtw.) 1951, Red Star

Ayshe (♀) (Hyb.) 1961, Red Star/Moscow (Privately Owned)

		Fakt (M.Wdg.) 1951, Red Star
	Grum (M.Wdg.) 1954, Red Star	
Ledi (M.Wdg.Hyb.)		Ufa (M.Wdg.) 1950, Red Star
1959,		Azot (Cx.) 1954, Red Star
Red Star/Moscow	Ginta (M.Wdg.Hyb.)	
(Privately Owned)	1956, Red Star (Privately Owned)	Hanka (M.Wdg.) 1952, Red Star

---

		Karat (Hyb.) 1964, Red Star
	Dzhek (Hyb.) 1966, Red Star	
Karu (Hyb.) 1970,		Ata (Hyb.) 1964, Red Star
St. Petersburg		Dasso f. Drahenshljuht (Schn.) 1960, Red Star
	Alma (Hyb.) 1966, Red Star/St. Petersburg (Privately Owned)	
		Aida (Hyb.) 1964 (Privately Owned)

Kroshka, Krezi (♀) (Hyb.) 1976, St. Petersburg (Privately Owned)

		Dzhek (Hyb.) 1966
	Karu (Hyb.) 1970, St. Petersburg	
Vaksa (Hyb.) 1973,		Alma (Hyb.) 1966
St. Petersburg		Nayt (Hyb.) 1964, Red Star
(Privately Owned)	Dar Ritsa (Hyb.) 1968 (Privately Owned)	
		Ditta (Hyb.) 1964, Red Star/Moscow

Bim I (Hyb.), Red Star

Ayman (Hyb.) 1964, Red Star (Privately Owned)

Foka (Hyb.) 1960, Red Star

Nayda (Hyb.) 1961, Red Star

Alfa (Hyb.), Red Star

Uran (Hyb.) 1966, Red Star

Alfa (Hyb.) 1961, Red Star

Sherif (♂) (Hyb.) 1977, St. Petersburg (Privately Owned)

Alkara (Hyb.) 1973, Moscow (Privately Owned)

Chard-Han (Hyb.) 1969 (Privately Owned)

Rom (Hyb.) 1963, Moscow (Privately Owned)

Chanita (Hyb.) 1966, Red Star

Karolina (Hyb.) 1970, St. Petersburg

Dzhek (Hyb.) 1966, Red Star

Alma (Hyb.) 1966, Red Star/St. Petersburg

Chingiz Rhan (Hyb.) 1969 (Privately Owned)

Rom (Hyb.) 1963 (Privately Owned)

Tyapa (Hyb.) 1964, Moscow (Privately Owned)
Lada Tag (Hyb.) 1969, Moscow (Privately Owned)

Chanita (Hyb.) 1964, Red Star

Karat (Hyb.) 1964, Red Star

Teya (Cx.) 1961, Red Star

Tan Irza (♀) (Hyb.) (Privately Owned)

Zitta (Hyb.), Moscow (Privately Owned)

Karat (Hyb.) 1964, Red Star

Foka (Hyb.) 1960, Red Star

Nayda (Hyb.) 1961, Red Star

Adi (Hyb.) 1964, Moscow (Privately Owned)

Dik (Hyb.) 1958, Red Star

Ayshe (Hyb.) 1961, Red Star/Moscow (Privately Owned)

Dasso f. Drahenshljuht (Schn.) 1960, Red Star
- Ajax f. Kliatal SchH III (Schn.) 1954, Germany
  - Unknown
  - Unknown
- Azra f. Notr-Dam (Schn.) Germany
  - Unknown
  - Unknown

Terri (♂), Lira (♀)1966, Red Star, Alma (♀) (Hyb.), Red Star/ St. Petersburg

Aida (Hyb.) 1964, Red Star/Moscow
- Dik (Hyb.) 1958, Red Star (Privately Owned)
  - Haytar (Cx.) 1952, Red Star
  - Vishnya (M.Wdg.Hyb.) 1956, Red Star
- Ayshe (Hyb.) 1961, Red Star (Privately Owned)
  - Demon (Hyb.) 1957, Red Star/Saratov (Privately Owned)
  - Ledi (M.Wdg.Hyb.) 1959, Red Star (Privately Owned)

Karat (Hyb.) 1964, Red Star
- Foka (Hyb.) 1960, Red Star
  - Vah (Cx.) 1956, Red Star
  - Bara (Hyb.) 1957, Red Star
- Nayda (Hyb.) 1961, Red Star
  - Brayt (M.Wdg.Hyb.) 1956, Red Star
  - Nelma (Hyb.) Red Star

Zitta (♀) (Hyb.), Moscow (Privately Owned)

Adi (Hyb.) 1964, Moscow (Privately Owned)
- Dik (Hyb.) 1958, Red Star
  - Haytar (Cx.) 1952, Red Star
  - Vishnya (M.Wdg.Hyb.) 1956, Red Star
- Ayshe (Hyb.) 1961, Red Star/Moscow (Privately Owned)
  - Demon (Hyb.) 1957, Red Star/Saratov (Privately Owned)
  - Ledi (M.Wdg.Hyb.) 1959, Red Star/Moscow (Privately Owned)

		Nayt (Hyb.) 1964, Red Star
	Karay (Hyb.) 1967, St. Petersburg	
Irtish (Hyb.) 1976,		Ditta (Hyb.) 1964, Red Star
Tallin, Estonia		Karay (Hyb.) 1967, St. Petersburg
(Privately Owned)	Irisha (Hyb.) 1970, St. Petersburg	
		Ayna (Hyb.) 1967, St. Petersburg

Zorro (♂), Zolli (♀) (Hyb.) 1978, St. Petersburg (Privately Owned)

		Dzhek (Hyb.) 1966, Red Star
	Karu (Hyb.) 1970, St. Petersburg (Privately Owned)	
Kroshka (Hyb.) 1976, St. Petersburg? (Privately Owned)		Alma (Hyb.) 1966, Red Star
		Karu (Hyb.) 1970, St. Petersburg
	Vaksa (Hyb.) 1973, St. Petersburg (Privately Owned)	
		Dar Ritsa 1968 (Hyb.) (Privately Owned)

1963: Family Lines Based on Hybrid Dzhessi (Female) (Hybrid, Demon × Hybrid, Ledi)

		Aray (Cx.) 1954, Red Star
	Gay (Cx.), Red Star	Borka (Cx.) 1955, Red Star
Tom (Hyb.) 1964, Red Star		Tuman (Hyb.) Red Star
	Dina (Hyb.) Moscow (Privately Owned)	Fimka (Unkn.) (Privately Owned)

Arma (♀) (Hyb.) 1966?, Red Star

		Arras (Hyb.) 1954, Red Star
	Demon (Hyb.) 1957, Red Star/Saratov (Privately Owned)	Chomga (Cx.) 1953, Red Star
Dzhessi (Hyb.) 1963, Red Star		Grum (M.Wdg.) 1954, Red Star
	Ledi (M.Wdg.Hyb.) 1959, Red Star (Privately Owned)	Ginta (M.Wdg.Hyb.) 1956, Red Star

Abbreviations: ♀, bitch; ♂, dog; Aired., Airedale; C.Ovch., Caucasian Ovcharka; C.A.Ovch., Central Asian Ovcharka; Cx., Crossbreed; E.E.Shep., East European Shepherd; G.G.Dane, German Great Dane; Hyb., Hybrid; M.Dvr, Moscow Diver; M.Dog, Moscow Dog; M.Wdg., Moscow Waterdog; Newf., Newfoundland; R.S.Hnd., Russian Spotted Hound; Rtw., Rottweiler; Schn., Schnauzer; S.R.Ovch., South Russian Ovcharka.

		Beniamino (Rtw.) 1949, Red Star
	Arras (Hyb.) 1954, Red Star	
		Hizha [Hinga] (Cx.) 1952, Red Star
Demon (Hyb.) 1957, Red Star/Saratov (Privately Owned)		Roy (Schn.) 1947?, Red Star
	Chomga (Cx.) 1953, Red Star	
		Femka (Rtw.) 1951, Red Star

Dzhessi (♀) (Hyb.) 1963, Red Star

		Fakt (M.Wdg.) 1951, Red Star
	Grum (M.Wdg.) 1954, Red Star	
		Ufa (M.Wdg.) 1950, Red Star
Ledi (M.Wdg.Hyb.) 1959, Red Star/Moscow (Privately Owned)		Azot (Cx.) 1954, Red Star
	Ginta (M.Wdg.Hyb.) 1956, Red Star	
		Hanka (M.Wdg.) 1952, Red Star

		Roy (Schn.) 1947?, Red Star
	Vah (Cx.) 1956, Red Star	
		Una (Rtw.) 1950, Red Star
Viy (Hyb.) 1960, Red Star		Brayt (M.Wdg.Hyb.) 1956, Red Star
	Bara (Hyb.) 1957, Red Star	
		Appa (Hyb.) 1954, Red Star

Sarra (♀) (Hyb.) 1966, Red Star (Privately Owned)

		Arras (Hyb.) 1954, Red Star
	Demon (Hyb.) 1957, Red Star/Saratov (Privately Owned)	
		Chomga (Cx.) 1953, Red Star
Dzhessi (Hyb.) 1963, Red Star		Grum (M.Wdg.) 1954, Red Star
	Ledi (M.Wdg.Hyb.) 1959, Red Star (Privately Owned)	
		Ginta (M.Wdg.Hyb.) 1956, Red Star

1964: Family Lines Based on Hybrid Nayt (Male) (Hybrid, Shaytan × Hybrid, Teya)

		Rams I (Hyb.) 1966, Red Star
	Artosha (Hyb.) 1971	
	(Privately Owned)	Alba (Hyb.) 1968, Moscow (Priv. Own.)
Len Klaus (Hyb.)		
1974		Vud (Hyb.) 1967 (Privately Owned)
(Privately Owned)	Kleopatra (Hyb.) 1971	
	(Privately Owned)	Miledi (Hyb.) (Privately Owned)

Le Kuchum (♂) (Hyb.) 1977 (Privately Owned)

		Dik (Hyb.) 1958, Red Star
	Vud (Hyb.) 1967	
	(Privately Owned)	Velta (Hyb.) 1964, Red Star
Leda (Hyb.)		
Red Star		Karat (Hyb.) 1964, Red Star
(Privately Owned)	Chara(Hyb.) 1968,	
	Red Star	Irda (Hyb.) 1962, Red Star

Abbreviations: ♀, bitch; ♂, dog; Aired., Airedale; C.Ovch., Caucasian Ovcharka; C.A.Ovch., Central Asian Ovcharka; Cx., Crossbreed; E.E.Shep., East European Shepherd; G.G.Dane, German Great Dane; Hyb., Hybrid; M.Dvr, Moscow Diver; M.Dog, Moscow Dog; M.Wdg., Moscow Waterdog; Newf., Newfoundland; R.S.Hnd., Russian Spotted Hound; Rtw., Rottweiler; Schn., Schnauzer; S.R.Ovch., South Russian Ovcharka.

		Foka (Hyb.) 1960, Red Star
	Rams I (Hyb.) 1966, Red Star	
Artosha (Hyb.) 1971		Dega (Hyb.) 1962, Red Star
(Privately Owned)		Topaz (Hyb.) 1967, Red Star
	Alba (Hyb.) 1969, Moscow (Privately Owned)	
		Changa (Cx.) 1962, Red Star

Len Klaus (♂) (Hyb.) 1974 (Privately Owned)

		Dik (Hyb.) 1958, Red Star
	Vud (Hyb.) 1967 (Privately Owned)	
Kleopatra (Hyb.) 1971		Velta (Hyb.) 1964, Red Star (Priv. Own.)
(Privately Owned)		Nayt (Hyb.) 1964, Red Star/Moscow (Privately Owned)
	Miledi (Hyb.) (Privately Owned)	
		Dzhina (Hyb.) 1965 (Privately Owned)

		Chubarik (Cx.) 1953, Red Star
	Dik (Hyb.) 1956, Red Star	
Shaytan (Hyb.) 1958, Red Star		Chadra (Cx.) 1953, Red Star
		Roy (Schn.) 1947?, Red Star
	Ahta (Cx.) 1954, Red Star	
		Una (Rtw.) 1950, Red Star

Nayt (♂) (Hyb.) 1964, Red Star/Moscow (Privately Owned)

		Roy (Schn.) 1947?, Red Star
	Vah (Cx.) 1956, Red Star	
Teya (Cx.) 1961, Red Star		Una (Rtw.) 1950, Red Star
		Roy (Schn.) 1948?, Red Star
	Basta (Cx.) 1955, Red Star	
		Urma (Rtw.) 1950, Red Star

1964: Family Lines Based on Hybrid Tom (Male) (Crossbreed, Gay × Hybrid, Dina)

		Linch (Rtw.) (Cx.)
	Karen 1 (Cx.) 1963, Red Star	Dila (Cx.) 1958, Red Star
Bezeviht (Cx.) 1967, Red Star (Privately Owned)		Geyni (Rtw.) 1955, Red Star
	Ila (Cx.) 1960, Red Star	Dila (Cx.) 1958, Red Star

Adolf (♂) (Rtw.) (Cx.), Red Star (Privately Owned)

		Kastor (Rtw.) 1947, Red Star
	Farno (Rtw.) 1951, Red Star	Birma (Rtw.) Moscow
Lasta (Rtw.) (Cx.), Red Star		Uteshay (R.S.Hund.), Red Star
	Chuta (Cx.), Red Star	Uza (Rtw.) 1950, Red Star

Abbreviations: ♀, bitch; ♂, dog; Aired., Airedale; C.Ovch., Caucasian Ovcharka; C.A.Ovch., Central Asian Ovcharka; Cx., Crossbreed; E.E.Shep., East European Shepherd; G.G.Dane, German Great Dane; Hyb., Hybrid; M.Dvr, Moscow Diver; M.Dog, Moscow Dog; M.Wdg., Moscow Waterdog; Newf., Newfoundland; R.S.Hnd., Russian Spotted Hound; Rtw., Rottweiler; Schn., Schnauzer; S.R.Ovch., South Russian Ovcharka.

Tom (Hyb.) 1964,
Red Star

Gay (Cx.)

Aray (Cx.) 1954

Borka (Cx.) 1955

Dina (Hyb.)

Tuman (Hyb.)

Fimka (Unkn.)

Cherri, Nensi (♀), Dzhim (♂) (Hyb.) 1967? (Privately Owned)

Dzhina (Hyb.) 1965
(Privately Owned)

Daks (Hyb.) 1962

Foka (Hyb.) 1960

Lada Tag (Hyb.) 1959, (Privately Owned)

Nora* (Hyb.) 1962,
Moscow
(Privately Owned)

Ditter f. Drahenshljuht† (Schn.) 1960,
Red Star

Vanda (Hyb.) 1957, Red Star/Moscow
(Privately Owned)

*Coat colour "cloudy"
†Pepper and salt colour

Tom (Hyb.) 1964,
Red Star

Gay (Cx.), Red Star

Aray (Cx.) 1954, Red Star

Borka (Cx.) 1955, Red Star

Dina (Hyb.), Moscow
(Privately Owned)

Tuman (Hyb.), Red Star

Fimka (Unkn.) (Privately Owned)

Dinka (♀), Osman (♂) (Hyb.), 1967, Red Star (Privately Owned)

Adi (Hyb.) 1964,
Red Star

Dik (Hyb.) 1958,
Red Star
(Privately Owned)

Haytar (Cx.) 1952, Red Star

Vishnya (M.Wdg.Hyb.) 1956, Red Star

Ayshe (Hyb.) 1961, Red
Star (Privately Owned)

Demon (Hyb.) 1957, Red Star/Saratov
(Privately Owned)

Ledi (M.Wdg.Hyb.) 1959, Red Star
(Privately Owned)

	Ajax v. Kliatal (Schn.)	Unknown
Dasso f.		Unknown
Drahenshljuht		Unknown
(Schn.) 1960	Azra f. Notr-Dam	
Red Star	(Schn.)	Unknown

Dzhaga (♂), Lassi (♀) (Hyb.), 1965

		Brayt (M.Wdg.Hyb.) 1956, Red Star
	Bars [Baron] (Hyb.), Red Star	Chonga (Cx.) 1953, Red Star
Berta (Hyb.) 1961, Red Star		Araj (Unkn.) (Privately Owned)
	Fimka (Unkn.) (Privately Owned)	Unknown

		Dzhim (Hyb.) 1966, Red Star/Moscow (Privately Owned)
	Dan Zhan (Hyb.) 1970, Moscow (Privately Owned)	Dzhoya (Hyb.) 1967, Red Star/Moscow (Privately Owned)
Char-Tuman (Hyb.) 1973, Ekaterinburg (Privately Owned)		Rom (Hyb.) 1963 (Privately Owned)
	Chara (Hyb.) 1969 (Privately Owned)	Chanita (Hyb.) 1966, Red Star/Moscow (Privately Owned)

Dzherri (♀) (Hyb.) 1979, Ekaterinburg (Privately Owned)

		Deyv (Hyb.) Red Star/Chelyaybinsk (Privately Owned)
	Shaytan (Hyb.) Chelyaybinsk (Privately Owned)	Kara (Hyb.) (Privately Owned)
Rika (Hyb.) 1973 (Privately Owned)		Tom (Hyb.) 1964, Red Star
	Cherri (Hyb.) 1967? (Privately Owner)	Dzhina (Hyb.) 1965, (Privately Owner)

		Beniamino (Rtw.) 1949, Red Star
Arras (Hyb.) 1954, Red Star		
		Hizha [Hinga] (Cx.) 1952, Red Star
Demon (Hyb.) 1957, Red Star/Saratov (Privately Owned)		Roy (Schn.) 1947?, Red Star
	Chomga (Cx.) 1953, Red Star	
		Femka (Rtw.) 1951

Dzhessi (♀) (Hyb.) 1963, Red Star

		Fakt (M.Wdg.) 1951, Red Star
Grum (M.Wdg.) 1954, Red Star		
		Ufa (M.Wdg.) 1950, Red Star
Ledi (M.Wdg.Hyb.) 1959, Red Star (Privately Owned)		Azot (Cx.) 1954, Red Star
	Ginta (M.Wdg.Hyb.) 1956, Red Star	
		Hanka (M.Wdg.) 1952, Red Star

		Vah (Cx.) 1956, Red Star
Foka (Hyb.) 1960, Red Star		
		Bara (Hyb.) 1957, Red Star
Karat (Hyb.) 1964, Red Star		Brayt (M.Wdg.Hyb.) 1956, Red Star
	Nayda (Hyb.) 1961, Red Star	
		Nelma (Hyb.) Red Star

Dzhim (♂) (Hyb.) 1968, Novocherkassk (Privately Owned)

		Gay (Cx.), Red Star
Tom (Hyb.) 1964, Red Star		
		Dina (Hyb.) Moscow
Nora (Hyb.) 1966, Red Star (Privately Owned)		Bul (Hyb.) 1956, Red Star
	Irda (Hyb.) 1962, Red Star	
		Binta (Cx.) 1955, Red Star

Karat (Hyb.) 1964,
Red Star

  Foka (Hyb.) 1960,
  Red Star

    Vah (Cx.) 1956, Red Star

    Bara (Hyb.) 1957

  Nayda (Hyb.) 1961,
  Red Star

    Brayt (M.Wdg.Hyb.) 1956

    Nelma (Hyb.)

Dzhim (♂) Chanita, Vita (♀) (Hyb.) 1966, Red Star (Privately Owned)

Teya (Cx.) 1961,
Red Star

  Vah (Cx.) 1956,
  Red Star

    Roy (Schn.) 1947?, Red Star

    Una (Rtw.) 1950, Red Star

  Basta (Cx.) 1955,
  Red Star

    Roy (Schn.) 1947?, Red Star

    Urma (Rtw.) 1950, Red Star

Tom (Hyb.) 1964,
Red Star

  Gay (Cx.), Red Star

    Aray (Cx.) 1954, Red Star

    Borka (Cx.) 1955, Red Star

  Dina (Hyb.), Moscow
  (Privately Owned)

    Tuman (Hyb.), Red Star

    Fimka (Unkn.) (Privately Owned)

Dzhim (♂), Chanita (Hyb.) yr?, Red Star

Panta (Cx.) 1965,
Red Star

  Karen 1 (Cx.) 1963,
  Red Star

    Linch (Rtw.) 1960, Red Star

    Dila (Cx.) 1958, Red Star

  Ilma (Cx.) 1960,
  Red Star

    Geyni (Rtw.) 1955, Red Star

    Dila (Cx.) 1958, Red Star

			Aray (Cx.) 1954, Red Star
		Gay (Cx.), Red Star	
			Borka (Cx.) 1955, Red Star
	Tom (Hyb.) 1964, Red Star		
			Tuman (Hyb.) 1954?, Red Star
		Dina (Hyb.), Moscow (Privately Owned)	
			Fimka (Unkn.) (Privately Owned)

Dzhoya (♀) (Hyb.) Tuman (♂) 1967, Red Star (Privately Owned)

			Arras (Hyb.) 1954, Red Star
		Demon (Hyb.) 1957, Red Star/Saratov (Privately Owned)	
			Chomga (Cx.) 1953, Red Star
	Dega (Hyb.) 1962, Red Star		
			Negus (Hyb.) (Privately Owned)
		Galka (Hyb.) (yr?) (Privately Owned)	
			Yaga (Hyb.) (yr?), Red Star

			Unknown
		Armin f. Tize Turm (Rtw.)	
			Unknown
	Geyni (Rtw.) 1955, Red Star		
			Unknown
		Kora f. Schneidenplatz (Rtw.)	
			Unknown

Ila, Ilma (♀) (Cx.) 1960, Red Star

			Kastor (Rtw.) 1947, Moscow
		Farno (Rtw.) 1951, Red Star	
			Birma (Rtw.) Moscow
	Dila (Cx.) 1958, Red Star		
			Uteshay (R.S.Hund.), Red Star
		Chuta (Cx.) Red Star	
			Uza (Rtw.) 1950, Red Star

		Topaz (Hyb.) 1967, Red Star
	Kapitan Flint (Hyb.) 1969, Red Star/Moscow (Privately Owned)	Sekki (Hyb.) Red Star
Zhan Grey (Hyb.) 1976, Red Star (Privately Owned)		Tuman (Hyb.) 1967, Red Star (Privately Owned)
	Chara (Hyb.) 1972, Red Star (Priv. Own.)	Nayda (Hyb.) 1966, Red Star (Priv. Own.)

Kim Boy (♂) (Hyb.) 1979, Germany (Privately Owned)

		Bechel (Hyb.) 1966, Red Star
	Barhan-Zhan (Hyb.) 1969, Moscow (Privately Bred/Owned)	Adzhi-Shahra (Hyb.) 1964, Moscow (Privately Bred/Owned)
Tim Ilza (Hyb.) 1975, Moscow (Priv. Bred/Owned)		Dzhaga (Hyb.) 1965, Red Star
	Radzh-Mira (Hyb.) 1971, Kaunas, Lithuania (Privately Owned)	Raksha (Hyb.) Red Star Kaunas, Lithuania (Privately Owned)

		Gay (Cx.), Red Star
	Tom (Hyb.) 1964 (Privately Owned)	Dina (Hyb.) (Privately Owned)
Tuman (Hyb.) 1967, Red Star (Privately Owned)		Demon (Hyb.) 1957, Red Star/Saratov (Privately Owned)
	Dega (Hyb.) 1962, Red Star (Priv. Own.)	Galka (Hyb.) (Privately Owned)

Lada (♀)1970, Red Star (Privately Owned)

		Linch (Rtw.) 1960, Red Star (Privately Owned)
	Karen 1 (Cx.) 1963, Red Star (Privately Owned)	Dila (Cx.) 1958, Red Star (Priv. Own.)
Panta (Cx.) 1965, Red Star (Privately Owned)		Geyni (Rtw.) 1955 (Privately Owned)
	Ilma (Cx.) 1960, Red Star (Priv. Own.)	Dila (Cx.) 1958, Red Star (Priv. Own.)

		Topaz (Hyb.) 1967, Red Star
	Kapitan Flint (Hyb.) 1969, Red Star/Moscow (Privately Owned)	Sekki (Hyb.), Red Star
Zhan Grey (Hyb.) 1976 (Privately Owned)		Tuman (Hyb.) 1967, Red Star
	Chara (Hyb.) 1972, Red Star (Priv. Own.)	Nayda (Hyb.) 1966, Red Star

Log-Magri (♀) (Hyb.) 1980, Red Star

		Bezeviht (Cx.) 1967, Red Star (Privately Owned)
	Adolf (Rtw.) (Cx.), Red Star (Privately Owned)	Lasta (Rtw.), Red Star
Lir Lita (Hyb.) 1976 (Privately Owned)		Chuk (Hyb.) 1968, Red Star
	Aza (Hyb.) 1973 (Privately Owned)	Changa (Cx.) 1962, Red Star (Priv. Own.)

		Aray (Cx.) 1954, Red Star
	Gay (Cx.), Red Star	Borka (Cx.) 1955, Red Star
Tom (Hyb.) 1964, Red Star		Tuman (Hyb.) 1967, Red Star
	Dina (Hyb.), Moscow (Privately Owned)	Fimka (Unkn.)

Lord (♂) (Hyb.) 1966, Red Star (Privately Owned)

		Vah (Cx.) 1956, Red Star
	Foka (Hyb.) 1960, Red Star	Bara (Hyb.) 1957, Red Star
Dina I (Hyb.) 1964, Red Star		Brayt (Hyb.) 1956, Red Star
	Nayda (Hyb.) 1961, Red Star (Priv. Own.)	Nelma (Hyb.), Red Star

		Aray (Cx.) 1954
Gay (Cx.)		
		Borka (Cx.) 1955
Tom (Hyb.) 1964, Red Star		
		Tuman (Hyb.)
Dina (Hyb.)		
		Fimka (Unkn.)

Nora (♀) (Hyb.) 1966, Red Star (Privately Owned)

		Roy (Schn.) 1947?, Red Star
Bul (Hyb.) 1956, Red Star		
		Aza (Hyb.) 1954
Irda (Hyb.) 1962, Red Star		
		Farno (Rtw.) 1951
Binta (Cx.) 1955, Red Star		
		Charva (Cx.) 1953

		Sultan-3 (Rtw.) 1956, Red Star
Linch (Rtw.) (Cx.), 1960, Red Star		
		Malva (Rtw.) (Cx.), Red Star
Karen 1 (Cx.) 1963, Red Star		
		Farno (Rtw.) 1951, Red Star
Dila (Cx.) 1958, Red Star		
		Chuta (Cx.), Red Star

Panta (♀) (Cx.) 1965, Red Star

		Armin f. Tize Turm (Rtw.)
Geyni (Rtw.) 1955, Moscow		
		Kora f. Schneidenplatz (Rtw.)
Ilma (Cx.) 1960, Red Star		
		Farno (Rtw.) 1951, Red Star
Dila (Cx.) 1958, Red Star		
		Chuta (Cx.), Red Star

Dzhim (Hyb.) 1968,
Novocherkassk
(Privately Owned)

Karat (Hyb.) 1964,
Red Star

Foka (Hyb.) 1960, Red Star

Nayda (Hyb.) 1961, Red Star

Nora (Hyb.) 1966,
Red Star (Priv. Own.)

Tom (Hyb.) 1964, Red Star

Irda (Hyb.) 1962, Red Star

Poldi Char (♀) (Hyb.) 1972, Novocherkassk (Privately Owned)

Chari (Hyb.) 1969,
Novocherkassk
(Privately Owned)

Bechel (Hyb.) 1966,
Red Star
(Privately Owned)

Karat (Hyb.) 1964, Red Star

Ila (Cx.) 1960, Red Star

Ayda (Hyb.) 1964
(Privately Owned)

Dik (Hyb.) 1958, Red Star/Moscow
(Privately Owned)
Ayshe (Hyb.) 1961, Red Star/Moscow
(Privately Owned)

Kapitan Flint (Hyb.)
1969,
Red Star/Moscow
(Privately Owned)

Topaz (Hyb.) 1967,
Red Star

Tom (Hyb.) 1964, Red Star

Lada (Hyb.) 1964, Red Star

Sekki (Hyb.) 1962,
Red Star

Demon (Hyb.) 1957, Red Star/Saratov
(Privately Owned)
Arsa, Red Star

Sello Un (♂), Latvia; Sunika Un, Santa Un (♀) (Hyb.) 1973, Moscow (Privately Owned)

Ulma (Hyb.),
Red Star
(Privately Owned)

Topaz (Hyb.) 1967,
Red Star

Tom (Hyb.) 1964, Red Star

Lada (Hyb.) 1964, Red Star

Dina II (Hyb.) 1967,
Red Star

Nayt (Hyb.) 1964, Red Star
(Privately Owned)
Ditta (Hyb.) 1964, Moscow
(Privately Owned)

Aray (Cx.) 1954,
Red Star

Roy (Schn.) 1947?, Red Star

Urma (Rtw.) 1950, Red Star

Gay (Cx.),
Red Star

Borka (Cx.) 1955,
Red Star

Roy (Schn.) 1947?, Red Star

Urma (Rtw.) 1950, Red Star

Tom (♂) (Hyb.) 1964

Tuman (Hyb.), Red Star

Aray (Cx.) 1954, Red Star

Htora (Cx.) 1952, Red Star

Dina (Hyb.),
Moscow
(Privately Owned)

Fimka (Unkn.)
(Privately Owned)

Araj (Unkn.) (Privately Owned)

Unknown

Gay (Cx.) 1961,
Red Star

Aray (Cx.) 1954, Red Star

Borka (Cx.) 1955, Red Star

Tom (Hyb.) 1964,
Red Star

Dina (Hyb.) 1961?,
Moscow

Tuman (Hyb.) 1956?, Red Star

Fimka (Unkn.)

Topaz (♂) (Hyb.) 1967, Red Star

Nord (Hyb.) 1962,
Red Star

Brayt (M.Wdg.Hyb.) 1956, Red Star

Ira (Cx.), Red Star

Lada (Hyb.) 1964,
Red Star

Alfa (Hyb.) 1961,
Red Star

Chuk (M.DogHyb.) 1956, Red Star

Volga (M.Wdg.Hyb.) 1956, Red Star

Bim II (Hyb.) 1979, Red Star

Charli 1 (Hyb.) Red Star

Rams I (Hyb.) 1966, Red Star (Privately Owned)
Chada (Hyb.) 1968, Red Star

Sabina-Diana (Hyb.) 1973, Red Star

Barhan-Zhan (Hyb.) 1979, Moscow (Privately Owned)
Rema Greza (Hyb.) 1970 (Priv. Own.)

Vanish (♂) (BRT) 1987, Red Star/Moscow (Privately Owned)

Log-Magri (Hyb.) 1980, Red Star

Zhan Grey (Hyb.) 1976 (Privately Owned)

Kapitan Flint (Hyb.) 1969, Red Star (Privately Owned)
Chara (Hyb.) 1972, Red Star (Priv. Own.)

Lir Lita (Hyb.) 1976 (Privately Owned)

Adolf (Rtw.) (Cx.) Red Star (Privately Owned)
Aza (Hyb.) 1973 (Privately Owned)

Dzhaga (Hyb.) 1965, Red Star (Privately Owned)

Dasso f. Drahenshljuht (Schn.) 1960, Red Star

Ajax Vom Kliatal SchH III (Schn.) 1954, Germany
Azra f. Notr-Dam (Schn.) Germany

Berta (Hyb.) 1961, Red Star

Bars [Baron] (Hyb.), Red Star

Fimka (Unk.) (Privately Owned)

Vesta (♀) (Hyb.) 1973, Red Star

Yuna (Hyb.), Red Star

Tuman (Hyb.) 1967, Red Star (Privately Owned)

Tom (Hyb.) 1964, Red Star
Dega (Hyb.) 1962, Red Star

Yuta [Yutta], (Hyb.) 1968, Red Star

Tom (Hyb.) 1964, Red Star
Rokki (Hyb.), Red Star

Viy (♂) Varta (♀) (Hyb.) 1979, Red Star

- Lo-Rom (Hyb.) 1973, Red Star
  - Dan Zhan (Hyb.) 1970 (Privately Owned)
    - Dzhim (Hyb.) 1966, Red Star
    - Dzhoya (Hyb.) 1967, Red Star (Priv.O.)
  - Rayma (Hyb.) 1970 (Privately Owned)
    - Tuman (Hyb.) 1967, Red Star (Privately Owned)
    - Rynda (Hyb.) 1966 (Privately Owned)
- Vesta (Hyb.) 1973, Red Star
  - Dzhaga (Hyb.) 1965, Red Star (Privately Owned)
    - Dasso f. Drahenshljuht (Schn.) 1960, Red Star
    - Berta (Hyb.) 1961, Red Star
  - Yuna (Hyb.), Red Star
    - Tuman (Hyb.) 1967, Red Star (Privately Owned)
    - Yuta (Hyb.) 1968, Red Star

Yarrey (♂) (Hyb.) 1973, Chebarkul (Privately Owned)

- Irbis (Hyb.) 1970, St. Petersburg.
  - Karay (Hyb.) 1967, St. Petersburg
    - Nayt (Hyb.) 1964, Red Star
    - Ditta (Hyb.) 1964, Red Star
  - Ayna (Hyb.) 1967, St. Petersburg
    - Karat (Hyb.) 1964, Red Star
    - Stesha (Hyb.) 1965, St. Petersburg
- Unga (Hyb.) 1970, Red Star (Privately Owned)
  - Dzhaga (Hyb.) 1965, Red Star
    - Dasso f. Drahenshljuht (Schn.) 1960, Red Star
    - Berta (Hyb.) 1961, Red Star
  - Yuta [Yutta] (Hyb.) 1968, Red Star
    - Tom (Hyb.) 1964, Red Star
    - Rokki (Hyb.) Red Star

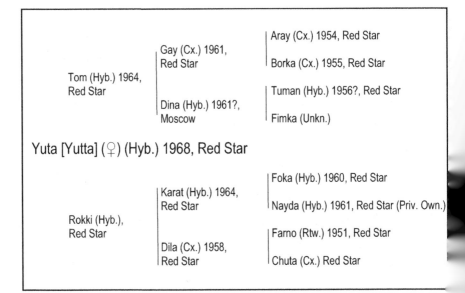

Yuna (♀) (Hyb.), Red Star

		Gay (Cx.) Red Star
	Tom (Hyb.) 1964, Red Star	
Tuman (Hyb.) 1967,		Dina (Hyb.) (Privately Owned)
Red Star		Demon (Hyb.) 1957, Red Star/Saratov
(Privately Owned)	Dega (Hyb.) 1962,	(Privately Owned)
	Red Star	Galka (Hyb.) (Privately Owned)

		Gay (Cx.) Red Star
	Tom (Hyb.) 1964, Red Star	
Yuta (Hyb.) 1968,		Dina (Hyb.) Moscow (Privately Owned)
Red Star		Karat (Hyb.) 1964, Red Star
	Rokki (Hyb.),	
	Red Star	Dila (Cx.) 1958, Red Star

Yuta [Yutta] (♀) (Hyb.) 1968, Red Star

		Aray (Cx.) 1954, Red Star
	Gay (Cx.) 1961, Red Star	
Tom (Hyb.) 1964,		Borka (Cx.) 1955, Red Star
Red Star		Tuman (Hyb.) 1956?, Red Star
	Dina (Hyb.) 1961?,	
	Moscow	Fimka (Unkn.)

		Foka (Hyb.) 1960, Red Star
	Karat (Hyb.) 1964, Red Star	
Rokki (Hyb.),		Nayda (Hyb.) 1961, Red Star (Priv. Own.)
Red Star		Farno (Rtw.) 1951, Red Star
	Dila (Cx.) 1958,	
	Red Star	Chuta (Cx.) Red Star

		Tom (Hyb.) 1964, Red Star
	Topaz (Hyb.) 1967, Red Star	
Kapitan Flint (Hyb.)		Lada (Hyb.) 1964, Red Star (Priv. Own.)
1969,		Demon (Hyb.) 1957, Red Star/Saratov
Red Star/Moscow	Sekki (Hyb.) Red Star	
(Privately Owned)	(Privately Owned)	Arsa, Red Star (Privately Owned)

Zhan Grey (♂) (Hyb.) 1976, Red Star (Privately Owned)

		Tom (Hyb.) 1964, Red Star
	Tuman (Hyb.) 1967, Red Star	
Chara (Hyb.) 1972,	(Privately Owned)	Dega (Hyb.) 1962, Red Star
Red Star		Karat (Hyb.) 1964, Red Star
(Privately Owned)	Nayda (Hyb.) 1966,	
	Red Star	
	(Privately Owned)	Teya (Cx.) 1961, Red Star

1964: Family Lines Based on Hybrid Karat (Male) (Hybrid, Foka × Hybrid, Nayda)

		Foka (Hyb.) 1960, Red Star
	Daks (Hyb.) 1962, Red Star/ Moscow	Lada Tag (Hyb.) 1959, Red Star
Alf (Hyb.) 1966 (Privately Owned)	(Privately Owned)	Ditter f. Drahenshljuht (Schn.) 1960,
	Veda (Hyb.) 1962 (Privately Owned)	Red Star
		Vanda (Hyb.) 1957, Red Star/Moscow (Privately Owned)

Argo (♂) (Hyb.) 1971 (Privately Owned)

		Foka (Hyb.) 1960, Red Star
	Karat (Hyb.) 1964, Red Star	Nayda (Hyb.) 1961, Red Star (Priv. Own.)
Blek-Veda (Hyb.) 1968, Red Star/Sarov (Privately Owned)		Demon (Hyb.) 1957, Red Star/Saratov (Privately Owned)
	Sekki (Hyb.) 1962, Red Star	Arsa (Hyb.) Red Star

Abbreviations: ♀, bitch; ♂, dog; Aired., Airedale; C.Ovch., Caucasian Ovcharka; C.A.Ovch., Central Asian Ovcharka; Cx., Crossbreed; E.E.Shep., East European Shepherd; G.G.Dane, German Great Dane; Hyb., Hybrid; M.Dvr, Moscow Diver; M.Dog, Moscow Dog; M.Wdg., Moscow Waterdog; Newf., Newfoundland; R.S.Hnd., Russian Spotted Hound; Rtw., Rottweiler; Schn., Schnauzer; S.R.Ovch., South Russian Ovcharka.

		Karat (Hyb.) 1964, Red Star
	Dzhim (Hyb.) 1966, Red Star /Moscow	
Dan Zhan (Hyb.)	(Privately Owned)	Teya (Cx.) 1961, Red Star
1970, Moscow		Tom (Hyb.) 1964, Red Star
(Privately Owned)	Dzhoya (Hyb.) 1967	
	Red Star/Moscow (Priv.)	Dega (Hyb.) 1962, Red Star

Atos (♂) (Hyb.) 1978, Red Star (Privately Owned)

		Tom (Hyb.) 1964, Red Star
	Tuman (Hyb.) 1967, Red Star	
Lera (Hyb.) 1972, Red Star		Dega (Hyb.) 1962, Red Star
	Nayda (Hyb.) 1966, Red Star	Karat (Hyb.) 1964, Red Star
		Teya (Cx.) 1961, Red Star

		Vah (Cx.) 1956, Red Star
	Foka (Hyb.) 1960, Red Star	
Karat (Hyb.) 1964, Red Star		Bara (Hyb.) 1957, Red Star
	Nayda (Hyb.) 1961, Red Star	Brayt (M.Wdg.Hyb.) 1956, Red Star
		Nelma (Hyb.) Red Star

Ayna, St. Petersburg, Arni, Arisha, Ada, Atika, Arta (♀), Ayaks [Ajaks], Moscow, Antey, St. Petersburg (♂) (Hyb.) 1967 (Privately Owned)

		Haytar (Cx.) 1952
	Dik (Hyb.) 1958, Red Star	
Stesha (Hyb.) 1965, St. Petersburg		Vishnya (M.Wdg.Hyb.) 1956, Red Star
	Nastya (Hyb.) St. Petersburg (Privately Owned)	Foka (Hyb.) 1960, Red Star
		Lada Tag (Hyb.) 1959, Moscow (Privately Owned)

		Vah (Cx.) 1956, Red Star
	Foka (Hyb.) 1960, Red Star	
		Bara (Hyb.) 1957, Red Star
Karat (Hyb.) 1964, Red Star		
		Brayt (M.Wdg.Hyb.) 1956, Red Star
	Nayda (Hyb.) 1961, Red Star (Priv. Own.)	
		Nelma (Hyb.), Red Star

Bechel (♂) (Hyb.) 1966, Red Star (Privately Owned)

		Armin f. Tize Turn (Rtw.)
	Geyni (Rtw.) 1955, Red Star	
		Kora f. Schneidenplatz (Rtw.)
Ila (Cx.) 1960, Red Star		
		Farno (Rtw.) 1951, Red Star
	Dila (Cx.) 1958, Red Star	
		Chuta (Cx.), Red Star

		Vah (Cx.) 1956, Red Star
	Foka (Hyb.) 1960, Red Star	
		Bara (Hyb.) 1957, Red Star
Rams I (Hyb.) 1966, Red Star (Privately Owned)		Demon (Hyb.) 1957, Red Star/Saratov (Privately Owned)
	Dega (Hyb.) 1962, Red Star	
		Galka (Hyb.) (Privately Owned)

Charli 1 (♂) (Hyb.), Red Star

		Foka (Hyb.) 1960, Red Star
	Karat (Hyb.) 1964, Red Star	
		Nayda (Hyb.) 1961, Red Star
Chada (Hyb.) 1968, Red Star		
		Demon (Hyb.) 1957, Red Star/Saratov (Privately Owned)
	Sekki (Hyb.) 1962, Red Star	
		Arsa (Hyb.) Red Star

Dzhim (Hyb.) 1966,
Red Star/Moscow
(Privately Owned)

Karat (Hyb.) 1964,
Red Star

Foka (Hyb.) 1960, Red Star

Nayda (Hyb.) 1961, Red Star (Priv. Own.)

Teya (Cx.) 1961,
Red Star

Vah (Cx.) 1956, Red Star

Basta (Cx.) 1955, Red Star

Dan Zhan (♂) (Hyb.) 1970, Moscow (Privately Owned)

Dzhoya (Hyb.) 1967,
Red Star
(Privately Owned)

Tom (Hyb.) 1964,
Red Star

Gay (Cx.), Red Star

Dina (Hyb.), Moscow (Privately Owned)

Dega (Hyb.) 1962,
Red Star

Demon (Hyb.) 1957, Red Star/Saratov
(Privately Owned)

Galka (Hyb.) (Privately Owned)

Demon (Hyb.) 1957,
Red Star/Saratov
(Privately Owned)

Arras (Hyb.) 1954,
Red Star

Beniamino I (Rtw.) 1949, Red Star

Hizha [Hinga] (Cx.) 1952, Red Star

Chomga (Cx.) 1953,
Red Star

Roy (Schn.) 1947?, Red Star

Femka (Rtw.) 1951, Red Star

Dega (♀) (Hyb.) 1962, Red Star

Galka (Hyb.)
(Privately Owned)

Negus (Hyb.)
(Privately Owned)

Demon (Hyb.) 1957, Red Star/Saratov

Unknown

Yaga (Hyb.),
Red Star

Demon (Hyb.) 1957, Red Star/Saratov
(Privately Owned)

Mirta (Hyb.) 1960, Red Star

		Vah (Cx.) 1956, Red Star
	Foka (Hyb.) 1960, Red Star	Bara (Hyb.) 1957, Red Star
Karat (Hyb.) 1964		Brayt (M.Wdg.Hyb.) 1956, Red Star
	Nayda (Hyb.) 1961, Red Star (Priv. Own.)	Nelma (Hyb.), Red Star

Dzhek (♂) (Hyb.) 1966, Red Star (Privately Owned)

		Aray (Cx.) 1954, Red Star
	Gay (Cx.), Red Star	Borka (Cx.) 1955, Red Star
Ata (Hyb.) 1964, Red Star		Tuman (Hyb.), Red Star
	Dina (Hyb.), Moscow (Privately Owned)	Fimka (Unkn.) (Privately Owned)

		Vah (Cx.) 1956, Red Star
	Foka (Hyb.) 1960, Red Star	Bara (Hyb.) 1957
Karat (Hyb.) 1964, Red Star		Brayt (M.Wdg.Hyb.) 1956, Red Star
	Nayda (Hyb.) 1961, Red Star (Priv. Own.)	Nelma (Hyb.), Red Star

Dzhim (♂) (Hyb.) 1966

		Roy (Schn.) 1947?, Red Star
	Vah (Cx.) 1956, Red Star	Una (Rtw.) 1950, Red Star
Teya (Cx.) 1961, Red Star		Roy (Schn.) 1947?, Red Star
	Basta (Cx.) 1955, Red Star	Urma (Rtw.) 1950, Red Star

		Arras (Hyb.) 1954, Red Star
Negus (Hyb.) (Privately Owned)	Demon (Hyb.) 1957, Red Star/Saratov (Privately Owned)	Chomga (Cx.) 1953, Red Star
	Unknown	Unknown
		Unknown

Galka (♀) (Hyb.) (yr?), Red Star

		Arras (Hyb.) 1954, Red Star
Yaga (Hyb.), Red Star	Demon (Hyb.) 1957, Red Star/Saratov (Privately Owned)	Chomga (Cx.) 1953, Red Star
	Mirta (Hyb.) 1960, Red Star	Chuk (M.Dog/Hyb.) 1956, Red Star
		Volga (M.Wdg./Hyb.) 1956, Red Star

		Daks (Hyb.) 1962, Red Star/Moscow
Argo (Hyb.) 1971 (Privately Owned)	Alf (Hyb.) 1966 (Privately Owned)	(Privately Owned) Veda (Hyb.) 1962 (Privately Owned)
	Blek-Veda (Hyb.) 1968, Red Star	Karat (Hyb.) 1964, Red Star
		Sekki (Hyb.) 1962, Red Star

Grey f. Raakzeje [Raakze] (♂), Nizhniy Novgorod, Gabi (♀) (Hyb.) 1977, Moscow? (Privately Owned)

		Ekso f. Rozeggers-Haus (Schn.), Germany
Silva-Bagira (Hyb.) 1974, Nizhniy Novgorod	Akbar f. Raakze (Schn.), Red Star	Britta f. Haus Brekker (Schn.), Germany
	Adel (Hyb.) (Privately Owned)	Ayaks [Ajaks] (Hyb.) 1967, Moscow
		Lada (Unkn.) (Privately Owned)

		Roy (Schn.) 1947?, Red Star
	Vah (Cx.) 1956, Red Star	Una (Rtw.) 1950, Red Star
Foka (Hyb.) 1960, Red Star		Brayt (M.Wdg.Hyb.) 1956, Red Star
	Bara (Hyb.) 1957, Red Star	Appa (Hyb.) 1954, Red Star

Karat (♂) (Hyb.) 1964, Red Star

		Azart [Crossbreed] 1954, Red Star
	Brayt (M.Wdg.Hyb.) 1956, Red Star	Hanka (M.Wdg.) 1962, Red Star
Nayda (Hyb.) 1961, Moscow (Privately Owned)		Haytar (Cx.) 1952, Red Star
	Nelma (Hyb.), Red Star	Gayda (Hyb.) 1956, Red Star

		Vah (Cx.) 1956, Red Star
	Foka (Hyb.) 1960, Red Star	Bara (Hyb.) 1957
Karat (Hyb.) 1964, Red Star		Brayt (M.Wdg.Hyb.) 1956, Red Star
	Nayda (Hyb.) 1961, Red Star (Priv. Own.)	Nelma (Hyb.), Red Star

Nayda, Red Star, Chanita, Vita (♀) Dzhim (♂) (Hyb.) 1966, Red Star (Privately Owned)

		Roy (Schn.) 1947?, Red Star
	Vah (Cx.) 1956, Red Star	Una (Rtw.) 1950, Red Star
Teya (Cx.) 1961, Red Star		Roy (Schn.) 1947?, Red Star
	Basta (Cx.) 1955, Red Star	Urma (Rtw.) 1950, Red Star

		Karat (Hyb.) 1964, Red Star
	Dzhim (Hyb.) 1966, Red Star /Moscow (Privately Owned)	Teya (Cx.) 1961, Red Star
Dan Zhan (Hyb.) 1970, Moscow (Privately Owned)		Tom (Hyb.) 1964, Red Star
	Dzhoya (Hyb.) 1967 Red Star/Moscow (Priv.)	Dega (Hyb.) 1962, Red Star

Ped-Shvarc (♂) Ped-Shanel, Ped-Shelli (♀) (Hyb.) 1974, Moscow (Privately Owned)

		Dasso f. Drahenshljuht (Schn.) 1960, Red Star
	Reks (Hyb.), Red Star/Moscow (Privately Owned)	Gloriya (Hyb.) 1959, Red Star/Moscow (Privately Owned)
Dezi (Hyb.) 1971		Nord (Hyb.) 1962, Red Star
	Lada (Hyb.) 1968, Red Star/Moscow (Priv.)	Nelli (Hyb.) 1966, Red Star

		Foks f. Klaynkirhhaim-Bad SchH I (Schn.)
	Ekso f. Rozeggers-Haus SchH III (Schn.) Germany 988	Ambare f. Rozeggers-Haus (Schn.)
Akbar f. Raakze (Schn.), Nizhnly Novgorod/Moscow		Bero v.d. Wallwitzburg (Schn.) Germany
	Britta f. Haus Brekker (Schn.) Germany 02544	Elke f.d. Raiter Brukke (Schn.) Germany

Silva-Bagira (♀) (Hyb.) 1974, Nizhnly Novgorod

		Karat (Hyb.) 1964, Red Star
	Ayaks [Ajaks] (Hyb.) 1962, Moscow	Stesha (Hyb.) 1965, St. Petersburg
Adel (Hyb.) (Privately Owned)		Anzor (Unkn.) (Privately Owned)
	Lada (Unkn.) (Privately Owned)	Nika (Unkn.) (Privately Owned)

	Rom (Hyb.) 1963 (Privately Owned)	Tyapa (Hyb.) 1959, Red Star/Moscow (Privately Owned)
Chingiz Rhan (Hyb.), 1969 (Privately Owned)		Lada Tag (Hyb.) 1959, Moscow (Priv.)
	Chanita (Hyb.) 1966, Red Star/Moscow (Privately Owned)	Karat (Hyb.) 1964, Red Star
		Teya (Cx.) 1961, Red Star

Tap Arto (♂) (Hyb.) 1975 (Privately Owned)

	Dzherri (Hyb.) 1969 (Privately Owned)	Dzhim (Hyb.) 1966, Red Star/Moscow (Privately Owned)
Tapa (Hyb.) 1971, (Privately Owned)		Nensi (Hyb.) 1967 (Privately Owned)
	Charmi (Hyb.) 1969 (Privately Owned)	Rom (Hyb.) 1963 (Privately Owned)
		Chanita (Hyb.) 1966, Red Star/Moscow (Privately Owned)

	Rom (Hyb.) 1963 (Privately Owned)	Tyapa (Hyb.) 1959, Red Star/Moscow (Privately Owned)
Chingiz Rhan (Hyb.), 1969 (Privately Owned)		Lada Tag (Hyb.) 1959, Moscow (Priv.)
	Chanita (Hyb.) 1966, Red Star/Moscow (Privately Owned)	Karat (Hyb.) 1964, Red Star
		Teya (Cx.) 1961, Red Star

Zitta (♀) (Hyb.) (Privately Owned)

	Karat (Hyb.)1964, Red Star	Foka (Hyb.) 1960, Red Star
Vita (Hyb.) 1966, Red Star (Privately Owned)		Nayda (Hyb.) 1961, Red Star (Priv. Own.)
	Teya (Cx.) 1961, Red Star	Vah (Cx.) 1956, Red Star
		Basta (Cx.) 1955, Red Star

1967: Family Lines Based on Hybrid Vud (Male) (Hybrid, Dik × Hybrid, Velta)

Ned-Nays (Hyb.) 1975, Moscow (Privately Owned)	Dan Zhan (Hyb.) 1970, Moscow (Privately Owned)	Dzhim (Hyb.) 1966, Red Star (Privately Owned)
		Dzhoya (Hyb.) 1967, Red Star (Priv.)
	Neda (Hyb.) 1972 (Privately Owned)	Tishka (Hyb.) 1967, Moscow
		Lada (Hyb.) 1968, Red Star

Arna (♀) (Hyb.) 1979 (Privately Owned)

Dzhilda (Hyb.), Red Star (Privately Owned)	Vud (Hyb.) 1967 (Privately Owned)	Dik (Hyb.) 1958, Red Star
		Velta (Hyb.) 1964, Red Star
	Chara (Hyb.) 1968, Red Star	Karat (Hyb.) 1964, Red Star
		Irda (Hyb.) 1962, Red Star

Abbreviations: ♀, bitch; ♂, dog; Aired., Airedale; C.Ovch., Caucasian Ovcharka; C.A.Ovch., Central Asian Ovcharka; Cx., Crossbreed; E.E.Shep., East European Shepherd; G.G.Dane, German Great Dane; Hyb., Hybrid; M.Dvr, Moscow Diver; M.Dog, Moscow Dog; M.Wdg., Moscow Waterdog; Newf., Newfoundland; R.S.Hnd., Russian Spotted Hound; Rtw., Rottweiler; Schn., Schnauzer; S.R.Ovch., South Russian Ovcharka.

			Haytar (Cx.) 1952, Red Star
	Dik (Hyb.) 1958, Red Star (Privately Owned)		Vishnya (M.Wdg.Hyb.) 1956, Red Star
Vud (Hyb.) 1967, Red Star (Privately Owned)			Vah (Cx.) 1956, Red Star
	Velta (Hyb.) 1964, Red Star (Priv. Own.)		Meggi (Hyb.) 1961, Red Star

Rams 2 (♂) (Hyb.) (Privately Owned)

			Vah (Cx.) 1956, Red Star
	Viy (Hyb.) 1960, Red Star (Privately Owned)		Bara (Hyb.) 1957, Red Star
Diva (Hyb.), Red Star (Privately Owned)			Dik (Hyb.) 1958, Red Star (Privately Owned)
	Dzhan (Hyb.) 1964, (Privately Owned)		Ayshe (Hyb.) 1961, Red Star (Priv. Own.)

			Foka (Hyb.) 1960 Red Star
	Rams I (Hyb.) 1966, Red Star		Dega (Hyb.)
Charli 1 (Hyb.) Red Star			Karat (Hyb.) 1964 Red Star
	Chada (Hyb.) 1968, Red Star		Sekki (Hyb.) 1962, Red Star

Shvarts 2 (♂) (Hyb.) 1977, Red Star (Privately Owned)

			Dik (Hyb.) 1958, Red Star (Privately Owned)
	Vud (Hyb.) 1967 (Privately Owned)		Velta (Hyb.) 1964, Red Star (Priv. Own.)
Kerri (Hyb.) Red Star			Karat (Hyb.) 1964, Red Star
	Chara (Hyb.) 1968, Red Star		Irda (Hyb.) 1962, Red Star

```
                                                       | Roy (Schn.) 1947?, Red Star
                               | Haytar (Cx.) 1952,
                               | Red Star             | Sotta (Aired.) 1949, Red Star
         Dik (Hyb.) 1958,
         Red Star                                     | Azart (Cx.) 1954, Red Star
         (Privately Owned)     | Vishnya (M.Wdg.Hyb.)
                               | 1956, Red Star        | Hanka (M.Wdg.) 1952, Red Star
```

Vud (♂) (Hyb.) 1967, Moscow (Privately Owned)

```
                                                       | Roy (Schn.) 1947?, Red Star
                               | Vah (Cx.) 1956,
                               | Red Star             | Una (Rtw.) 1950, Red Star
         Velta (Hyb.) 1964,
         Red Star                                     | Ditter f. Drahenshljuht (Schn.) 1960,
         (Privately Owned)     | Meggi (Hyb.) 1961,    | Red Star
                               | Red Star             | Gayda (Hyb.) 1956, Red Star
```

1967: Family Lines Based on Hybrid Tuman (Male) (Hybrid, Tom × Hybrid, Dega)

		Topaz (Hyb.) 1967, Red Star
	Kapitan Flint (Hyb.)	
	1969, Red Star	Sekki (Hyb.) Red Star
Zhan Grey (Hyb.)	(Privately Owned)	
1976		Tuman (Hyb.) 1967, Red Star
(Privately Owned)	Chara (Hyb.) 1972,	
	Red Star	Nayda (Hyb.) 1966, Red Star

Baska (♀) (Hyb.) 1981 (Privately Owned)

		Unknown
	Chernish (Unk.)	
	(Privately Owned)	Unknown
Dzhenni (Unkn.)		
1975 (Priv. Own.)		Unknown
	Alpha-Malyshka (Unkn.)	
	(Privately Owned)	Unknown

Abbreviations: ♀, bitch; ♂, dog; Aired., Airedale; C.Ovch., Caucasian Ovcharka; C.A.Ovch., Central Asian Ovcharka; Cx., Crossbreed; E.E.Shep., East European Shepherd; G.G.Dane; German Great Dane; Hyb., Hybrid; M.Dvr, Moscow Diver; M.Dog, Moscow Dog; M.Wdg., Moscow Waterdog; Newf., Newfoundland; R.S.Hnd., Russian Spotted Hound; Rtw., Rottweiler; Schn., Schnauzer; S.R.Ovch., South Russian Ovcharka.

		Gay (Cx.), Red Star
	Tom (Hyb.) 1964, Red Star	Dina (Hyb.) Moscow
Tuman (Hyb.) 1967, Red Star		Demon (Hyb.) 1957, Red Star/Saratov
	Dega (Hyb.) 1962, Red Star	Galka (Hyb.)

Dina (♀), Timur (♂) (Hyb.), Red Star (Privately Owned)

		Linch (Rtw.) 1960, Red Star
	Karen 1 (Cx.) 1963, Red Star	Dila (Cx.) 1958, Red Star
Panta (Cx.) 1965, Red Star		Geyni (Rtw.) 1955, Moscow
	Ilma (Cx.) 1960, Red Star	Dila (Cx.) 1958, Red Star

		Gay (Cx.), Red Star
	Tom (Hyb.) 1964, Red Star	Dina (Hyb.) Moscow
Tuman (Hyb.) 1967, Red Star		Demon (Hyb.) 1957, Red Star/Saratov (Privately Owned)
	Dega (Hyb.) 1962, Red Star	Galka (Hyb.) (Privately Owned)

Kras-Boss (♂) Karina-Un (♀) (Hyb.) 1971?, Red Star

		Tom (Hyb.) 1964, Red Star
	Topaz (Hyb.) 1967, Red Star	Lada (Hyb.) 1964, Red Star
Ulma (Hyb.), Red Star (Privately Owned)		Nayt (Hyb.) 1964, Red Star
	Dina II (Hyb.) 1967, Moscow (Priv. Own.)	Ditta (Hyb.) 1964, Moscow

Tuman (Hyb.) 1967,
Red Star

 Tom (Hyb.) 1964,
 Red Star

  Gay (Cx.), Red Star

  Dina (Hyb.), Moscow (Privately Owned)

 Dega (Hyb.) 1962,
 Red Star

  Demon (Hyb.) 1957, Red Star/Saratov
  (Privately Owned)

  Galka (Hyb.) (Privately Owned)

Maur (♂) (Hyb.) (yr?), Red Star/Ekaterinburg (Privately Owned)

Sekki (Hyb.) 1962,
Red Star

 Demon (Hyb.) 1957,
 Red Star/Saratov
 (Privately Owned)

  Arras (Hyb.) 1954, Red Star

  Chomga (Cx.) 1953, Red Star

 Arsa (Hyb.),
 Red Star

  Azart (Cx.) 1954, Red Star

  Arsa (Hyb.) 1954, Red Star

Set (Hyb.) 1971
(Privately Owned)

 Karay (Hyb.) 1967,
 St. Petersburg
 (Privately Owned)

  Nayt (Hyb.) 1964, Red Star

  Ditta (Hyb.) 1964, Red Star

 Arni (Hyb.) 1967
 (Privately Owned)

  Karat (Hyb.) 1964, Red Star

  Stesha (Hyb.) 1965, St. Petersburg

Olesya, Ora, Oyta (♀), Oksay, Om (♂) (Hyb.) 1973, St. Petersburg

Zhulya (Hyb.) 1970,
St. Petersburg

 Tuman (Hyb.) 1967,
 Red Star

  Tom (Hyb.) 1964, Red Star

  Dega (Hyb.) 1962, Red Star

 Raksha (Hyb.) Red Star/
 Kaunas Lithuania

  Karat (Hyb.) 1964, Red Star

  Irda (Hyb.) 1962, Red Star

Tuman (Hyb.) 1967, Red Star
- Tom (Hyb.) 1964, Red Star
  - Gay (Cx.), Moscow
  - Dina (Hyb.), Red Star
- Dega (Hyb.) 1962, Red Star
  - Demon (Hyb.) 1957, Red Star/Saratov
  - Galka (Hyb.) (Privately Owned)

Rema Greza (♀) (Hyb.) 1970 (Privately Owned)

Rynda (Hyb.) 1966 (Privately Owned)
- Daks (Hyb.) 1962, Red Star
  - Foka (Hyb.) 1960, Red Star
  - Lada Tag (Hyb.) 1959, Red Star
- Veda (Hyb.) 1962 (Privately Owned)
  - Ditter f. Drahenshljuht (Schn.) 1960, Red Star
  - Vanda (Hyb.) 1957, Red Star

Barhan-Zhan (Hyb.) 1969 (Privately Owned)
- Bechel (Hyb.) 1966, Red Star
  - Karat (Hyb.) 1964, Red Star
  - Ila (Cx.) 1960, Red Star
- Adzhi-Shahra (Hyb.) 1964, Moscow (Priv.)
  - Dik (Hyb.) 1958, Red Star
  - Ayshe (Hyb.) 1961, Red Star

Seggi, Setti, Sabina-Diana (♀) (Hyb.) 1973, Moscow

Rema Greza (Hyb.) 1970 (Privately Owned)
- Tuman (Hyb.) 1967, Red Star
  - Tom (Hyb.) 1964, Red Star
  - Dega (Hyb.) 1962, Red Star
- Rynda (Hyb.) 1966 (Privately Owned)
  - Daks (Hyb.) 1962, Red Star
  - Veda (Hyb.) 1962 (Privately Owned)

Tsorn (♂) (Hyb.) 1977, Red Star

Oksay (Hyb.) 1973, St. Petersburg (Privately Owned)	Set (Hyb.) 1971 (Privately Owned)	Karay (Hyb.) 1967, St. Petersburg (Privately Owned)
		Arni (Hyb.) 1967 (Privately Owned)
	Zhulya (Hyb.) 1970, St. Petersburg	Tuman (Hyb.) 1967, Red Star
		Raksha (Hyb.) Red Star/Kaunas
Oyta (Hyb.) 1973 (Privately Owned)	Set (Hyb.) 1971 (Privately Owned)	Karay (Hyb.) 1967, St. Petersburg
		Arni (Hyb.) 1967
	Zhulya (Hyb.) 1970, St. Petersburg (Priv.)	Tuman (Hyb.) 1967, Red Star
		Raksha (Hyb.) Red Star/Kaunas, Lithuania

Tuman (♂) (Hyb.) 1956, Red Star

Aray (Cx.) 1954, Red Star	Roy (Schn.) 1947?, Red Star	Zorab (Schn.)
		Ledi (Schn.), Red Star
	Urma (Rtw.) 1950, Red Star	Kastor (Rtw.) 1947, Moscow
		Birma (Rtw.), Moscow
Htora (Cx.) 1952, Red Star	Roy (Schn.) 1947?, Red Star	Zorab (Schn.)
		Ledi (Schn.), Red Star
	Sotta (Aired.) 1949, Red Star	Bil f. Askania (Aired.) 1944, Moscow
		Teffi (Aired.), Moscow

Tom 1964,
Red Star

Gay (Cx.) Red Star
- Aray (Cx.) 1954, Red Star
- Borka (Cx.) 1955, Red Star

Dina (Hyb.), Moscow (Privately Owned)
- Tuman (Hyb.), Red Star
- Fimka (Unkn.) 1951? (Privately Owned)

Tuman (♂) (Hyb.) 1967, Red Star

Dega (Hyb.) 1962, Red Star

Demon (Hyb.) 1957, Red Star (Privately Owned)
- Arras (Hyb.) 1954, Red Star
- Chomga (Cx.) 1953, Red Star

Galka (Hyb.) (Privately Owned)
- Negus (Hyb.) (Privately Owned)
- Yaga (Hyb.), Red Star

Timur (Hyb.), Red Star (Privately Owned)

Tuman (Hyb.) 1967, Red Star
- Tom (Hyb.) 1964, Red Star
- Dega (Hyb.) 1962, Red Star

Panta (Cx.) 1965, Red Star
- Karen 1 (Cx.) 1963, Red Star
- Ilma (Cx.) 1960, Red Star

Virta, Verda, Vietta (♀), Vajs (♂) (Hyb.) (yr?), Red Star

Vayda (Hyb.), Red Star (Privately Owned)

Vays (Hyb.) 1969, Moscow (Privately Owned)
- Lord (Hyb.) 1966, Red Star
- Roksa (Hyb.) 1966, St. Petersburg (Priv.)

Chada (Hyb.) 1968, Red Star
- Karat (Hyb.) 1964 Red Star
- Sekki (Hyb.) 1962 Red Star

1975: Family Lines Based on Hybrid Tap Arto (Male) (Hybrid, Chyingiz Rhan × Hybrid, Tapa)

		Tyapa (Hyb.) 1959, Red Star
	Rom (Hyb.) 1963	
	(Privately Owned)	Lada Tag (Hyb.) 1959, Moscow (Priv.)
Chingiz Rhan (Hyb.),		
1969	Chanita (Hyb.) 1966,	Karat (Hyb.) 1964, Red Star
(Privately Owned)	Red Star/Moscow	
	(Privately Owned)	Teya (Cx.) 1961, Red Star

Tap Arto (♂) (Hyb.) 1975 (Privately Owned)

		Dzhim [Hyrid] 1966 Red Star/Moscow
	Dzherri (Hyb.) 1969	(Privately Owned)
	(Privately Owned)	Nensi (Hyb.) 1967 (Privately Owned)
Tapa (Hyb.) 1971 ,		
(Privately Owned)		Rom (Hyb.) 1963 (Privately Owned)
	Charmi (Hyb.) 1969	
	(Privately Owned)	Chanita (Hyb.) 1966, Red Star/Moscow
		(Privately Owned)

Abbreviations: ♀, bitch; ♂, dog; Aired., Airedale; C.Ovch., Caucasian Ovcharka; C.A.Ovch., Central Asian Ovcharka; Cx., Crossbreed; E.E.Shep., East European Shepherd; G.G.Dane, German Great Dane; Hyb., Hybrid; M.Dvr, Moscow Diver; M.Dog, Moscow Dog; M.Wdg., Moscow Waterdog; Newf., Newfoundland; R.S.Hnd., Russian Spotted Hound; Rtw., Rottweiler; Schn., Schnauzer; S.R.Ovch., South Russian Ovcharka.

1976: Family Lines Based on Hybrid Mashka (Female) (Hybrid, Urban × Hybrid, Masha)

		Karay (Hyb.) 1967, St. Petersburg
	Set (Hyb.) 1971,	(Privately Owned)
	St. Petersburg	Arni (Hyb.) 1967 (Privately Owned)
Urban (Hyb.) 1974	(Privately Owned)	
(Privately Owned)		Skif (Hyb.) 1965 (Privately Owned)
	Lusha (Hyb.) 1971	
	(Privately Owned)	Dar Ritsa (Hyb.) 1968 (Privately Owned)

Mashka (♀) (Hyb.) 1976, Sweden (Privately Owned)

		Tom (Hyb.) 1964, Red Star
	Lord (Hyb.) 1966,	
	Red Star	Dina I (Hyb.) 1964, Red Star
Masha (Hyb.) 1971	(Privately Owned)	
(Privately Owned)		Nayt (Hyb.) 1964, Red Star
	Beta (Hyb.) 1969,	(Privately Owned)
	St. Petersburg	Dega (Hyb.) 1963, Red Star
	(Privately Owned)	(Privately Owned)

Abbreviations: ♀, bitch; ♂, dog; Aired., Airedale; C.Ovch., Caucasian Ovcharka; C.A.Ovch., Central Asian Ovcharka; Cx., Crossbreed; E.E.Shep., East European Shepherd; G.G.Dane, German Great Dane; Hyb., Hybrid; M.Dvr, Moscow Diver; M.Dog, Moscow Dog; M.Wdg., Moscow Waterdog; Newf., Newfoundland; R.S.Hnd., Russian Spotted Hound; Rtw., Rottweiler; Schn., Schnauzer; S.R.Ovch., South Russian Ovcharka.

1977: Family Lines Based on Hybrid Lord (Male) (Hybrid, Atos × Hybrid, Virta)

		Dik (Hyb.) 1958, Red Star
	Tishka (Hyb.) 1967, Red Star	(Privately Owned)
	(Privately Owned)	Nora* (Hyb.) 1962 (Privately Owned)
Atos (Hyb.) (yr?), Red Star		
		Karat (Hyb.) 1964, Red Star
	Chara (Hyb.) 1968, Red Star	
		Irda (Hyb.) 1962, Red Star

Lord (♂) (Hyb.) 1977, Red Star (Privately Owned)

		Tuman (Hyb.) 1967, Red Star
	Timur (Hyb.) Red Star (Privately Owned)	
		Panta (Cx.) 1965, Red Star
Virta (Hyb.), Red Star		
		Vays (Hyb.) 1969 (Privately Owned)
	Vayda (Hyb.), Red Star (Privately Owned)	
		Chada (Hyb.) 1968, Red Star

*Cloudy coat

1979, 1982, 1983: Family Lines Based on Offspring of Hybrid Mashka (Female) (Hybrid, Urban × Hybrid, Masha)

		Karay (Hyb.) 1967, St. Petersburg
	Ivan-Sf (Hyb.) 1976,	(Privately Owned)
	Finland	Irisha (Hyb.) 1970, St. Petersburg (Priv.)
Jolkas Genij (Hyb.)	(Privately Owned)	
1978		Max [Max-Nim] (Hyb.) 1970, Finland
(Privately Owned)	Jolkas Dobrusa (Hyb.)	(Privately Owned)
	1976, Sweden (Priv.)	Anastasia (Hyb.) 1972, Finland (Priv.)

Calov (♂) 1979, Netherlands, Cacsha (♀) (Hyb.), Sweden (Privately Owned)

		Set (Hyb.) 1965, St. Petersburg
	Urban (Hyb.) 1974	(Privately Owned)
	(Privately Owned)	Lusha (Hyb.) 1971 (Privately Owned)
Mashka (Hyb.) 1976,		
Sweden		Lord (Hyb.) 1966, Red Star
(Privately Owned)	Masha (Hyb.) 1974	
	(Privately Owned)	Beta (Hyb.) 1969, St. Petersburg (Priv.)

Abbreviations: ♀, bitch; ♂, dog; Aired., Airedale; C.Ovch., Caucasian Ovcharka; C.A.Ovch., Central Asian Ovcharka; Cx., Crossbreed; E.E.Shep., East European Shepherd; G.G.Dane, German Great Dane; Hyb., Hybrid; M.Dvr, Moscow Diver; M.Dog, Moscow Dog; M.Wdg., Moscow Waterdog; Newf., Newfoundland; R.S.Hnd., Russian Spotted Hound; Rtw., Rottweiler; Schn., Schnauzer; S.R.Ovch., South Russian Ovcharka.

		Atos (Hyb.) Red Star
	Larsen (Hyb.) 1977, Red Star	
		Dan-Yamika (Hyb.) 1974, Moscow (Priv.)
Hrabrij Foka (Hyb.)	(Privately Owned)	
1980, Sweden		Dan Zhan 1970, Moscow
(Privately Owned)	Dali (Hyb.) 1976	(Privately Owned)
	(Privately Owned)	Rin-Deza (Hyb.) 1974, Moscow (Priv.)

Gritt (♂) 1982, Grisja (♀) (Hyb.), Netherlands (Privately Owned)

		Set (Hyb.) 1965, St. Petersburg
	Urban (Hyb.) 1974	(Privately Owned)
	(Privately Owned)	Lusha (Hyb.) 1971 (Privately Owned)
Mashka (Hyb.) 1976,		
Sweden		Lord (Hyb.) 1966, Red Star
(Privately Owned)	Masha (Hyb.) 1974	
	(Privately Owned)	Beta (Hyb.) 1969, St. Petersburg (Priv.)

		Karay (Hyb.) 1967, St. Petersburg
	Ivan-Sf (Hyb.) 1976,	(Privately Owned)
	Finland	Irisha (Hyb.) 1970, St. Petersburg (Priv.)
Deiko (Hyb.) 1980,	(Privately Owned)	
Sweden		Max [Max-Nim] [Hybrid 1970, Finland
(Privately Owned)	Jolkas Donetska (Hyb.)	(Privately Owned)
	1976, Sweden (Priv.)	Anastasia (Hyb.) 1972, Finland (Priv.)

Harpo (♂) (Hyb.) 1983, Sweden (Privately Owned)

		Set (Hyb.) 1965, St. Petersburg
	Urban (Hyb.) 1974	(Privately Owned)
	(Privately Owned)	Lusha (Hyb.) 1971 (Privately Owned)
Mashka (Hyb.) 1976,		
Sweden		Lord (Hyb.) 1966, Red Star
(Privately Owned)	Masha (Hyb.) 1974	
	(Privately Owned)	Beta (Hyb.) 1969, St. Petersburg (Priv.)

1980: Family Lines Based on Hybrid Panta (Female) (Hybrid, Tsorn × Hybrid, Charda)

		Dan Zhan (Hyb.) 1970, Moscow
	Lo-Rom (Hyb.) 1973,	(Privately Owned)
	Red Star	Rayma (Hyb.) 1970 (Privately Owned)
Atos (Hyb.) 1980,		
Magnitogorsk		Barhan-Zhan (Hyb.) 1969, Moscow
(Privately Owned)	Sabina-Diana (Hyb.)	(Privately Owned)
	1973, Red Star	Rema Greza (Hyb.) 1970 (Priv. Own.)

O Bim (♂) (Hyb.) 1982, Magnitogorsk (Privately Owned)

		Oksay (Hyb.) 1973, St. Petersburg
	Tsorn (Hyb.) 1977,	(Privately Owned)
	Red Star	Oyta (Hyb.) 1973 (Privately Owned)
Panta (Hyb.) 1980,		
Magnitogorsk		Roy (Hyb.) Red Star
(Privately Owned)	Charda (Hyb.),	
	Red Star	Chara (Hyb.) 1968, Red Star

		Set (Hyb.) 1971, St. Petersburg
	Oksay (Hyb.) 1973,	(Privately Owned)
	St. Petersburg	Zhulya (Hyb.) 1970, St. Petersburg (Priv.)
Tsorn (Hyb.) 1977,	(Privately Owned)	
Red Star		Set (Hyb.) 1971, St. Petersburg
	Oyta (Hyb.) 1973	(Privately Owned)
	(Privately Owned)	Zhulya (Hyb.) 1970, St. Petersburg (Priv.)

Panta (♀) (Hyb.) 1980, Magnitogorsk (Privately Owned)

		Dan Zhan (Hyb.) 1970, Moscow
	Roy (Hyb.),	(Privately Owned)
	Red Star	Alfa (Hyb.) 1961, Red Star
Charda (Hyb.),		
Red Star		Karat (Hyb.) 1964, Red Star
	Chara (Hyb.) 1968,	
	Red Star	Irda (Hyb.) 1962, Red Star

Addendum

1978: Family Lines Based on Giant Schnauzer (Females) Ledi and Anni f. Raakzeje

		Gainar v. Virker Park (Schn.), Moscow
	Grey (Hyb.) 1979	(Privately Owned).
	(Privately Owned)	Rada (Hyb.) 1976 (Privately Owned)
Wojtek Dzsek		
(Hyb.), Hungary		Bars (Hyb.) 1970, Red Star (Priv. Own.)
(Privately Owned)	Shel Biruta (Hyb.) 1978,	
	Moscow (Priv. Own.)	Ped Shelli (Hyb.) 1974, Moscow (Priv.)

Amur Z Ro-Da-Gu (♂), Czech Republic, Amurka Z Ro-Da-Gu (♀) (Hyb.), Hungary 1985 (Privately Owned)

		King (Hyb.) 1975, Ukraine
	Lord (Hyb.) 1978,	(Privately Owned)
	Odessa	Kerri (Hyb.) 1973, Odessa (Priv. Own.)
Bajka (Hyb.) 1981,	(Privately Owned)	
Czech Republic		Din-Dzhin (Hyb.) 1976, Odessa
(Privately Owned)	Dzhina (Hyb.) 1979	(Privately Owned)
	(Privately Owned)	Lada (Hyb.) 1976 (Privately Owned)

Abbreviations: ♀, bitch; ♂, dog; Aired., Airedale; C.Ovch., Caucasian Ovcharka; C.A.Ovch., Central Asian Ovcharka; Cx., Crossbreed; E.E.Shep., East European Shepherd; G.G.Dane, German Great Dane; Hyb., Hybrid; M.Dvr, Moscow Diver; M.Dog, Moscow Dog; M.Wdg., Moscow Waterdog; Newf., Newfoundland; R.S.Hnd., Russian Spotted Hound; Rtw., Rottweiler; Schn., Schnauzer; S.R.Ovch., South Russian Ovcharka.

		Unknown
Ekso f. Rozeggers-Haus [Exo v. Roseggerhaus] SchH III (Schn.), Germany 988	Foks f. Klaynkirhhaim-Bad SchH I (Schn.) Germany Sr86	Unknown
		Unknown
	Ambare f. Rozeggers-Haus (Schn.) Germany Sr844	Unknown

Anni f. Raakzeje (♀) (Schn.), Red Star

		Unknown
Britta f. Haus Brekker [Britta v. Haus Brekker] (Schn.) Germany 02544	Bero v.d. Wallwitzburg SchH III (Schn.) Germany Ddr1881	Unknown
	Elke f.d. Raiter Brukke [Elka v.d. Reiterbrücke] SchH III (Schn.) Germany DDR1957	Unknown
		Unknown

		Foks f. Klaynkirhhaim-Bad SchH I (Schn.) Germany Sr867
Artus v. Sachsenring SchH III (Schn.)	Ekso f. Rozeggers-Haus [Exo v. Roseggerhaus] SchH III (Schn.) Germany 988	Ambare f. Rozeggers-Haus (Schn.) Germany Sr844
	Burga V.Stefanidrunnen (Schn.) Germany GDR	Bero Von Der Wallwitzburg SchH III (Schn.) Germany DDR1881
		Unknown

Gainar v. Virker Park (Schn.), Moscow (Privately Owned)

		Unknown
Hella v.d. Wallwitzburg (Schn.) GDR Germany	Unknown	Unknown
		Unknown
	Unknown	Unknown

	Roy (Schn.) 1947?, Red Star	Zorab (Schn.)
Azart (Cx.) 1954, Red Star		Ledi (Schn.), Red Star
	Una (Rtw.) 1950, Red Star	Kastor (Rtw.) 1947, Moscow
		Birma (Rtw.), Moscow

Kerri (♀) (Cx.) 1958 (Privately Owned)

	Chudniy (Cx.) 1953, Red Star	Roy (Schn.)1947, Red Star
Kemi (Cx.) 1955, Moscow (Privately Owned)		Uda (Rtw.) 1950, Red Star
	Kal'ma (Schn.) 1949, Moscow (Privately Owned)	Boj (Schn.) 1947?, Red Star
		Mira (Schn.) (Privately Owned)

	Bars (Hyb.) 1970, Red Star (Privately Owned)	Agat (Hyb.) 1964, Red Star
Bes (Hyb.) 1979 (Privately Owned)		Chara (Hyb.) 1968, Red Star
	Gayde (Hyb.), Red Star (Privately Owned)	Kuchum (Hyb.) Red Star
		Anni f. Raakzeje (Schn.), Red Star

Nord (♂) (Hyb.) 1985, Moscow (Privately Owned)

	Sem (Hyb.) 1979 (Privately Owned)	Dan Grey (Hyb.) 1975 (Privately Owned)
Dolli Bek (Hyb.) 1982 (Privately Owned)		Gil-Assol (Hyb.) 1974 (Privately Owned)
	Dalila (Hyb.) 1978 (Privately Owned)	Artosha (Hyb.) 1971 (Privately Owned)
		Dzherri (Hyb.) 1974 (Privately Owned)

```
                          Nerhan (Hyb.) 1973     | Nord (Hyb.) 1968, Red Star/Moscow
                          (Privately Owned)       (Privately Owned)
    Blord (Hyb.) 1979                            | Bella (Hyb.) 1968 Moscow (Priv. Own.)
    (Privately Owned)
                          Re-Dzhessi (Hyb.) 1976 | Danchar (Hyb.) 1972 (Privately Owned)
                          (Privately Owned)       Setti (Hyb.) 1976 (Privately Owned)
```

Reda, Rena (♀) (Hyb.) 1982 (Privately Owned)

```
                          Gainar v. Virker Park  | Artus v. Sachsenring (Schn.)
                          (Schn.), Moscow          Hella v.d. Wallwitzburg (Schn.)
    Nora (Unk.)           (Privately Owned)
    (Privately Owned)                            | Unknown
                          Unknown
                                                   Unknown
```

```
                          Kalyan (Schn.) 1949    | Boj (Schn.) 1947?, Red Star
                          (Privately Owned)        Mira (Schn.) (Privately Owned)
    Bagor (Cx.) 1955,
    Red Star                                     | Roy (Schn.) 1947?, Red Star
                          Chadra (Cx.) 1953,
                          Red Star                 Una (Rtw.) 1950, Red Star
```

Tjapa (♀) (Hyb.) 1956, Red Star

```
                          Roy (Schn.) 1947?,     | Zorab (Schn.)
                          Red Star                 Ledi (Schn.) Red Star
    Mukha (Cx.) 1953,
    Red Star/Moscow                              | Negus f. Mangeym [Newf.] 1943,
    (Privately Owned)                              Red Star
                          Tiza (M.Wdg.) 1949,      Karabashka (C.Ovch.), Red Star
                          Red Star
```

		Artus v. Sachsenring (Schn.)
	Gainar v. Virker Park	
	(Schn.), Moscow	Hella v.d. Wallwitzburg (Schn.)
Grey (Hyb.) 1979,	(Privately Owned)	
Hungary		Adolf (Hyb.), Red Star (Privately Owned)
(Privately Owned)	Rada (Hyb.) 1976	
	(Privately Owned)	Aza (Hyb.) 1973 (Privately Owned)

Wojtek Dzsek (♂) (Hyb.) (1980s), Hungary (Privately Owned)

		Agat (Hyb.) 1964, Red Star
	Bars 1970, Red Star	
	(Privately Owned)	Chara (Hyb.) 1968, Red Star
Shel Biruta 1978,		
Moscow		Dan Zhan (Hyb.) 1970, Moscow
(Privately Owned)	Ped Shelli (Hyb.) 1974,	(Privately Owned)
	Moscow (Priv. Own.)	Dezi (Hyb.) 1971 (Privately Owned)

		Unknown
	Kris f. Rortrayh (Schn.)	
Jaguar (Schn.) 1982,	1980, Pedigree No.7635	Unknown
Pedigree No.1250,	GDR (Privately Owned)	
Moscow	Ugra Zhulen (Schn.)	Unknown
(Privately Owned)	1974, Ped. No.251-74	
	(Privately Owned)	Unknown

Zeman (♂) (Hyb.) 1984, (Privately Owned)

		Dan Zhan (Hyb.) 1970, Moscow
	Atos (Hyb.) 1978,	(Privately Owned)
	Red Star	Lera (Hyb.) 1972, Red Star
Linda (Hyb.) 1980	(Privately Owned)	
(Privately Owned)		Bars (Hyb.) 1970, Red Star
	Rada (Hyb.)	(Privately Owned)
	(Privately Owned)	Unknown

Acknowledgements

IN *THE CREATION OF THE Black Russian Terrier*, I have endeavoured to inform readers about the origin and the development of the breed from the 1940s until the 1970s, then touching into the 1980s. I wish to acknowledge and recognize those who have shared information, and those who have played major roles in the development of the Breed.

Although extensive attempts were made to identify the early participants, this proved difficult due to the lack of availability of early documentation and credits. I offer my sincere apologies for any inadvertently missed acknowledgement. Every precaution was taken in the preparation of this study, and the author assumes no responsibility for errors or omissions. Neither is any responsibility assumed for damages resulting from the use or misuse of information contained herein.

My sincere thanks and gratitude go to Yuri Semenov, owner/author of *Virtual Breed Database of the Black Russian Terrier* for clarification on the use of Database content for the English language. Mr. Semenov's Database [www.brtinfo.ru] was made possible through the work and dedication of many people.

I wish to highlight the special contributions of the following people:

- Yuri Semenov, Moscow
- Kirillova Natalia, Novosibirsk
- Lushnikova Natalia, Nizhniy Novgorod
- Ashastina Tatiana, Moscow
- Erugin Vjacheslav Konstantinovich, Moscow
- Terentyeva Anna, Ural
- Bochkovskaya Aleksandra, Ukraine
- Sharapova Elena Borisovna, Moscow
- Fastov Eugeniy, Estonia

- Krasova Olga, St.Peterburg
- Gertsman Elvira, Samara
- Fedyuk Natalia, Samara
- Danilenko Marina, Samara
- Goratchek Alexandra, Sweden
- Vatolina Olga, Penza
- Lifshits Veronica, Angarsk
- Zakharova Larisa vladislavovna, St. Petersburg
- Medvedskiy Victor, Rostov-na-Donu
- Leontyeva Marina, Moscow
- Nedelko Irina, Vladivostok
- Shuster Marina, Nikolaev
- Pavlenko Irina, Khabarovsk
- Patrycja Spotan, Poland
- Katarzyna Sokolska, Poland
- Ivan Stalev, Bulgaria
- Lashkova Olga Nikolaevna, Novosibirsk

Appreciation goes to Y.A. Lakatos, L.S. Osipova, and I.L. Filina for their research and study of the Breed`s development in Russia, and for sharing with the Black Russian Terrier fancy.

Special thanks and my profound gratitude are expressed:

- to Irina Nedeljko, Vladivostok, Russia, for graciously providing permission to display her Black Russian Terriers on the front and back covers of this volume, *Moscow Families.*
- to Svetlana Beolgurova, Novosibirsk, Russia for permission to use her photographs on the front and back covers.
- to Cindi Stumm, Aristes Black Russian Terrier Kennel, Brooks, California, USA, for kindly giving permission to include a photograph of Mikk, the stunning GCH Aristes Paint It Black .
- to my designer, Sherrill Wark of Crowe Creations, for professional advice, editing, patience, and final touches.

With nearly sixty years' experience within the world of dogs, Donald B. Anderson was drawn by destiny to the Black Russian Terrier in 2004. This interest was initiated by information that this "new dog" had been created by the Russian military under Stalin's rule, following WWII. The captivating attraction was that its format was founded on Anderson's beloved Giant Schnauzer breed. This discovery was the driving force that hurtled him head on into a complex labyrinth of dead ends, closed doors and false promises — the nightmare of research projects.

His professional approach to the world of dogs, bolstered by a 40-year career in international conference organization and high level international protocol, served well in establishing contacts and working relationships, over time, within the world of the Black Russian Terrier. Despite the inevitable challenges in breaking the perceived Russian codes of secrecy, Anderson has garnered a phenomenal amount of information.

In 1961 he began showing Bullmastiffs in Eastern Ontario and in1967 introduced the Giant Schnauzer to Canada. He boldly took on the dog-fancy establishment of the day, being ostracized for refusing to crop the ears of his Giants. Only one young female, Jannel, in his Prestigia Kennel, was cropped and she came that way. He was obviously ahead of his time.

In 1966, he began a 46-year (part time) research project on the history of a native Canadian breed, the Tahltan Bear Dog. Anderson has acquired a great deal of data, including "one of a kind" documents and personal letters from long-departed breeders and owners of that now extinct breed.

Over the years, Donald Anderson has collaborated with the Canadian Museum of Natural History, the Provincial Museum of Natural History of British Columbia and the Canadian Kennel Club. The National Museum honoured him by giving permission to photograph the only preserved specimen of the Tahltan Bear Dog in existence. The Tahltan Bear Dog was determined to be extinct in the mid 1970s.

Donald B. Anderson is the holder of Her Majesty Queen Elizabeth II Silver Jubilee Medal. He also is the recipient of Awards of Excellence for Exemplary Professionalism in the Federal Public Service of Canada. He holds a Degree in Law and Security Administration.

Made in the USA
Monee, IL
20 February 2021